INTRODUCTION TO THE ADMINISTRATION OF JUSTICE

D0403559

INTRODUCTION TO THE ADMINISTRATION OF JUSTICE

an overview of the justice system and its components

THOMAS F. ADAMS

*Dean, Applied Arts and Sciences and Instructor
Administration of Justice Educational Program*

SANTA ANA COLLEGE

PRENTICE-HALL, INC., Englewood Cliffs, N.J.

Library of Congress Cataloging in Publication Data

ADAMS, THOMAS FRANCIS, 1927-
  Introduction to the administration of justice.

  Includes bibliographies.
  1. Criminal justice, Administration of—United States. I. Title.
KF9223.A927   364   74-4476
ISBN 0-13-477810-3

Prentice-Hall Series in Law Enforcement
James D. Stinchcomb, *Editor*

© 1975 by PRENTICE-HALL, INC.,
Englewood Cliffs, New Jersey

10 9 8 7 6 5 4 3 2 1

Printed in the United States of America

PRENTICE-HALL INTERNATIONAL, INC., *London*
PRENTICE-HALL OF AUSTRALIA, PTY. LTD., *Sydney*
PRENTICE-HALL OF CANADA, LTD., *Toronto*
PRENTICE-HALL OF INDIA PRIVATE LIMITED, *New Delhi*
PRENTICE-HALL OF JAPAN, INC., *Toyko*

Dedicated to Brian
My son and good friend

Contents

Preface

The System of Justice Administration in the United States is directly involved in the maintenance of ordered liberty in a free society. It touches the lives of every single individual who lives in this society. In this text, it is my sincere wish that you, the reader and the student, will have a better understanding of the system and how it works as a direct result of my efforts at writing the book, and the many unnamed individuals who must share the credit for any success that we may experience. I stand alone for any of the errors and misinformation, because many sources were accurate prior to my interpretation.

The book consists of twelve major parts, each divided into a separate chapter. Beginning with a general overview of the total Justice System, the next chapters address the explanations of crime and a discussion of the needs for the system as it is and should be, and a discussion of the nature and extent of the crime challenge. Although crime is a major problem in the United States, I choose to address it as a challenge, which seems to be a more positive approach.

Each of the components of the System—Law Enforcement, the Courts, and Corrections—are explained in terms of the many philosophies involved in their organization and operation, and the manner in which they are operated in our complex society. Although not intended as an historical exposition, one brief chapter is devoted to the system's evolution, principally to provide the reader with an understanding of how the system reached its present state of development, and where some of our so-called "modern concepts" had their real beginning.

The latter part of the book addresses the important considerations of selection and professional preparation for the several components of the system, a chapter on ethics and professionalism, a discussion of the critical matter of the Constitutions of the United States and the respective states and their relationship to the administration of justice; the relationships of the several agencies of the System and the community; and a final chapter devoted to a few words about trends for the future of the Justice System.

This book is intended as a text for introducing the student to the exciting and fascinating study of the System of Justice Administration and its many components; a guided tour through the world of law enforcement, the courts, and the corrections components of probation, parole, and the correctional institutions.

T.F. ADAMS
Santa Ana

1

Administration of Justice: The System

Introduction

Throughout the United States there is a unique system of law enforcement and criminal justice. Literally thousands of agencies with similar objectives and responsibilities are linked together into a conglomeration of interrelated bureaus, divisions, and departments of law enforcement, investigation, corrections, prosecution, defense, probation, parole, regulation, direction, and assistance. Although many of them have quite similar objectives and responsibilities, few of these agencies are identical. Throughout this fascinating array of people and their agencies, most commonly known as the criminal justice system, there seems to run a common thread of public service with a crime-free society the unattainable—yet sought after—ultimate goal.

The system of criminal justice has often been labeled a "nonsystem" because so many of the agencies are totally autonomous and independent, although their legal responsibilities and/or geographical jurisdictions may be contiguous or in some cases may even overlap. An example of such criticism may be found in a recent committee report of the American Bar Association:

> The American criminal justice system is rocked by inefficiency, lack of coordination, and an obsessive adherence to outmoded practices and procedures. In many respects, the entire process might more aptly be termed a non-system, a feudalistic confederation of several independent components often working at cross purposes. A disproportionate allocation

of funds to police works to the detriment of other constituent agencies, such as the courts and correction facilities.[1]

Although not as critical of the effectiveness of the system, a federal commission report similarly appraised the agency relationships in the system:

> This study finds that, generally, the collective operations of police, public prosecutors, public defense counsels, courts and corrections establishments do not constitute a well articulated system. Those operations do not reflect clearly assigned responsibilities, supported by ample and strategic allocation of resources and affording—indeed, guaranteeing—protection for all citizens. While this report necessarily focuses on the intergovernmental relations problems impinging on the criminal justice system, no analysis of its institutional parts can, or should, avoid the basic judgment that much of it, in fact, is a "non-system." Police, prosecution, courts, and corrections function too frequently in isolation, or in ways that are counterproductive to each other.[2]

With no attempt to find fault with—or to pass judgment upon—the system of administration of justice (or "nonsystem" if you choose), we shall devote this introductory chapter to an explanation of the various agencies and their working relationships, their goals and objectives, and society's expectations. As a prelude to such a discussion, it is, perhaps, appropriate to review the legal basis for the criminal justice system in this conglomeration of governments that comprise the United States and its component parts. Thus, let us examine the phenomenon known as *police power.*

Police Power

Primary police power, or the power of the government to regulate the conduct of the people with respect to public health, welfare, safety, morals, and general prosperity, and to impose punitive sanctions upon those who fail to comply with such regulations, rests with the individual sovereign states. Except for relatively limited authority of the federal government, the respective states enact and enforce laws that provide

---

[1] American Bar Association, *New Perspectives on Urban Crime,* Spec. 31, Committee on Crime Prevention and Control (Chicago: American Bar Association, 1972), p. 7.

[2] Advisory Commission on Intergovernmental Relations, *State-Local Relations in the Criminal Justice System* (Washington, D.C.: Government Printing Office, 1971), p. 13.

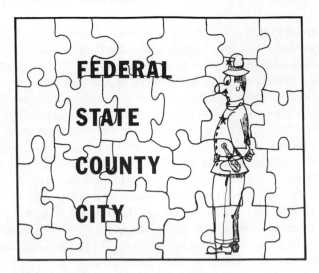

The "system" as many people perceive it.

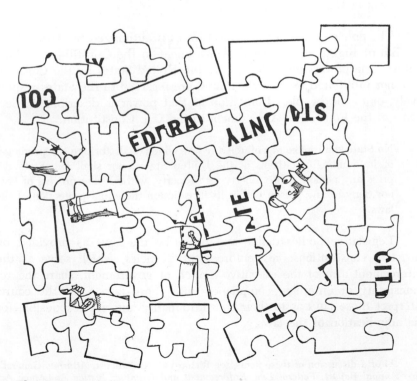

The system as it is.

for the activities of the several components of the criminal justice system: law enforcement, the courts, and corrections.

The federal police power is described in three clauses of the U.S. Constitution, which refer to the powers of Congress to enact criminal laws. Article I, Section 8, Clause 6 empowers the Congress to provide for the punishment of counterfeiting the securities and "current Coin of the United States." Clause 10 of the same section empowers Congress "to define and punish Piracies and Felonies committed on the high seas, and Offenses against the Law of Nations." The third reference to federal crimes is found in Article III, Section 3, which defines treason: "Treason against the United States, shall consist only in levying War against them, or in adhering to their Enemies, giving them Aid and Comfort."

The overall authority of the Congress to enact federal criminal laws derives from Article I, Section 8, Clause 18 of the U.S. Constitution, which states that the Congress shall have power:

> To make all Laws whch shall be necessary and proper for carrying into Execution the foregoing Powers, and all other Powers vested by this Constitution in the Government of the United States, or in any Department or Officer thereof.[3]

The police power of the several states is authorized by Article X of the Bill of Rights, or the Tenth Amendment to the Constitution, which states: "The powers not delegated to the United States by the Constitution, nor prohibited by it to the States, are reserved to the States respectively, or to the people." Limitation of that power is described in Section I of the Fourteenth Amendment to the U.S. Constitution:

> No State shall make or enforce any law which shall abridge the privileges or immunities of citizens of the United States; nor shall any State deprive any person of life, liberty, or property, without due process of law; nor deny to any person within its jurisdiction the equal protection of the laws.

Legislative bodies define and prescribe the laws as provided by the state constitutions; law enforcement agencies, which serve as the enforcement arm of the executive branch of government, share the responsibility of enforcing compliance with those laws; and the courts interpret those laws as to their constitutionality and are responsible for the adjudication of the laws.

---

[3] For a discussion of these items, see Richard G. Kleindienst, *Attorney General's First Annual Report, Federal Law Enforcement and Criminal Justice Assistance Activities* (Washington, D.C.: Government Printing Office, 1972), pp. 26–27.

State Police Power as Interpreted by the Courts

An early case involving state police powers may be found in a Supreme Court case that examined interstate commerce: *New York, New Haven, and Hartford Railroad Company* v. *New York:* 165 United States, 628 (1897). The issue involved a New York State law forbidding use of coal or wood stoves or furnaces for heating passenger coaches on all trains operating in the state. In sustaining the statute, the Court applied five main tests:

1. Was the nature of the subject being regulated such that it would require uniform national regulations? The Court found "not necessarily" though it was a matter on which governments might be expected to legislate.

2. Had Congress enacted legislation with which the New York statute was in conflict? The Court said "No."

3. Did the matter concern the health, safety, morals, convenience, or welfare of the inhabitants of New York State—in other words, did it come with the police power of the state? The Court ruled "Yes."

4. Did the state statute apply to both interstate and intrastate commerce, or did it discriminate against interstate commerce? The law did not single out and unreasonably burden interstate commerce, according to the Court.

5. Was the regulation reasonable, or did it impose an unreasonable burden on interstate commerce? On page 631 of that case Justice Harlan wrote "While the Laws of the States must yield to acts of Congress passed in execution of the powers conferred upon it by the Constitution, the mere grant to Congress of the power to regulate commerce did not, of itself and without legislation by Congress, impair the authority of the States to establish such reasonable regulations as were appropriate for the protection of the health, lives and safety of their people." [4]

Law Enforcement

For the purpose of discussion in this text, we shall address the basic three components of the criminal justice system as (1) law enforcement, (2) courts, and (3) corrections. Each component is comprised of many parts. The law enforcement—or police—component includes all law enforcement and investigative agencies that are directly or indirectly in-

---

[4] Jewell Case Phillips, Henry J. Abraham, and A. M. Ewing Cortez, *Essentials of National Government*, 3rd ed. (Cincinnati: Van Norstrand Reinhold Co., 1971), pp. 348–349.

volved in the process of identifying and apprehending individuals who are suspected of disobeying some law or administrative regulation as well as those involved in the arrest or some form of summoning process that causes individuals to be brought before the court to answer to charges.

Objectives of Law Enforcement. In order to strive toward accomplishment of their goals of peace and order in the community, the many thousands of agencies and their personnel have certain objectives they must attempt to accomplish. Those objectives include the following:

a. Provide benevolent services in cooperation with other agencies, which will include giving directions, providing counseling services, rescue and emergency first aid medical services, and generally assisting people.

b. Mediate domestic and other disputes as well as other forms of crisis intervention for the purpose of preserving peace and preventing crime.

c. Attend public gatherings and protect the rights of the people to assemble peaceably upon ascertaining that the gathering is lawful and peaceful.

d. Investigate allegations of criminal acts and take appropriate measures to identify, arrest, and bring to a fair trial those persons who are responsible for those crimes.

e. Enforce the laws and ordinances that are enacted on authority of the police power of the government to assure the public health, welfare, safety, morals, and convenience, and the powers of the federal government by the Constitution and its amendments.

f. Investigate the causes and effects of traffic collisions for the purpose of promoting safety, education of the public, and assistance in street and highway engineering.

g. Investigate conditions and other matters related to licensing and other regulatory concerns of the jurisdiction involved.

h. Regulate vehicular and pedestrian traffic to expedite its flow free from congestion and other hazards. This will include enforcement of the traffic laws.

i. Patrol the jurisdiction to observe and take effective action to prevent and repress criminal and antisocial behavior and to maintain the peace in the community.

j. Investigate complaints and calls for assistance in those matters that involve the legal and traditional responsibilities of the department.

k. Prepare reports and maintain records essential to the effective operation and management of the department.

l. Maintain a property and evidence storage facility for the safe-keeping and return of lost and stolen property and control of evidence according to a system assuring procedurally correct presentation in court.

m. Discover as soon as possible predelinquency and delinquent acts by children and youths and take effective action to deter development of criminal and other asocial behavior patterns.

n. Assure an effective balance of vice control in accordance with the community standards through investigation and enforcement activities.

o. Interact with the various segments and individuals in the community and explain the various functions of the department and its responsibilities in the administration of justice.

p. Act as master-at-arms in the court, maintain order, and provide other services as required by the judge.

q. Operate the jail—if one is maintained by the department—and provide related services.

Objectives of each agency in the law enforcement component of the system are unique in many respects. Jurisdictions and scope of responsibility are different. Frequent reference is made to so-called "levels" of government and to corresponding "levels" of law enforcement, as if there were some sort of hierarchy in ranking of federal, state, and local law enforcement and investigative agencies. There is no such hierarchy. Federal agencies that are charged with law enforcement and investigative responsibilities are restricted to the exercise of very limited powers although their geographical jurisdictions may be national or international in size or scope. State agencies have statewide jurisdiction with specific investigative and enforcement functions, such as a highway patrol force, or with a specific location, such as a state college or university police department. The county and municipal police agencies have very specific geographical limitations on their jurisdictions, but are usually charged with almost endless law enforcement and investigative responsibilities involving laws of the city, county, state, and federal governments.

Federal agencies with police responsibilities include the following:

Secret Service, charged with protection of the nation's currency and the President; Internal Revenue Service, a tax-related function; Bureau of Alcohol, Tobacco, and Firearms, principally involved in bombs and contraband weapons; Bureau of Narcotics and Dangerous Drugs, focused on illicit and licit distribution of drugs throughout the world; the highly publicized Federal Bureau of Investigation, charged with investigative functions including interstate flight to avoid prosecution and bank robbery statutes; and literally dozens of special purpose agencies.

State police agencies include, among others: Alcoholic Beverage Control, a licensing and regulating agency involving the alcoholic beverage industries; Highway Patrol, charged with highway safety and law enforcement on the state's highways and expressways; Motor Vehicles, with dual responsibilities of licensing drivers and vehicles and regulation of agencies in the motor vehicle industry; Professional and Vocational Standards, with jurisdiction involving enforcing minimum standards among a wide variety of professional practitioners such as doctors, chiropractors, attorneys, insurance agents, veterinarians, pharmacists, nurses, dentists, and many others; and hundreds of other special purpose police agencies such as Parks and Recreation, Fish and Game, Industrial Relations, Horse Racing, Fire Marshal, Forestry, Aviation, Social Welfare, State College and University Police, ad infinitum.

The law enforcement/police component of the criminal justice system involves at least 50 federal agencies, 200 state agencies, and 39,750 local agencies directly involved in law enforcement in the United States, according to the U.S. Bureau of the Budget in 1966.[5]

The Courts

The courts throughout the United States are—like the police—organized (or "disorganized") in a fashion similar to the interrelationships of the local, state, and federal governments, each operating within its own separate sphere of authority and responsibility. The local courts at the municipal and county level, and numbering into the many thousands, have primary jurisdiction over criminal cases of misdemeanor and felony categories that involve municipal, county, and state laws. An appeals process through progressively higher court levels provides for certain issues to be appealed through the state court system to the state supreme court, and, in some cases, to the U.S. Supreme Court.

---

[5] President's Commission on Law Enforcement and the Administration of Justice, *Task Force Report: The Police* (Washington, D.C.: Government Printing Office, 1967), p. 7.

The federal court system consists of the U.S. Supreme Court, the appellate courts, and the Courts of First Instance, the district courts. Jurisdiction of the Supreme Court includes appeals in matters of constitutionality, controversies involving certain public officials, and other matters in which a state is a party to a legal action. The courts of appeal, eleven in number, hear appeals from the district courts. Other special purpose appeals courts include the Court of Systems and Patent Appeals and the Court of Military Appeals. At the trial level in federal courts are ninety-three district courts, the Court of Claims, Customs Court, and Courts Martial for the military services.

State court systems have several levels of jurisdiction, ranging from the small township justice court to the state supreme court. At the local level is the justice court, the city court, or the municipal court. The exact type and designation varies from state to state. The smaller or less populous court district may call for a designation of lesser stature than a court district with a greater population, with the justice court being the lower designation and the municipal court the higher designation. These courts handle misdemeanor criminal cases, small claims, and other civil cases involving less than $2,000 to $3,000. The higher category of these two courts—municipal court—usually handles the preliminary hearing phase of the felony crime process to determine whether the case should be tried in superior court.

Superior court is the trial court for the county or parish for all felony offenses; this court also serves as an appeals court for cases decided upon in the lower courts, and handles litigation involving greater amounts of damages sought for redress than the lower courts can handle. Juvenile court is usually a separate division of the civil division of the superior court, and the probation officer of the county and his (her) deputies serve under direction of this court as well. Special departments of the superior court include probate to handle matters involving wills and related administrative matters, guardianship, domestic relations, adoptions, and a psychiatric department to deal with matters involving the mentally ill and others needing treatment, including addicts, inebriates, and mentally disordered sex offenders.

The grand jury, a vestige of eleventh-century English criminal justice, performs in a quasi-judicial role. Appointed by the court to serve for a specified period of time, usually not more than one year, grand juries operate for both federal and state judicial systems. Initially recommended by judges, then selected by lot, these individuals who allegedly represent the communities they serve investigate various matters and recommend actions that should be taken to improve community and government operations. In criminal matters, the prosecutor (district or county attorney, or other government prosecutor) presents evidence and introduces witnesses to the grand jury. The jurors make whatever inquiries they consider essential and in accordance with prescribed procedures as interpreted to them by the prosecutor. Their vote determines whether or not certain people should be held to answer in superior court for the charges they specify. In the absence of such a grand jury proceeding, this function is performed by a municipal court judge in a preliminary hearing. When remanded by the grand jury, the action is called an *indictment*. When remanded to the higher court by a lower court judge, the action is called an *information*. In either case the district prosecutor handles the prosecution.

In addition to the formalized court system, many states have an assortment of other bodies that perform judicial roles. Arbitration boards in matters of liability claims and various types of disputes between people make decisions that have the same effect as though they were made by a court. Commissions charged with professional and vocational standards appoint hearing officers, who take testimony and examine evidence to make recommendations to the commission, which, in turn, takes action that likewise has a courtlike effect, such as the temporary or permanent loss of a license and the right to continue practicing in that profession or occupation.

Court officers include all of the attorneys who practice law in the courts. Prosecutors, who represent the People through the respective governments, are charged with proving guilt in accordance with the Constitution, and they include the Attorney General of the United States and the respective states, U.S. attorneys, corporation counsels, district attorneys, county and city prosecutors, and others with similar responsibilities. The accused are assured legal counsel by virtue of the Fifth and Sixth Amendments to the Constitution, which provide for "due process" and representation by counsel.[6] In the event the defendant is indigent and cannot provide for his own counsel, one will be provided by the court for him. In order to provide competent counsel for indigent defendants on a consistent basis, the professional, government-employed public defender has taken his place as a regular member of the criminal justice system.

Peace officers who serve as part of the Court's component of the system include the sheriff, marshal, and constable, who serve as bailiffs of the court and ministerial officers to carry out the instructions of the court. These officers may also serve as law enforcement officers for the executive branch of government as well, such as the sheriff who has full

---

[6] See Articles V and VI of the Bill of Rights. For further elaboration and detailed explanation of these rights see Gideon V. Wainright (372 U.S. 335), Escobedo v. Illinois (378 U.S. 478), Massiah v. United States (377 U.S. 210), Miranda v. Arizona (384 U.S. 436); and for an elaboration of this right to emphasize a juvenile's rights under similar conditions see Gault v. Arizona (387 U.S. 1).

police authority and responsibility for the unincorporated and other specified areas of the county. The specific roles each of these three officers play are almost identical, except that the courts they serve are different. For example, the sheriff serves the superior court, the marshal serves the municipal court (except the U.S. Marshal, who serves the U.S. courts), and the constable serves the lower justice courts by direction of the justice of the peace.

The probation officer and his deputies serve at the pleasure of the superior court. Their role is to conduct presentence investigations and to make recommendations to the court regarding decisions relative to confinement and alternatives with a view to punishment and rehabilitation, and to supervise those individuals who have been placed on probation with a specified program of supervised freedom as prescribed by the court.

The district courts of appeal meet at various locations throughout the state, sometimes on a circuit-court basis, meeting for several months each year at several locations. Cases originating in the municipal courts and justice courts are taken, on appeal, through the superior court to the district courts of appeal. Except when otherwise provided, appeals from superior court are likewise taken to the district courts of appeal. The appellate courts hear cases on appeal in criminal matters, contesting elections, eminent domain, and various contested matters of civil law.

The state supreme court is the highest court in each state provided for by the several state constitutions, with jurisdiction generally as follows:

    a. In all superior court cases in equity.

    b. In cases at law involving title or possession of real estate, tax legality, impost, assessment, toll, or municipal fine.

    c. In all probate matters as provided by law.

    d. In criminal cases in which a sentence of death has been prescribed, and the automatic appeal examines only questions of law.

    e. Over writs of mandamus, certiorari, prohibition, habeas corpus, and all other necessary writs.

    f. Over matters before the district courts of appeal when the Supreme Court orders such matters to be transferred to it from that court.

    g. Over applicants to the State Bar when found qualified by the Bar Examiners of the State Bar and in matters of disciplinary action on recommendation of the Board of Governors of the State Bar.[7]

Still to be considered along with the Court's component of the criminal justice system, yet separate and distinct from it, is the Court of Impeachment, which consists of the U.S. Senate. Other ministerial mat-

---

[7] Sections 3, 4, 21, and 26, Article VI, California State Constitution.

ters of the courts are related to such bodies as a judicial council, which is concerned with policy matters of the practices and procedures in the courts; and the Commission on Judicial Qualifications and Judicial Council, which is concerned with qualification and appointment of competent judges, and their retention or removal for cause.

Corrections

The corrections component of the criminal justice system serves a population described by the Corrections Task Force:

> The jails, workhouses, penitentiaries, and reformatories of the nation admit, control, and release an estimated 3 million individuals each year. On an average day, approximately 1.3 million people . . . are under correctional authority in the United States, roughly one-third of whom being in institutions and the balance on parole or probation.[8]

Federal institutions in the correctional system include a network of facilities at thirty-eight locations throughout the nation.[9] That number includes six penitentiaries, a medical center, behavioral research center, intermediate and short-term adult institutions; centers for young adults, youths and juveniles; and community treatment centers. The Federal Bureau of Prisons is also planning the development of eight Metropolitan Federal Correctional Centers to replace traditional jails, most of which are obsolete and overcrowded.[10]

Throughout the fifty states there are approximately 432 correctional institution systems, including over 1,200 separate facilities for adults and juveniles.[11] As of March 1970, there were 4,037 locally administered jails (city and county).[12]

Probation and parole systems in the United States, many operating as combination probation and parole organizations, including the federal probation system, totalled 1,647 in 1966.[13]

[8] President's Commission on Law Enforcement and the Administration of Justice, *Task Force Report: Corrections* (Washington, D.C.: Government Printing Office, 1967).

[9] Federal Bureau of Prisons, *Biennial Report 1970–71* (Washington, D.C.: U.S. Department of Justice, 1971), p. 1.

[10] *Ibid.*, p. 24.

[11] Herman Piven and Abraham Alcabes, *The Crisis of Qualified Manpower for Criminal Justice: An Analytic Assessment with Guidelines for New Policy* (Washington, D.C.: Government Printing Office, 1969), vol. 2, *Correctional Institutions,* p. 7.

[12] Federal Bureau of Prisons: *Biennial Report 1970–71,* p. 24.

[13] Piven and Alcabes, *The Crisis of Qualified Manpower for Criminal Justice: An Analytic Assessment with Guidelines for New Policy,* vol. 1, *Probation/Parole,* p. 6.

Definitions. As indicated in the summary of the many facilities, it is evident that the term *corrections* encompasses a multitude of functions, people, concepts, and ideals. Corrections generally involves the rehabilitation—or correcting—phase of the process through which an individual must proceed once he has been determined guilty of a crime and inducted into the justice system. There are three basic parts to this component, although the first and third are quite similar. Those three parts are probation, institutions, and parole.

Probation involves the placement of a convicted offender (or an adjudicated delinquent juvenile) under supervision in the community in lieu of incarceration, under conditions prescribed by the court, and under the control of a probation officer.[14] Probation involves a suspension of sentence, and it is conditional for a specified period of time. Probation may actually be granted in place of a prison sentence, during which time the individual may be sentenced to a short term in a county jail followed by a period of time under supervised liberty. Conditions of probation are prescribed by the court and agreed to by the probationer as a condition of the assignment to probation. The conditions may include any or all of the following:

1. Observing all laws.
2. Keeping and developing good habits.
3. Keeping a good work or school record.
4. Associating only with approved persons.
5. Changing marital status only after consultation with the probation officer.
6. Abiding by all of the restrictions imposed by the judge who granted probation.

Correctional Institutions

JUVENILE INSTITUTIONS

Juveniles are detained in a variety of places, but they are not considered as having been convicted at any time. The philosophy of the juvenile courts has been to return the child to his parents as soon as possible whenever practicable. First and minor offenders may be returned home with no incarceration, or they may be remanded to the custody of county probation officials or a state institution.

[14] Center for Law Enforcement and Corrections, *Probation, Parole and Pardons: A Basic Course,* Training Module 6913 (University Park, Pa.: Pennsylvania State University, 1969), p. 4.

When the court remands the juvenile to custody for his first time, he may go to a local juvenile home or a camp of some type. Subsequent incarcerations for the juvenile repeater may result in his being sent to a state institution or camp for a longer period of time and then eventually home again for probation or parole.

During recent years, more than ever before it seems, criticism of the correctional institutions has been vocal, and it has been quite incisive. The correctional institutions have been involved in a constant crisis, as may be verified by reference almost any day to the newspaper. Prisons have been the breeding grounds for a criminal culture. As an example of the many reports that follow inspections of correctional institutions, the following assessment of youth corrections appeared in the annual report, *Federal Activities in Juvenile Delinquency, Youth Development, and Related Fields*.[15]

The field of youth corrections faces two problems. First, funds and facilities are inadequate to the demands placed on correctional institutions by the community. Second, the validity of the techniques of present day corrections has been seriously challenged.

Even with its swing away from large institutions to smaller correctional facilities, the correctional process still segregates and labels those in custody. It still stands as the last resort—the end of the line—for those unfortunate enough to enter its jurisdiction.

ADULT INSTITUTIONS

Adults are sentenced either to a city or county jail or to a state or federal penal institution for a prescribed period of time. Jail sentences are set by the judge for a specific period of time, and the defendant serves that time, less good behavior and earned time off for such voluntary acts as donating blood. Some states have "straight" sentences for felony imprisonment in state institutions that are prescribed by the judge in the same manner as one would be sent to the county jail. Other states, including California, have the "indeterminate sentence" that provides for the judge remanding the subject to prison for "the sentence prescribed by law," which is later established by a corrections board or similar committee.

The purpose for sentencing a convicted person to prison include the following:

[15] U.S. Department of Health, Education and Welfare, *Federal Activities in Juvenile Delinquency, Youth Development, and Related Fields* (Washington, D.C.: Government Printing Office, 1971).

1. The people desire changed persons to emerge after serving a period of time in prison. Their habit patterns should, according to this philosophy, be sufficiently different after isolation from the law-abiding society, for they have had the opportunity to develop new skills and improve their academic education so that they can seek lawful outlets to satisfy their needs and desires.

2. Segregation from society is a means whereby the offender can be separated from his victims for an extended period of time, and during that time he cannot commit his crime again.

3. The victim and the people in the community want retribution and revenge.

During his term of imprisonment the individual is prepared in some way for his eventual release back into the social milieu from which he came. The return is a fact, but when and under what conditions is where the problem begins. Ideally, the individual should return to freedom after having "paid his debt to society" and never repeat his criminal depredations. There is no magic formula for determining at precisely what point an individual has been appropriately punished, or rehabilitated, and is ready to return to society. Criminal codes provide for terms of imprisonment, presumably in proportion to the seriousness of the crime. In some jurisdictions, as mentioned earlier, the final determination of the exact length of time the prisoner must spend in the institution is left to a prison board, or a board of review, and the sentence prescribed by a judge is "indeterminate."

The indeterminate sentence is a procedure whereby the sentencing judge merely sentences the individual to prison. The penal code prescribes the punishment as "one to ten years" for example. Once in prison, the subject is placed under the jurisdiction of the department of corrections. A board of review, comprised of persons usually appointed by a governor, reviews the subject's case and establishes a more definite time within the broader limits as originally prescribed. For example, a man sentenced to "one to fourteen" may have his sentence set by the board at three years before his case may come up for review and consideration for parole.

The convicted person may leave prison at the end of his completed sentence and be done with it. But there are other legal ways that he may leave. One method is for the president or governor of the state to grant him a pardon, which causes the person to be released with full civil rights restored. Another method is a commutation, or reduction of sentence, by executive order. Amnesty is a pardon applied to a group of prisoners by executive order, and it is seldom used to any great extent. The most common method for exit is by parole.

Parole

Paroles are granted by federal, state, or county boards from the various institutions. Following release from prison, the parolee from a federal or state prison is placed under the supervision of a parole officer. A county jail parolee may be placed under the supervision of a probation officer. The role of the parole officer is basically the same as that of a probation officer in most cases. Both probation officer and parole officer, or "agent," are case managers who serve as "change agents" with the principal objective of assisting the individuals under their supervision to rehabilitate themselves and redirect their lives in more meaningful and lawful pursuits to avoid repeating their crimes and having to return to the courts as defendants.

The distinction between probation and parole is that in the case of parole the individual is considered "still in custody" and only on leave from the institution during the period of time he is on his good behavior. He lives under the threat of immediate return to prison if he does not live according to the strict rules that are prescribed for him. The conditions of parole are also similar to those for the person on probation, but the two should not be confused. Probation refers to the term spent by the individual in lieu of a term of imprisonment. Parole follows imprisonment and is merely considered as a continuation of that prison sentence while outside the walls of the institution. Recent developments, however, have made it necessary for more formal procedures to be followed, including hearings with representation by counsel, prior to return to prison for parole violations.

Goals and Objectives of Corrections

Correctional goals and objectives should be defined as clearly as possible—and reviewed and redefined whenever necessary—so that management of this component of the system and its separate parts may be accomplished more effectively. Following is a statement of goals and objectives prepared by the Organization of State Correctional Services in the Control and Treatment of Crime and Delinquency, Board of Corrections for the State of California in 1967, and reproduced to serve simply as an example of how such a statement may be adapted as a guideline for action:

Goals of Corrections:

1. PREVENTION—To minimize the frequency with which law violators are recruited from the non-criminal population. Accordingly, the effectiveness of preventive efforts is measured by the volume of first offenses, that is, the rate of criminal recruitment.

2. CORRECTION—To minimize the frequency which law violations are committed by persons who have prior records of criminality. Success of the corrective effort is, therefore, measured by various kinds of recidivism rates.

Objectives of Youth and Adult Corrections:

Achievement of the goals of corrections requires establishment of more specific "targets" or "objectives" of the system. These objectives are:

1. TO ASSIST THE CRIMINAL AND JUVENILE COURTS AND THE QUASI-JUDICIAL PAROLE BOARDS TO MAKE EFFECTIVE DECISIONS REGARDING DISPOSITION OF OFFENDERS SUBJECT TO THE COURT'S OR PAROLE BOARD'S JURISDICTION.

   This objective is accomplished by:

   a. Application of established standards in the determination of detention status of adults detained in jail and juveniles detained in juvenile hall.

   b. Clinical and investigative techniques culminating in reports with recommendations which evaluate the characteristics of the offender, the offense, and the feasibility of probation of other sentencing dispositions.

   c. Providing paroling authorities with information for the determination of sentence and of parole date and conditions, which information is based largely on evaluation of the attitudes, skills and demonstrated performance of the subject in a controlled environment and after progress in an appropriate rehabilitation or treatment program.

2. TO ADMINISTER THE SENTENCING DISPOSITIONS OF THE COURTS BY CONTROL OF COMMITTED OFFENDERS IN THE INSTITUTIONS AND/OR ON PROBATION OR PAROLE.

   This objective is accomplished by:

   a. Control in the institutions:
      (1) Classifying inmates in accordance with security requirements;
      (2) Maintaining safety and order within a secure perimeter; and,
      (3) Providing for basic human needs and maintaining morale through good human relations.

   b. Control in the community:
      (1) Classifying probationers and parolees in accordance with control requirements;
      (2) Enforcing the conditions of parole; and,
      (3) Investigating, evaluating, and reporting probation and parole performance.

3. PREPARE COMMITTED OFFENDERS FOR RETURN TO THE COMMUNITY AS USEFUL PERSONS BY PROMOTING AND SUSTAINING CHANGES IN ATTITUDE AND BEHAVIOR.
This objective is accomplished by:

a. Providing programs in accordance with needs individually determined and reviewed.

   (1) Work programs in the institution and on-parole employment compatible with his aptitudes, training, and consistent with his social and legal situation;

   (2) Resocialization programs; to include both clinical and custodial aspects of the therapeutic community;

   (3) Educational programs; consistent with appraisal of aptitudes, interests, and educational objectives;

   (4) Spiritual programs; to include religious services and guidance;

   (5) Medical service programs; to maintain good health and physical condition through medical and dental care; and,

   (6) Leisure time programs; encouraging the use of leisure time for self-improvement and wholesome recreation.

b. Developing and maintaining the offender's link to the community to the maximum extent compatible with control requirements.

   (1) Encouraging legitimate communications with family, friends, and the community;

   (2) Fostering contact with prospective employers and other persons concerned with vocational planning;

   (3) Assisting in resolving personal problems of parents and dependents of the offender.

4. UTILIZE INCARCERATED OFFENDERS' MANPOWER AND CORRECTIONAL FACILITIES FOR THE PUBLIC BENEFIT.
This objective is accomplished by:

a. Providing work for subjects in production of goods and repair of equipment for governmental use.

b. Providing subjects for work in:

   (1) Fire fighting;

   (2) Forestry and road maintenance operations;

   (3) Maintenance of beaches and parks and development of outdoor recreational areas; and,

   (4) Public assistance in civil defense and disaster work.

5. FIND THE CAUSES AND THE MEANS FOR PREVENTION AND TREATMENT OF DELINQUENCY AND CRIMINAL BEHAVIOR AND TO PARTICIPATE IN THE DEVELOPMENT OF CRIMINAL LAW.
This objective is accomplished by:

a. Conducting basic research in the behavioral sciences related to the causation of delinquency, crime, and the modification of deviant behavior.

b. Applying experimental program models designed to modify the behavior of wars, inmates, and parolees.

c. Evaluating program effectiveness through accepted research methods.

   d. Communicating to the Governor, the Legislature, the Courts, and
   the public in general, analysis of the effects of the administration
   of criminal justice in the control of crime, and providing leadership
   towards the making of improvements.[16]

Critical Evaluation of the Justice System

Throughout the text we shall approach the study of the system of administration of justice in a positive manner, working within the framework of thought that the system is beset with many lingering and seem-
ingly insoluble problems but that the best way to address those problems
is to identify them and then squarely face each of them and act upon
them as challenges to be met rather than problems to be feared. Consider the following critical statements as challenges:

   The increasing incidence of violent crime in the streets of our great
   cities, . . . has begun to create doubts that our criminal justice apparatus, as now constituted, can adequately satisfy those essential goals of
   a free society.

   Two very broad options are open to us as a nation. We could permit
   the governmental machinery for the administration of justice to continue to deteriorate, relegating us ultimately to primitive self-help crime
   control remedies. Lynch mobs and vigilante groups are no strangers in
   American history. Such an option is abhorrent and the very antithesis
   of our democratic system. Rather, we must renew our commitment to
   achieve crime control by orderly and lawful means through the criminal
   justice process. Such a commitment requires more than the expression of
   noble ideas. It requires strong and immediate action to reexamine criti-
   cally the criminal justice process and to reshape it into an effective deterrent to violent crime in our city streets.[17]

Referring to its statement of concern for the health of our nation
as well as an estimated $16 billion per year loss by the business com-
munity, the Committee for Economic Development issued the following
appraisal of our criminal justice system.

   The Committee believes that the ineffectiveness of the present structure
   is rooted in the organizational and administrative chaos that character-
   izes the nation's uncoordinated system of criminal justice, and in the

---

[16] Law Enforcement Assistance Administration, *Correctional Planning and Resource Guide* (Washington, D.C.: Government Printing Office, 1969), pp. 19–22.
   [17] American Bar Association Special Committee on Crime Prevention and Control, *New Perspectives on Urban Crime* (Chicago: American Bar Association, 1972),
p. 9.

management weaknesses prevailing in agencies at all levels. The Committee therefore proposes a complete administrative overhaul of the criminal justice system and a redistribution of responsibility functions, and financial support among the various levels of government.[18]

The American Bar's Committee on Crime Prevention and Control offered its explanation of reasons for the "failure of the existing criminal justice system and its bankrupt crime control policies":

1. An antiquated, inefficient system without coordination that is overburdened with a heavier case load than it could handle.
2. A spiraling heroin addiction epidemic that contributes directly to urban crime and the overloading of the system.
3. A slow motion justice that defeats the goals of the system and demeans the entire process in the eyes of the public.[19]

The same committee of the Bar Association presented an example of the inadequacy of the system as follows:

Even if a criminal is apprehended, his chances of being seriously disciplined are low. According to New York City's Criminal Justice Plan for 1971: ". . . Of those arrested in 1968, the last year for which complete data is available for felonies or misdemeanors, only 32 percent were found guilty of *any charge*. Of the remainder, 56 percent were acquitted or had their cases dismissed, 11 percent failed to appear for trial and one percent received other dispositions. Of those found guilty, only 7.4 percent received any sentences of over one year in jail and only 50 percent were sentenced to any further time in jail." When considered with the low probability of arrest for most crimes, these figures make it clear that the *crime control system* in New York poses little threat to the average criminal.[20]

The committee suggested that the so-called "system" of criminal justice be converted into a real system:

The nation's criminal justice apparatus must be converted at all levels of government from a diffuse group of agencies, each acting without regard on a coordinated basis to achieve the common goal of crime control. The key word is "system," for the Task Force Report on Law and Law Enforcement to the National Commission on the Causes and Prevention of

---

[18] Committee for Economic Development, *Reducing Crime and Assuring Justice, A Statement on National Policy,* prepared by The Research and Policy Committee (New York: Committee for Economic Development, 1972), p. 7.

[19] ABA, *New Perspectives on Urban Crime,* p. 7.

[20] *Ibid.,* p. 7.

Representatives of the people. California State Senator George Deukmejian (left), Los Angeles District Attorney Joseph P. Busch, and Attorney General Euelle J. Younger discuss pending legislation involving the Justice System.
Photo courtesy of District Attorney, Los Angeles County.

Violence has aptly described the present criminal justice process as a "non-system" of criminal justice.[21]

The foregoing statements are representative of many study committees and commissions that have set out to appraise the system from many different points of vantage with a view to improvement of certain specialized areas within the system. Although many other studies had been made during previous years, one of the more extensive studies of the problems facing the administration of justice and one that capped off its findings with a comprehensive series of specific recommendations was the commission known popularly as the President's Crime Commission.

President's Crime Commission

On July 23, 1965 President Lyndon B. Johnson assembled together a panel of people representing divergent views and a variety of back-

[21] *Ibid.,* p. 13.

grounds and created a committee with a single objective: to study the criminal justice system for the purpose of making a series of recommendations for improvement of the system. Officially named the President's Commission on Law Enforcement and Administration of Justice, the commission, its consultants, and its staff compiled in a series of publications, task force reports, and its major publication, *Challenge of Crime in a Free Society,* a wealth of information that previously had been available to the people in piecemeal fashion. Little of the information was new, just the method of collecting and disseminating it and putting it into focus.

The President's Crime Commission made more than two hundred recommendations for change in every facet of the criminal justice system. Not only did the commission recommend action to be taken by the public segment of our society but also the private segment in a massive cooperative effort. All of these publications are available for nominal prices through the U.S. Government Printing Office and should find their way into your library.

For the purpose of this chapter's theme, some of the commission's most significant recommendations are recounted. Study the recommendations carefully and compare them with the actual policies and procedures of the various agencies in your own city, county, and state.

Crime in America

THE COMMISSION RECOMMENDS:

* Those cities that have not already done so should adopt centralized procedures for handling the receipt of reports of crime from citizens and institute and staff controls necessary to make those procedures effective.
* The present index of reported crime should be broken into two wholly separate parts, one for crimes of violence and the other for crimes against property.

Juvenile Delinquency and Youth Crime

THE COMMISSION RECOMMENDS:

* Efforts, both private and public, should be intensified to:
    Prepare youth for employment.
    Provide youth with information about employment opportunities.
    Reduce barriers to employment posed by discrimination, the misuse of criminal records, and maintenance of rigid job qualifications.
    Create new employment opportunities.

* To the greatest feasible extent, police departments should formulate policy guidelines for dealing with juveniles.
* All officers should be acquainted with the special characteristics of adolescents, particularly those of the social, racial, and other specific groups with which they are likely to come in contact.
* Custody of a juvenile (both prolonged street stops and station house visits) should be limited to instances where there is objective, specifiable ground for suspicion.
* Every stop that includes a frisk or an interrogation of more than a few preliminary identifying questions should be recorded in a strictly confidential report.
* Police forces should make full use of the central diagnosing and coordinating services of the Youth Services Bureau. Station adjustment should be limited to release and referral; it should not include hearings or the imposition of sanctions by the police. Court referral by the police should be restricted to those cases involving serious criminal conduct or repeated misconduct of a more than trivial nature.
* Communities should establish neighborhood youth-serving agencies —Youth Services Bureaus—located if possible in comprehensive neighborhood community centers and receiving juveniles (delinquent) referred by the police, the juvenile court, parents, schools, and other sources.
* Juvenile courts should make fullest feasible use of preliminary conferences to dispose of cases short of adjudication.
* The movement for narrowing the juvenile court's jurisdiction should be continued. (Specially, the commission recommends a list of changes, primarily limiting the jurisdiction of the juvenile court to only those acts of a juvenile that would be criminal acts if committed by an adult.)
* Counsel should be appointed as a matter of course wherever coercive action is a possibility, without requiring any affirmative choice by child or parent.
* Notice should be given well in advance of any scheduled court proceeding, including intake, detention, and waiver hearings, and should set forth the alleged misconduct with particularity.
* Adequate and appropriate separate detention facilities for juveniles should be provided.
* Legislation should be enacted restricting both authority to detain and the circumstances under which the detention is permitted.

The Police

THE COMMISSION RECOMMENDS:

* State legislatures should enact statutory provisions with respect to the authority of law enforcement officers to stop persons for brief questioning, including specifications of the circumstances and limitations under which stops are permissible.

* The police should formally participate in community planning in all cities.

* Police departments in all large communities should have community-relations machinery consisting of a headquarters unit that plans and supervises the department's community-relations programs. It should also have precinct units, responsible to the precinct commander, that carry out the programs. Community relations must be both a staff and a line function. Such machinery is a matter of the greatest importance in any community that has a substantial minority population.

* In each police precinct in a minority-group neighborhood there should be a citizen's advisory committee that meets regularly with police officials to work out solutions to problems of conflict between the police and the community. It is crucial that the committees be broadly representative of the community as a whole, including those elements who are critical or aggrieved.

* It should be a high-priority objective of all departments in communities with a substantial minority population to recruit minority-group officers and to deploy and promote them fairly. Every officer in such departments should receive thorough grounding in community-relations subjects. His performance in the field of community relations should be periodically reviewed and evaluated.

* Every jurisdiction should provide adequate procedures for full and fair processing of all citizen grievances and complaints about the conduct of any public officer or employee.

* Police departments should develop and enunciate policies that give police personnel specific guidance for the common situations requiring exercise of police discretion. Policies should cover such matters, among others, as the issuance of orders to citizens regarding their movements or activities, the handling of minor disputes, the safeguarding of rights of free speech and free assembly, the selection and use of investigative methods, and the decision whether or not to arrest in specific situations involving specific crimes.

* Each municipality, and other jurisdiction responsible for law enforcement, should carefully assess the manpower needs of its police agency on the basis of efficient use of all its personnel and should provide the resources required to meet the need for increased personnel if such a need is found to exist.

* Basic police functions, specially in large- and medium-sized urban departments, should be divided among three kinds of officers, here termed the "community service officer," the "police officer," and the "police agent."

* Police departments should recruit far more actively than they do now, with special attention to college campuses and inner-city neighborhoods.

* The ultimate aim of all police departments should be that all personnel with general enforcement powers have baccalaureate degrees.

* Police departments should take immediate steps to establish a

minimum requirement of a baccalaureate degree for all supervisory and executive positions.

* Until reliable tests are devised for identifying and measuring the personal characteristics that contribute to good police work, intelligence tests, thorough background investigations, and personal interviews should be used by all departments as absolute minimum techniques to determine the moral character and the intellectual and emotional fitness of police candidates.

* Police departments and civil service commisions should reexamine and, if necessary, modify present recruitment standards on age, height, weight, visual acuity, and prior residence. The appointing authority should place primary emphasis on the education, background, character and personality of a candidate for police service.

* Police salaries must be raised, particularly by increasing minimums. In order to attract college graduates to police service, starting and maximum salaries must be competitive with other professions and occupations that seek the same graduates.

* Salary proposals for each department within local government should be considered on their own merits and should not be joint with the demands of other departments within a city.

* Promotion eligibility requirements should stress ability above seniority. Promotion "lists" should be compiled on the basis not only of scores on technical examinations but on prior performance, character, educational achievement and leadership potential.

* Personnel to perform all specialized police functions not involving a need for general enforcement powers should be selected for their talents and abilities without regard to prior police service. Professional policemen should have the same opportunities as other professionals to seek employment where they are most needed. The inhibitions that civil service regulations, retirement plans, and hiring policies place on lateral entry should be removed. To encourage lateral movement of police personnel, a nationwide retirement system should be devised that permits the transferring of retirement credits.

* All training programs should provide instruction on subjects that prepare recruits to exercise discretion properly, and to understand the community, the role of the police, and what the criminal justice system can and cannot do. Professional educators and civilian experts should be used to teach specialized courses—law and psychology, for example. Recognized teaching techniques such as problem-solving seminars should be incorporated into training programs.

* Formal police training programs for recruits in all departments, large and small, should consist of an absolute minimum of 400 hours of classroom work spread over a four- to six-month period so that it can be combined with carefully selected and supervised field training.

* Entering officers should serve probation periods of, preferably, eighteen months and certainly no less than one year. During this period the recruit should be systematically observed and rated. Chief administrators should have the sole authority of dismissal during

the probation period and should willingly exercise it against unsatisfactory officers.

* Every general enforcement officer should have at least one week of intensive in-service training a year. Every officer should be given incentives to continue his general education or acquire special skills outside his department.

* Every state, through its commission on police standards, should provide financial and technical assistance to departments to conduct surveys and make recommendations for improvement and modernization of their organization, management, and operations.

* Every medium- and large-sized department should employ a skilled lawyer full time as its legal adviser. Smaller departments should arrange for legal advice on a part-time basis.

* Police departments must take every possible step to implement the guiding organizational principle of central control.

* Specialist staff units for such matters as planning, research, legal advice, and police personnel should include persons trained in a variety of disciplines and should be utilized to develop and improve the policies, operations, and administration of each function.

* Every department in a big or medium-sized city should organize key ranking staff and line personnel into an administrative board similar in function to a corporation's board of directors, whose duty would be to assist the chief and his staff units in developing, enunciating, and enforcing departmental policies and guidelines for the day-to-day activities of line personnel.

* Every department, regardless of size, should have a comprehensive program for maintaining police integrity and every medium- and large-sized department should have a well-manned internal investigation unit responsible only to the chief administrator. The unit should have both an investigative and preventive role in controlling dishonest, unethical, and offensive actions by police officers.

* Police departments should commence experimentation with a team-policing concept that envisions those with patrol and investigative duties combining under unified command with flexible assignments to deal with the crime problems in a defined sector.

* A comprehensive regulation should be formulated by every chief administrator to reflect the basic policy that firearms may be used only when the officer believes his life or the life of another is in imminent danger, or when other reasonable means of apprehension have failed to prevent the escape of a felony suspect whom the officer believes presents a serious danger to others.

* States should assume responsibility for assuring that areawide records and communications needs are provided.

* In every metropolitan area the central city or the state should provide laboratory facilities for the routine needs of all the communities in the area. State or multistate laboratories and the FBI laboratory should continue to provide the necessary research to make available to all laboratories more sophisticated means of analysis.

* Specialized personnel from state or metropolitan departments should assist smaller departments in each metropolitan area on major investigations and in specialized law enforcement functions.
* Each metropolitan area and each county should take action directed toward the pooling, or consolidation, of police services through the particular technique that will provide the most satisfactory law enforcement service and protection at lowest possible cost.
* Police standards commissions should be established in every state, and empowered to set mandatory requirements and to give financial aid to governmental units for the implementation of standards.

The Courts

THE COMMISSION RECOMMENDS:

* Felony and misdemeanor courts and their ancillary agencies—prosecutors, defenders, and probation services—should be unified.
  As an immediate step to meet the needs of the lower courts, the judicial manpower of these courts should be increased and their physical facilities should be improved so that these courts will be able to cope with the volume of cases coming before them in a dignified and deliberate way.
  Prosecutors, probation officers, and defense counsel should be provided in courts where these officers are not found, or their numbers are insufficient.
* The states and federal government should enact legislation to abolish or overhaul the justice of the peace and U.S. commissioner systems.
* Each State should enact comprehensive bail reform legislation. . . .
* Each community should establish procedures to enable and encourage police departments to release, in appropriate classes of cases, as many arrested persons as possible promptly after arrest upon issuance of a citation of summons requiring appearance.
* Prosecutors and defense counsel should in appropriate cases share information they secure independently at all points in the process when such sharing appears likely to lead to early disposition.
* Police, prosecutors, bar associations, and courts should issue regulations and standards as to the kinds of information that properly may be released to the news media about pending criminal cases by police officers, prosecutors, and defense counsel. These regulations and standards should be designed to minimize prejudicial statements by the media before or during trial, while safeguarding legitimate reporting on matters of public interest.
* States should reexamine the sentencing provisions of their penal codes with a view to simplifying the grading of offenses, and to removing mandatory minimum prison terms, long maximum prison

terms, and ineligibility for probation and parole. In cases of persistent habitual offenders of dangerous crimes, judges should have express authority to extend prison terms. Sentencing codes should include criteria designed to help judges exercise their discretion in accordance with clearly stated standards.

* The question whether capital punishment is an appropriate sanction is a policy decision to be made by each state. . . .

Corrections

THE COMMISSION RECOMMENDS:

* Parole and probation services should be available in all jurisdictions for felons, juveniles, and those adult misdemeanants who need or can profit from community treatment.
* Every state should provide that offenders who are not paroled receive adequate supervision after release unless it is determined to be unnecessary in a specific case.
* Probation and parole services should make use of volunteers and subprofessional aides in demonstration projects and regular programs.
* Probation and parole officials should develop new methods and skills to aid in reintegrating offenders through active intervention on their behalf with community institutions.
* Case loads for different types of offenders should vary in size and in type and intensity of treatment. Classification and assignment of offenders should be made according to their needs and problems.
* Correctional authorities should develop more extensive community programs providing special, intensive treatment as an alternative to institutionalization for both juvenile and adult offenders.
* Federal and state governments should finance the establishment of model, small-unit correctional institutions for flexible, community-oriented treatment.
* Graduated release and furlough programs should be expanded. They should be accompanied by guidance and coordinated with community treatment services.
* Located jails and misdemeanant institutions should be integrated into state correctional systems. They should not be operated by law enforcement agencies. Rehabilitative programs and other reforms should be instituted.
* Wherever possible, persons awaiting trial should be housed and handled separately from offenders.
* Universities and colleges should, with governmental and private participation and support, develop more courses and launch more research studies and projects on the problems of contemporary corrections.

Organized Crime

THE COMMISSION RECOMMENDS:

* At least one investigative grand jury should be impaneled annually at each jurisdiction that has major organized crime activity.
* Congress should enact legislation dealing specifically with wiretapping and bugging.
* Every attorney general in states where organized crime exists should form in his office a unit of attorneys and investigators to gather information and assist in prosecution regarding this criminal activity.
* Police departments in every major city should have a special intelligence unit solely to ferret out organized criminal activity and to collect information regarding the possible entry of criminal cartels into the area's criminal operations.
* The prosecutor's office in every major city should have sufficient manpower assigned full time to organize crime cases. Such personnel should have the power to initiate organized crime investigations and to conduct the investigative grand juries mentioned above.
* The federal government should create a central computerized office into which each federal agency would feed all of its organized crime intelligence.
* Groups should be created within the federal and state departments of justice to develop strategies and enlist regulatory action against businesses infiltrated by organized crime.
* Private business associations should develop strategies to prevent and uncover organized crime's illegal and unfair business tactics.
* Enforcement officials should provide regular briefings to leaders at all levels of government concerning organized crime conditions within the jurisdiction.

Narcotics and Drug Abuse

THE COMMISSION RECOMMENDS:

* Research should be undertaken devoted to early action on the further development of a sound and effective framework of regulatory and criminal laws with respect to dangerous drugs. In addition, research and educational programs concerning the effects of such drugs should be undertaken.
* The enforcement and related staff of the Bureau of Customs should be materially increased.
* The enforcement staff of the Bureau of Narcotics should be ma-

terially increased. Some part of the added personnel should be used to design and execute a long-range intelligence effort aimed at the upper echelons of the illicit drug traffic.

Drunkenness Offenses

THE COMMISSION RECOMMENDS:

* Drunkenness should not in itself be a criminal offense. Disorderly and other criminal conduct accompanied by drunkenness should remain punishable as separate crimes. The implementation of this recommendation requires the development of adequate civil detoxification procedures.
* Communities should establish detoxification units as part of comprehensive treatment programs.
* Research by private and governmental agencies into alcoholism, the problems of alcoholics, and methods of treatment should be expanded.

Science and Technology

THE COMMISSION RECOMMENDS:

* Police call boxes should be designated "public emergency call boxes," should be better marked and lighted, and should be left unlocked.
* Whenever practical, a single police telephone number should be established, at least within a metropolitan area and eventually over the entire United States, comparable to the telephone company's long-distance information number.
* Frequencies should be shared through the development of larger and more integrated police mobile radio networks.
* Police departments should undertake data collection and experimentation programs to develop appropriate statistical procedures for manpower allocation.
* A National Criminal Justice Statistics Center should be established in the Department of Justice. The center should be responsible for the collection, analysis, and dissemination of two basic kinds of data:
  Those characterizing criminal careers, derived from carefully drawn samples of anonymous offenders.
  Those on crime and the system's response to it, as reported by the criminal justice agencies at all levels.
* A federal agency should be assigned to coordinate the establishment of standards for equipment to be used by criminal justice agencies and to provide these agencies technical assistance.

* The federal government should encourage and support the establishment of operations research staffs in large criminal justice agencies.
* A major scientific and technological research program within a research institute should be created and supported by the federal government.
* Criminal justice agencies, such as state court and correctional systems and large police departments, should develop their own research units, staffed by specialists and drawing on the advice and assistance of leading scholars and experts in relevant fields.[22]

Summary

This chapter has been a brief introduction to various components of the criminal justice system. Tremendous increases in crime and the increased formalization of the system of dealing with juvenile delinquents and arrested criminals have progressively burdened every single part of the system. What may have worked in the past to address our problems in the administration of justice no longer works as well as was originally intended. Perhaps a lot of our methods did not work well in the past either, but we just pretended they did. Dramatic improvements in the system have been recommended and undoubtedly will be attempted by many sincere and dedicated professionals and paraprofessionals. President Richard M. Nixon at the opening session of the National Conference on the Judiciary [23] made the following remarks that echo the views of many professional practitioners:

> If we limit ourselves to calling for more judges, more police, more lawyers operating in the same system, we will produce more backlogs, more delays, more litigation, more jails, and more criminals. "More of the same" is not the answer. What is needed now is genuine reform—the kind of change that requires imagination and daring, that demands a focus on ultimate goals, just as you have indicated imagination and daring and are focusing on ultimate goals.
>
> . . . We must make it possible for each community to train its police to carry out their duties, using the most modern methods of detection and crime prevention. We must make it possible for the convicted criminal to receive constructive training while in confinement, instead of what he receives now usually—an advanced course in crime.

[22] President's Commission on Law Enforcement and the Administration of Justice, *Challenge of Crime in a Free Society* (Washington, D.C.: Government Printing Office, 1967).

[23] This conference was held in Williamsburg, Virginia, March 11, 1971.

The time has come to repudiate once and for all the idea that prisons are warehouses for human rubbish; our correctional systems must be changed to make them places that will correct and educate. Furthermore, we must strengthen the state court systems to enable them to fulfill their historic role as the tribunals of justice nearest and most responsive to the people.

A positive stance has been taken by many professional practitioners in the field of criminal justice, which is reflected in this quotation from the *Correctional Planning Guide,* published in 1969:

> Despite the seriousness of the crime problem today and the increasing challenge in the years ahead, the central conclusion of the Commission is that a significant reduction in crime is possible if the following objectives are vigorously pursued:
>
> *First,* society must seek to prevent crime before it happens by assuring all Americans a stake in the benefits and responsibilities of American life, by strengthening law enforcement, and by reducing criminal opportunities.
>
> *Second,* society's aim of reducing crime would be better served if the system of criminal justice developed a far broader range of techniques with which to deal with individual offenders.
>
> *Third,* the system of criminal justice must eliminate existing inequities if it is to achieve its ideals and win the respect and cooperation of all citizens.
>
> *Fourth,* the system of criminal justice must attract more people and better people—police, prosecutors, judges, defense attorneys, probation and parole officers, and corrections officials with more knowledge, expertise, initiative, and integrity.
>
> *Fifth,* there must be much more operational and basic research into the problems of crime and criminal administration, by those both ·within and without the system of criminal justice.
>
> *Sixth,* the police, courts, and correctional agencies must be given substantially greater amounts of money if they are to improve their ability to control crime.
>
> *Seventh,* individual citizens, civic and business organizations, religious institutions, and all levels of government must take responsibility for planning and implementing the changes that must be made in the criminal justice system if crime is to be reduced.[24]

Essential to the achievement of these objectives is the need to overcome the fragmentation, disunity, and operations of programs at cross-

[24] Law Enforcement Assistance Administration, *Correctional Planning and Resource Guide* (Washington, D.C.: Government Printing Office, 1969), p. 3.

purposes by the multitude of agencies and jurisdictions that are essential supports to law enforcement and corrections.

Exercises and Study Questions

1. Sketch a flow diagram of how the criminal justice system operates in your state.

2. Why is the criminal justice system so often called a "nonsystem"?

3. Where does the primary police power of government to legislate for the health and safety of the people lie?

4. What are the three basic components of the criminal justice system?

5. List at least three objectives of law enforcement that are not included in the list in this chapter.

6. Which has the greater scope of investigative and law enforcement responsibilities—a state or a municipal police agency? Why is this so?

7. What is the highest court in the state court system?

8. Under what conditions may an issue be appealed to the U.S. Supreme Court?

9. What Article of the Bill of Rights provides that the accused shall be represented by counsel in criminal prosecutions?

10. What are the three subunits of the corrections component of the criminal justice system?

11. What is the difference between probation and parole?

12. What is amnesty and who has the authority to grant it?

13. As you see it, what was the basic purpose for the establishment of the President's Commission on Law Enforcement and the Administration of Justice?

14. Recommended semester project: From the recommendations of the President's Commission on Law Enforcement and the Administration of Justice listed in this chapter, choose any twenty and list them. Write a brief explanation for each recommendation, as you see it. Then survey the local criminal justice agencies to see what changes, if any, have taken place. Prepare a report on your survey.

Suggested for Additional Study

President's Commission on Law Enforcement and the Administration of Justice, *Challenge of Crime in a Free Society.* Washington, D.C., Government Printing office, 1967. See also the *Task Force Reports* of this commission.

United States Constitution and the Constitution of the State in which you live.

2

Administration of Justice:
Explanation of Crime

Introduction

A utopian society is virtually impossible. By definition, such a society is
"impossibly and impractically ideal." A citizen's "pursuit of happiness"
is manifested in as many ways as there are people pursuing it in a free
country. Competition and conflict are intrinsic to a society that is characterized by dynamism, materialism, individualism, fierce loyalty to special interest groups, strong social pressures for prestige and affluence,
and differences of opinions and moral standards. Absolute conformity to
unrealistic mores of a nonexistent "perfect" society is neither desirable,
nor is it possible.

In 1806 Patrick Colquhoun observed in his *Treatise on the Police
of the Metropolis*[1] that crime in the London metropolitan area was the
result of bad laws, improper police methods, illness, depraved morals,
bad education, and criminal habits of the lower class of people.

In early America, Richard Quinney, researcher and professor of
criminology, reported:

> American thought is to equate crime with sin, pauperism, and immorality.
> Even when crime was recognized as a distinct phenomenon, it was
> usually regarded as an ill that had no place in social life. Crime was
> one of those conditions that fell within the domain of nineteenth-century
> reformism.[2]

[1] Patrick Colquhoun, *Treatise on the Police of the Metropolis* (London: J. Mow-
man, 1806).

[2] Richard Quinney, *The Problem of Crime* (New York: Dodd, Mead, & Co.,
1970), p. 50.

Criminologists Donald R. Taft and Ralph W. England discuss crime in today's society in their text:

> Both criminal law and crime in the United States express social values, even though not all specific laws are implementations of the mores of the people generally.
>
> Sometimes two sets of values are in conflict; sometimes crime and non-crime are different expressions of the same values. Group loyalty, for example, may be loyalty to a criminal gang or to a community. In American Society, restricted group loyalties are expected and approved. The property owner wishes to keep his property, the thief to take it away; but both value property, both personally seek the prestige which comes from possessing property, and both crave status in their immediate groups. In a society where material success is a major requisite to social status, there will be more crimes against property and more laws for the protection of property than in a society where less material basis for status is dominant.[3]

Theories of Crime Causes and Effects

Crime is related to various needs and how people go about satisfying those needs in many cases. The human maturation process includes a learning pattern. Behavior is governed to some extent by physical, psychological, and social needs and the manner in which the individual seeks to satisfy those needs. Basic physiological needs are for food, water, air, sexual activity, moderate temperature, rest and sleep, elimination of waste products, and reducing or avoiding pain.[4] Psychological needs include love, recognition, affiliation, prestige, popularity, self-esteem, a feeling of well-being, security, and a general freedom from mental and emotional pressures. Social needs may include luxury and comfort, better homes, newer and bigger automobiles, more and costlier clothing, jewelry, and more money to buy the items that serve those needs. Other social needs may include the need to dominate others or a need for power.

Psychologist Henry A. Murray[5] listed twenty basic needs to the individual's personality structure including many of those already listed. His list contains these additional needs:

[3] Donald R. Taft and Ralph W. England, Jr., *Criminology*, 4th Ed. (New York: Macmillan Co., 1964).

[4] Ernest R. Hilgard, *Introduction to Psychology* (New York: Harcourt Brace and Co., 1953), p. 104.

[5] Henry A. Murray, *Exploration in Personality* (New York: Oxford University Press, 1938), pp. 158–59.

Achievement: accomplish something difficult or different.

Aggression: overcome opposition, punish or revenge an injury.

Counteraction: overcome a defect or weakness or some difficult obstacle.

Defendance: vindicate the ego.

Defense: emulate a model, a modification of mimicry.

Exhibition: excite, amaze, fascinate, shock, or otherwise make an impression.

Sentience: seek and enjoy sensuous pleasures.

Succorance: be supported, protected, or advised.

As reported in *Psychology Today, An Introduction*,[6] Abraham Maslow, in *Motivation and Personality*[7] has listed five levels of needs and arranged them in heirarchical order, or a *heirarchy of needs* sequence. His thesis is that the more basic levels of needs must first be satisfied before the individual is able to function effectively to strive toward satisfaction of the next level of needs. From lower to higher categories, Maslow's heirarchy appears in the following sequence:

1.   Physiological: thirst, hunger, sex, relaxation, body integrity.
2.   Safety: orderly, safe, consistent, "just."
3.   Love and belongingness: human relationships.
4.   Esteem: achievement, competence, independence, freedom, reputatation, prestige.
5.   Self-actualization: exploitation of talents, capabilities, and potentialities.

As the child matures from childhood to adulthood, he progressively develops his own combination of needs and his own methods for seeking satisfaction of those needs. He learns by doing, by watching others, by studying the methods written and taught by others, and by trial and error. The child learns the many taboos of his own culture that frequently frustrate the drives involved in seeking his goals of satisfaction. The child learns that the pain of punishment may be avoided by minding his parents. As an adult, he learns that sexual satisfaction is sometimes gained by reciprocating for the satisfying experience by assumption of the responsibilities of supporting a wife and children. He also learns that basic sustenance is achieved with reasonably little effort or conflict, but certain minimum requirements must be met, such as work to earn money to spend.

The individual learns to share, to be patient, and to go about satis-

[6] *Psychology Today, An Introduction* (Del Mar, Calif.: CRM, Inc., 1970), pp. 151–52.

[7] Abraham Maslow, *Motivation and Personality* (New York: Harper and Row, Publishers, 1954).

fying those needs in an orderly manner in keeping with the customs and mores of the particular society in which he holds membership.

Frustrations are experienced by the individual, and he learns that he will never satisfy all of his needs. What he must learn is self-control and compromise. He learns to work for his money, study for his education, and to respect the rights and property of others if he is to have them respect his rights and property. He learns that some actions are right and other actions are wrong. There are laws, rules, customs, taboos, regulations, bans, and a variety of agents and agencies to enforce them. Through interaction with others, and with respect to all of these laws and regulations the individual has to obey, the majority of the population somehow manages to develop into law-abiding, socially acceptable members of society. However, many do not seek or attain their goals by lawful means for various reasons.

Cartesian Dichotomy

Rene Descartes (1596–1650), a French philosopher, introduced a theory on crime causes based on a doctrine of free will. Taft and England report:

> Descartes acknowledged that natural laws governed not only events external to man, but also events occurring within him, that is, his own bodily processes of growth, sustenance, and decay.[8]

Descartes' doctrine, which he called the Cartesian Dichotomy, was based on his thesis that the powers of reasoning and willing are divine gifts, setting man apart from all other forms of life.

> Descartes produced a doctrine which helped shape the eventual reformation of criminal law, provided an important rationalization for punishment, and produced an image of man's mental workings which prevails to this day.[9]

This theory appears to be reflected in the classical school theory, which also involves the concept of free choice.

Classical School

Cesare Beccaria (1738–1794) held that the occurrence of crime was based upon a theory of "pain avoidance." Beccaria postulated that a

[8] Taft and England, *Criminology*, p. 61.
[9] Taft and England, *Criminology*, p. 61.

would-be violator of the law weighed the pain or penalty of punishment in comparison with the benefits that he might gain from committing the crime.

> The classical school in criminology represents the culmination of eighteenth century humanitarian rationalism which preceded the application of scientific methods to the study of human behavior.[10]

In Beccaria's home, Italy, his ideas were not very warmly received. In England the theory "caught on" and for a time the classical theory was most prevalent there. There was no provision in punishments prescribed for crimes committed in error or as a result of extenuating circumstances, such as some degree of culpability on the part of the victim.

In 1765 Beccaria published his *Dei delitti e elle pene,* a treatise on crime and punishment that was translated in 1767.[11] His doctrine represented one of the first iterations of the Classical School on crime cause. Principal points of Beccaria's theory were:

> 1. Commission of crime was a matter of free choice on the part of the wrongdoer.
> 2. Hedonism exists in that every individual seeks a maximum of pleasure and avoids pain.
> 3. Punishment for crimes was to satisfy the need for retribution or vengeance but also to serve as a threat of punishment and thus as a deterrent to crimes of a similar nature being planned or considered by others.
> 4. The laws and their punishments had to be published for uniformity and for their deterrent value.
> 5. The length of sentences should be fixed by law and should be uniformly applied in accordance with the violations.
> 6. Children and the insane could not be charged as criminals.

Herbert A. Bloch and Gilbert Geis explained their view of Beccaria's school of thought:

> Permeating this doctrine was the powerful conception that man could determine his own destiny and political future by the controlled use of reason and the accumulation of knowledge based on rational discourse rather than on fear and superstition—a conception nurtured by a line of distinguished philosophers beginning with Thomas Hobbes.[12]

[10] Quinney, *The Problem of Crime,* p. 46.

[11] Quinney, *The Problem of Crime,* p. 46.

[12] Herbert A. Bloch and Gilbert Geis, *Man, Crime, and Society,* 2nd ed. (New York: Random House, 1970), p. 85.

Jeremy Bentham (1742–1832), an English philosopher and jurist, "engendered the so-called Classical School," according to Taft and England:

> Almost totally divorced from theological dogma, this school maintained (1) that the seriousness of crimes should be measured by their respective social harm rather than by their "sinfulness" or other transcendental qualities and (2) that crime is caused by the *rational* efforts of men to augment their pleasures and to minimize their pains.[13]

Bentham's philosophy was to establish:

> . . . for each crime a punishment whose pains would outweigh any possible pleasure to be gained from them and by assuring the certain and swift administration of justice, rational men, deterred by the realization that a net loss will inevitably result from a criminal act, will refrain from breaking the law.[14]

The Lombrosian Theory of Criminality

Cesare Lombroso (1836–1909) was another early Italian criminologist who focused his attention on the individual when attempting an explanation of crime. His basic premise was that a person was a "born criminal," or a criminal by heredity.

Lombroso, a professor of legal medicine at the University of Turin, classified criminals by their physical characteristics. According to his theory, there were three basic classes of criminals: born criminals, insane criminals, and criminaloids. The criminal was a degenerate, or defective in some way, an atavistic "throwback" to a more primitive and savage man.[15]

Quinney said of Lombroso and his contemporaries:

> Their approach to the study of crime was positivistic in that they utilize the point of view and methodology of the natural sciences. . . . While the Classical School emphasized the idea of the choice of right and wrong, the positive school placed the emphasis on the determination of conduct.[16]

[13] Taft and England, *Criminology,* pp. 61–62.
[14] Taft and England, *Criminology,* pp. 61–62.
[15] Quinney, *The Problem of Crime,* p. 59.
[16] Quinney, *The Problem of Crime,* p. 57.

Individual Explanations of Crime

Some theoreticians attributed crime to mental retardation or psychosis, epilepsy, emotional disturbances, or "moral insanity." For several hundred years the approach was to study crime causation or explanation by formulating a theory by which the criminals could be categorized and their behavior explained on the basis of such categorization. The trend during the past several decades has been to study each person as an individual rather than as a unit in a category.

There is no battery of tests that will identify a "born" or a potential criminal, which further negates a variety of hypotheses about propensities for criminality. Studies to date have shown that there is nothing substantial to report when comparing known criminals and persons who have no arrest records in several areas of study where such comparison has been attempted. There is no correlation in temperament, physical maturity, emotional maturity, and only a slight correlation indicated when the entire personality is surveyed by means of the Rorschach (ink blot) test. It has been found that the sociopath, or psychopathic personality, has a greater propensity for the formation of criminal behavior patterns if the individual so identified is allowed to develop these patterns.

The sociopath is described as extremely self-centered, impulsive, aggressive toward society, and having an attitude of omnipotence. He has no feelings of conscience, and he lacks what Freud defines as superego, which consists of a combination of conscience, fair-mindedness, empathy, and social sensitivity. To the true sociopath, only those laws that are agreeable to him and that he chooses to obey seem to restrict him in any way. Although not all sociopaths are criminals—or all criminals sociopaths—there is a predisposition to the formulation of criminal behavior patterns.

The modern sociologist's point of view regarding criminal behavior is that many factors with a variety of combinations go together to cause a person to commit a criminal act and then to go on to live his life as a criminal. Some early criminologists attempted to prove that single traits were determinants of criminal behavior. Let us look at some of the factors they attempted to authenticate with well-chosen source material.

Heredity. Specific families with extensive criminal histories, such as the "celebrated" Jukes family, were used to illustrate the point. Out of 1200 family members studied by Richard L. Dugdale in 1877, 140 were criminals, 7 of whom were convicted murderers, some 60 were thieves, and the balance were prostitutes. This study shows better than 10 percent criminality in one family.

Although Dugdale, who was an inspector for the New York Prison Association, presented his "evidence" of hereditary degeneracy, he wrote:

> The tendency of heredity is to produce an environment which perpetuates that heredity; thus, the licentious parent makes an example which greatly aids in fixing habits of debauchery of the child. The correction is change of environment.[17]

Heredity should not be ruled out completely by the serious student of crime and its causes. Many distinguished geneticists have made valuable contributions to the study of inherited traits, which indicate that heredity cannot be eliminated as a factor in the influence one's ancestors have on his personal behavior.[18]

Phrenology. Some attempts have been made to correlate criminality with the configuration of bumps or bone structure of the skull, with physical deformities, ugliness, and a variety of similar single factors. Current literature and news items occasionally refer to studies under way to evaluate social or criminogenic personality changes that accompany corrective plastic surgery. The impact of an individual's new self-image is sometimes dramatic and has ameliorative value.

Body Shape and Criminal Propensity. In 1949 William H. Sheldon published his *Varieties of Delinquent Youth*,[19] in which he used three basic types of body configurations as an explanation of differences in personality and behavior. He classified the "soft and round" body as *endomorphic*, the muscular and angular body as *mesomorphic*, and the thin and gaunt body as *ectomorphic*. He had studied 200 delinquent youths and reported that his study identified the mesomorphic and endomorphic individuals as having stronger tendencies toward delinquency than the ectomorphic youths. He also stated that the potential delinquent could be classified by this method by age six.

---

[17] Richard L. Dugdale, *The Jukes: A Study in Crime, Pauperism, Disease, and Heredity* (New York: G. P. Putnam and Sons, 1877).

[18] Summaries of studies of genetics may be found in virtually any psychology or biology text. An interesting explanation of behavior genetics may be found in *Psychology Today: An Introduction*, pp. 163–80.

[19] William H. Sheldon, *Varieties of Delinquent Youth* (New York: Harper and Brothers, 1949).

Biological Explanations of Crime.   The study of genetics is essential to the study of criminal behavior as has already been mentioned. Along similar veins of study, many serious researchers are seeking clues to physical characteristics of the criminal so that perhaps some alteration of those characteristics might serve to prevent development of "criminal personalities." Although studies have not yet proven the information scientifically significant, at least one 1969 article by J. I. Rodale reported several cases in which asocial behavior and an imbalance of blood sugar were found to have some correlation.[20]

XYY Chromosome Syndrome.   One more recent theory has received some publicity (1968–1969). It involves an XYY chromosomal structure in certain males, an excess of male characteristics and aggressive tendencies, and a stronger tendency to commit crimes of sexual aggression and violence.

An Australian murder case in 1968 was alleged by one press release to have been decided on the basis of this chromosomal imbalance, but later it was referred to by the attorney who prosecuted the case as the "myth of Melbourne."[21] In that case, the phenomenon was mentioned only once and had no significant effect on the decision. In an earlier murder case in France, a convicted murderer's sentence was for seven years instead of the usual fourteen. In that case the XYY syndrome was introduced into the trial, but the decision contained no statement about that factor. What did happen, however, was that this avenue of study pointed the way to further research that may significantly lead to additional explanations of crime from a biological standpoint.[22]

Low Mentality and Crime.   Theories of low mentality and criminal tendencies have been postulated at various times by criminologists. Henry H. Goddard, one of America's distinguished proponents of the psychological school of crime causation, related mental deficiency to crime. In 1914 he estimated that more than 50 percent of all criminals were feebleminded.[23] In a later book, Goddard stated:

[20] J. I. Rodale, "Does Sugar Make Criminals?" *Prevention,* April 1969, pp. 107–14.

[21] *Los Angeles Times,* Feb. 3, 1969, Sec. D, p. 3.

[22] A brief reference to this theory appears in *Psychology Today: An Introduction,* p. 507. See also National Institute for Mental Health, *Report on the XYY Chromosome Abnormality* (Washington, D.C.: Government Printing Office, 1970), p. 5, in which this statement appeared: ". . . it seems most important that rather critical legal, social policy and related decisions should not become firm or rigid prior to the development of more adequate and definitive research findings."

[23] Henry H. Goddard, *Feeblemindedness: Its Causes and Consequences* (New York: Macmillan Co., 1914), p. 37.

It is no longer to be denied that the greatest single cause of delinquency and crime is low-grade mentality, much of it within the limits of feeble-mindedness.[24]

Although it may be a popular view held by many observers, an experienced police practioner will discount the theory on the basis of his own investigations. Many crimes are the culmination of well-laid plans by intelligent individuals carried out with extreme cleverness and cunning. Many crimes of embezzlement and "confidence" type situations are sometimes beyond the comprehension and imagination of the average person.

Criminal Ecology

Social ecology has been a topic of serious study by criminologists for many years. Man's environment and the influences it plays on his behavior is considered one of the most significant of the crime cause factors that demands understanding by the professional criminal justice practitioner. Although the methods of statistical computation were undoubtedly crude when compared with our modern data systems, studies of criminal ecology were underway in the early 1800s.

Richard Quinney recounts that foremost among the ecology researchers of the 1830s was Alexander von Oeltingen of Germany, who addressed the problems of crime measurement in his *Moralstatistick*. Adolphe Que'telet studied the social nature of crime as reflected in crime statistics in Belgium. Using maps, A. M. Guerry, who was in charge of judicial statistics for Paris, analyzed crime rates for the various regions of France.

In England there were some studies of the social changes related to the urbanization of that country during the industrial development of the country.[25] Rowson W. Rowson published one study in 1839, *An Inquiry Into the Statistics of Crime in England and Wales*. Other English criminal ecology theorists of about the same era included Joseph Fletcher, Henry Mayhew, John Glyde, and John T. Burt.[26]

Fletcher's theory was that criminals were developed by a process of apprenticeship in certain neighborhoods, prisons, and jails. He opposed the argument that crime was caused by poverty, ignorance, and

[24] Henry H. Goddard, *Human Efficiency and Levels of Intelligence* (Princeton: Princeton University Press, 1920), p. 74.

[25] Quinney, *The Problem of Crime*, p. 47.

[26] Quinney, *The Problem of Crime*, p. 48.

population density. Mayhew's study involved a comparison of the locations where crimes were committed and the residences of criminals. Glyde studied population density in relationship to crime in Suffolk. In 1863, Burt suggested that criminals came from criminal classes that already existed.

In his excellent book, Quinney observed:

> The writers of this period, 1860 to 1885, viewed crime as a product of "disharmony" in the operation of social forces, "constituents," or institutions of society. . . . In their explanation of crime in terms of social conditions, most of the writers assumed that the operation of any one factor could only partially explain the phenomenon of crime. While they pointed to associations, they believed that a multiplicity of social causes operated to produce crime. Of the many factors considered, most popular in the explanation of crime were drinking, lack of trade education, desire for luxuries, poverty, oblivion of religious and moral principles, idleness, abnormal family relations, bad company, and, in general, civilizations.[27]

In the United States it became particularly evident in some of the larger cities that there were certain neighborhoods or larger parts of the city that had more crime and spawned a disproportionate percentage of delinquents and criminal law violators.

The Committee for Economic Development made the following statements regarding the ecology of crime:

> The highest crime rates, five to ten times those for rural areas, are found in the congested centers of great cities, in association with a long list of other social ills. Housing there is generally substandard, often unfit for habitation; unemployment is endemic, especially among the young; health and sanitation services are weak; many of the public schools are demoralized, with heavy drop-out rates; and deep poverty is pervasive.

> Relatively high rates of juvenile delinquency have occurred consistently over a long period of time in central city slum areas, regardless of their social and ethnic constituencies. Delinquent behavior is often considered "normal" and socially acceptable there, while non-delinquent behavior may seem abnormal. Many parents strive to overcome these influences, but family and social sanctions are ineffective against peer-group support for unlawful conduct. Spontaneous criminality and easy recruitment by organized syndicates frequently result.[28]

---

[27] Quinney, *The Problem of Crime*, p. 48.

[28] Research and Police Committee of the Committee for Economic Development, *Reducing Crime and Assuring Justice* (New York: Committee for Economic Development, 1972).

One of the pioneers in the study of criminal ecology in America was Clifford K. Shaw. The object of his study was the city of Chicago, Illinois. Actually, Shaw and his colleagues conducted a number of studies that were reported in detail in a series of publications.[29]

Shaw's long-term study involved his use of pin maps. He located on the maps the residences of approximately 56,000 delinquent children and adults of both sexes.

The studies by Shaw and others showed that certain neighborhoods housed disproportionate percentages of delinquent children and criminal adults. Those neighborhoods were characterized by disorganization and congestion and "anomie," an absence of social influence or controls. The neighborhoods were in the center of town, adjacent to industry and commerce. During the Industrial Revolution and the accompanying mass migration to the cities, the people who worked in the factories had to live nearby. The factories depended upon centralized steam power and transportation, and the result was an industrial community of low-priced housing for the laborers. The residential zone immediately adjacent to the factories served as a transition zone. As each new migrant group moved into the city, they resided in the area called Zone I in Shaw's study (a series of concentric circles starting at Zone I and numbered progressively higher as the zones moved out). As the people became more successful, they moved to better neighborhoods, then the next migrants moved in.

Shaw's study, covering a period of over twenty years, showed a succession of several minority groups: Swedish, Syrian, German, Polish, Irish, Jewish, Italian, and Negro. Other studies showed similar trends with New York's most recent immigration of Puerto Ricans. In each of these decadent neighborhoods, a delinquent subculture was developed and has been perpetuated throughout the years by the current residents. There has been a succession of conflicts between the cultures of the newcomers and the dominant groups already in residence. The newcomers have never been welcome, but the "street culture" has continued to be perpetuated and passed on from group to group although there is conflict between the groups.[30]

Taft and England expanded on Shaw's identification of the "criminal zones" and listed seven types of neighborhoods "that are significant for their influence on delinquency." Their list includes (paraphrased):

[29] Clifford K. Shaw, *Delinquency Areas*, 1927; *The Jock-Roller*, 1930; *Natural History of a Delinquent Career*, 1931; *Brothers in Crime*, 1938; *Juvenile Delinquency and Urban Areas*, 1942 (Chicago: University of Chicago Press).

[30] See Taft and England, *Criminology*, p. 156; and Quinney, *The Problem of Crime*, p. 82.

1. A poverty area with fairly normal family organization.

2. The slum, which involves poverty as well as anomie and a heterogeneous population.

3. An interstitial area similar to the slum and shut off from conventional society by some physical or social barrier and involving conflicts of culture in this sort of no man's land.

4. A rooming-house area characterized by impersonal relations.

5. The ghetto, an area occupied by a single minority group.

6. A vice area, a police-protected area where prostitution and gambling go on without intervention by the police.

7. A deteriorated rural area that serves as a hideout or rest area for city gangsters in this type of ghost town.[31]

Crime continues to be explained in terms of social ecology. In September 1970, a report on the training needs of the New York City Police Department explained it thusly:

> With the increasing growth of the suburbs, the central cities have suffered a retardation of population growth. As has well been documented, this demographic shift has left areas of blight and decay in the central cities and has accelerated the social deteriorations in areas of the central cities occupied by minority groups. Projected patterns of growth suggest, in the case of the New York metropolitan region, that these trends will continue. In net, there is rapid growth for the region and slow growth for the central city.[32]

As is the case in the study of crime theory, certain factors must be borne in mind that will temper any overconfidence that the student may invest in such a theory. About the ecological theory, Taft and England observe:

> Delinquent acts of little children may occur near their homes, and in that case their correlation in space may conceivably have some significance for causation. But adult professional crime in these days of easy transportation will occur whenever opportunity for profitable activity is the greatest, which may be hundreds of miles away from the criminals' homes. Hence maps of the home addresses of adult criminals at the time of their acts need not even suggest possible causal influences.

> All such studies are in serious difficulties. . . . What we really need to locate is not necessarily the current residence of a criminal but the location of the causes of his criminal patterns of behavior.[33]

[31] Taft and England, *Criminology*, pp. 165–68.

[32] *Police Training and Performance Study*, National Institute of Law Enforcement and Criminal Justice Study PR70–4 (Washington, D.C.: Government Printing Office, 1970), p. 2.

[33] Taft and England, *Criminology*, pp. 153–54.

Multiple Factor Theories

In 1925 Cyril Burt concluded

> Crime is assignable to no single universal source, nor yet to two or three: it springs from a wide variety, and usually from a multiplicity, of alternative and converging influences.[34]

John L. Gillin wrote in 1926 in the way of a social-psychological explanation:

> Hence there is a conspiracy of conditions which account for his becoming a criminal—conditions in his own constitutional make-up, in his early development, in his lack of training, in his poverty, and in the surrounding social atmosphere, including habits, customs, ideals, beliefs, and practices. The social conditions around him set the stage on which each of these factors plays its part and release in his conduct the good or evil in his nature. Thus, is the criminal made.[35]

Differential Association Explanation of Crime

The late Edwin H. Sutherland postulated his genetic explanation of crime, commonly known as his differential association theory and discussed in depth in *Principles of Criminology*.[36] The theory involves environmental influences, ecology, psychological considerations, and sociological principles. The principal premise of the theory is that criminal behavior is learned through interaction with others by means of the same mechanisms that are involved in any other learning process. In capsulated form, the explanation is summed up:

> The specific direction of motives and drives is learned from definitions of the legal codes as favorable or unfavorable. . . . Differential associations

---

[34] Cyril Burt, *The Young Delinquent* (New York: D. Appleton), p. 3.

[35] John L. Gillin, *Criminology and Penology* (New York: The Century Company, 1926), pp. 250–51.

[36] E. H. Sutherland and D. R. Cressey, *Principles of Criminology*, 5th ed. (Philadelphia: J. B. Lippincott Co., 1955), pp. 77–79. The theory first appeared in Sutherland's 3rd edition in 1939, pp. 5–7. Cressey has since updated his own views on this theory but has left it intact so that students may continue to use it as a point of discussion on crime cause theories.

may vary in frequency, duration, priority, and intensity. . . . and a person becomes delinquent because of an excess of definitions favorable to violation of law over definitions unfavorable to violation of law.

Learning crime in the same manner as learning in general prompts reflection on the process of learning itself. Consider the explanation of this process by John Dollard and Neal E. Miller:

> Four factors are exceedingly important in learning. These are: drive, cue, response, and reinforcement. The drive impels responses which are actually channelized by cues from other stimuli not strong enough to act as drives but more specifically distinctive than the drive. If the first response is not rewarded, this creates a dilemma in which the extinction of successive non-reinforced responses leads to so-called random behavior. If some one response is followed by reinforcement, the connection between the stimulus pattern and this response is strengthened, so that the next time the same drive and other cues are present this response is more likely to occur. Since reinforcements presumably produce their effect by reducing the strength of the drive stimulus, events cannot be rewarding in the absence of the appropriate drive. After the drive has been satiated by sufficient reward, the tendency to make the rewarded response is weakened so that other responses occur until the drive reappears.[37]

Reference Group Theory

Dr. Martin R. Haskell, criminologist at California State University, Long Beach, introduced a sociopsychological explanation of crime that he calls the reference group theory.[38] He offers six propositions as an explanation of this theory:

1. The family is the first personal reference group of the child.
2. The family is a normative reference group. (The norm conforms to the larger society.)
3. Prior to his participation in a delinquent act, the delinquent boy adopts a street group as a personal reference group.
4. The street group that becomes the personal reference group of the lower class boy in New York has a delinquent subculture.
5. A boy for whom the street group is a personal reference group is

[37] John Dollard and Neal E. Miller, *Personality and Psychotherapy—An Analysis in Terms of Learning, Thinking, and Culture* (New York: McGraw-Hill Book Co., Inc., 1950), p. 47.
[38] M. R. Haskell, "Toward a Reference Group Theory," *Social Problems*, Winter 1960–61.

likely, in the dynamic assessment preceding a delinquent act, to decide in favor of the delinquent act.

6. The individual tends, as a member of a personal reference group, to impart into its context attitudes and ways of behaving that he is currently holding in sociogroup life.

Additional Crime Incidence Factors

AGE AND CRIME

The national statistics show a direct correlation between youth and crime. It is a young man's folly, so it would seem to the observer of crime statistics. Commission of crime by the young, as shown by the statistics, is not new, and it seems to be related to the physical condition, amount of leisure time, and the economic dependence of the young offender. On a line graph, the crest would appear between eighteen and thirty years with a sharp rise and decline between nineteen and twenty-five. The drop is gradual to about thirty-five, then a sharp decline to age forty-five and above.

SEX RATIOS

In the United States women enjoy virtually the same freedom as men, while in other countries there are some women who enjoy no freedom at all. The crime rates for women in the United States are also higher than in other countries. The ratio of women arrested compared to men is about one to ten, and the types of crimes they commit have about the same ratio, except for those offenses that are associated with the sex difference.

RACIAL DIFFERENCES

The nonwhite criminal versus the white shows a disproportionate ratio, with the highest rate of arrests per thousand population appearing among the Negro. Attempts to show atavistic traits of the Negro offender have demonstrated no correlation, which indicates that the higher rate should be attributed to such factors as economic and environmental influences more than any "throwback to barbarism" or other expressions of bigotry. The National Advisory Commission on Civil Disorders commented on the statistics that show low-income black areas with "significantly higher crime rates than low-income white areas." [39] "This reflects," state Bloch and Geis, "the high degree of social disorganization in the Negro areas as well as the fact that poor Negroes, as a group, have lower incomes than poor whites, as a group."

The Report of the National Advisory Commission on Civil Disorders includes the following statement:

> The record before this Commission reveals that the causes of recent racial disorders are imbedded in a massive tangle of issues and circumstances—social, economic, political, and psychological—which arise out of the historical patterns of Negro-white relations in America.
>
> At the base of this mixture are three of the most bitter fronts of white racial attitudes:
>
> Pervasive discrimination and segregation. . . .
>
> Black migration and white exodus. . . .
>
> Black ghettos.[40]

In his book *Man's Most Dangerous Myth*, Ashley Montagu stated that the belief in racial superiority and inferiority is, according to most geneticists, wholly lacking in factual basis.[41]

CLIMATE AND UNUSUAL WEATHER CONDITIONS

The opportunity for more frequent people-to-people contacts, and thus more opportunities for criminal acts, will arise more often in the warmer climates than in the arctic. Unusual "hot spells" are also related to the greater incidence of crimes of violence. However, there are many factors other than heat that are involved, such as more personal interaction among people and more opportunities for conflict, increased leisure time, and greater amounts of alcoholic beverages consumed during the very hot days and nights.

One early theory by Peter Kropotkin was somewhat more complicated but had a more "scientific" flavor. Kropotkin's method was to predict crime by analysis of temperature and humidity:

> By the statistics of previous years one could foretell with astonishing exactness the number of crimes to be committed during the following year in every country in Europe. . . . merely by consulting the thermometer

[39] As reported by Bloch and Geis, *Criminology*, p. 267.

[40] Report of the National Advisory Commission on Civil Disorders (Washington, D.C.: Government Printing Office, 1968), pp. 9–11.

[41] Ashley Montagu, *Man's Most Dangerous Myth* (New York: Columbia University Press, 1942).

and hygrometer. Take the average temperature of the month and multiply it by seven, then add the average humidity, multiply again by two and you will obtain the number of homicides that are committed during the month.[42]

COMPOSITION OF THE POPULATION

Age, race, and sex ratios in a community are directly related to crime rates. A homogeneous community of longstanding stability will have less conflict than the dynamic community with a wide variety of racial, ethnic, and cultural differences. The younger population will have had less time to attain the stability level of the older members of the community.

RELATIONSHIP OF THE POLICE TO THE COMMUNITY

The method of selection and retention of the police officers has a direct relationship to the image of the entire department and the attitudes of both the citizenry and the police officers themselves. The number of policemen per thousand population has a direct bearing upon the effectiveness of the police. Enforcement policies as articulated by the chief have a similar impact on the community.

Commissioner Patrick V. Murphy of the New York City Police Department stated in 1970:

> The police service relies on the theory that we are essentially an honest and peaceful society, and that most people voluntarily comply with the law. The presumption that we are a peace-loving people may be a fallacy.[43]

Although taken out of context of the entire speech, the rhetoric reflects the question asked repeatedly by many administrators: How are we to address the increasingly difficult challenge of the mushrooming crime problem? If we are not to presume the majority of the people we serve to be peaceful and law-abiding, then are the police to become an army of occupation? Within the framework of our present existence, there must be a considerable amount of mutual trust and respect.

---

[42] Reported by Bernaldo de Quiras, *Modern Theories of Criminology* (Boston: Little, Brown, & Co., 1911), p. 34.

[43] From a speech in December 1970, as reported in the *Los Angeles Times*, December 13, 1970, Sec. H, p. 1.

SOCIAL ATTITUDES

Contempt or disregard for the law has been a trend in many communities: One has only to read a newspaper to see that flagrant acts of criminal behavior occur under the guise of so-called peaceful demonstrations or similar affairs. A vocal minority is involved in such lawlessness, but they are capable of being a troublesome minority. The general attitude of the community will be reflected in the actions of the juries and the courts in such cases when arrests are made. "Moral holidays" occur when certain acts that would otherwise be considered crimes are sometimes allowed to occur because of the "temper of the crowd" or the spirit of the occasion. Halloween has been regarded by many people as a moral holiday when certain minor acts of vandalism may be considered "in the spirit of the day."

Bookies and operators of houses of prostitution may earn hundreds of dollars a day, and sometimes considerably more, but they may receive suspended sentences or be required to pay small fines when found guilty of their crimes. The action is explained by a statement such as "they didn't hurt anyone," or "their victims were just as guilty as they were," or "it's only a minor crime." All of these factors are directly related to the incidence rates of all crimes in any given community. The community with a consensus that indicates a desire for a corruption-free government will reflect that attitude in the people who hold office in that community.

ECONOMIC AND SOCIAL CRISES

Personal acquisition of property and vigorous business practices perpetuate an attitude of competition. Personal prestige is gauged by many people on the basis of personal wealth. Some people cannot acquire such wealth by legal means, and will cheat, steal, and amass great fortunes in other unethical and illegal ways. White-collar criminals use their businesses and professions as a means to acquire wealth by criminal means, and the professional and career criminals make a business or profession out of crime. Many criminals in all three categories of crime—white-collar, professional, and career—have been eulogized. Witness the influence of peddlers and politicians who have been staunchly defended in spite of their flagrant criminal acts and hailed as heroes.

Contrary to what one might believe would occur during an economic depression, the rates of property crimes do not rise. Instead, they go down. One reason for this downward trend may be that there is a less significant difference between the relative wealth of the classes. In times of affluence, the gap is greater, and the crime rates go up.

There is a correlation between the economic stature of the arrested criminal and his crimes; although, the fact that he is impoverished is not a sure predictor that the poor man will commit crimes. Most criminologists theorize that the correlation is more likely to be the result of the living patterns of the poor and their environment of frequent contacts with the delinquent subculture that exists in impoverished areas.

Commissioner Murphy, in the same speech referred to earlier in this chapter, stated:

> George Bernard Shaw once wrote that security cannot exist where the danger of poverty hangs over everyone's head. Poverty degrades the poor and infects with its degradation the whole neighborhood in which they live. And whatever can degrade a neighborhood can degrade an entire civilization. In this context, poverty is a burden not only on the poor but also on every intermediate level of our social and economic structure.

MOBILITY

The basic family group is not static in most of the growing urban communities and no longer serves as the primary reference group for many individuals. Mass communication and transportation have caused the individual to become a part of the larger society in general instead of his own family and neighborhood. He seeks entertainment, employment, and recreation wherever he chooses, and he may move away from home with no provocation. He may move to a city where he is comparatively free from the social and ethical pressures imposed by his peers and those who have exercised authority over him. Community responsibility is lacking in the transient. Although he may not become a criminal, the transient has no social ostracism to face if he does.

Types of Criminal Behavior

When one studies crime, its causes, effects, and all of the many related aspects, it is also necessary to study the types of criminal law violator. The most distinctive method used to study the criminal is to study him as an entity unto himself, an individual who commits an act or is guilty of an omission that is defined in the legal codes as a criminal offense. This individualistic approach is not invalid, but for the busy police science student and police practitioner this method is too time-consuming. A less exacting but still valid method for studying the criminal is by category. When using this method, however, one must not lose sight of the fact that the subcategories vary with personal differences.

The categories that we shall consider in this chapter are the "circumstantial" or first offender, the career criminal, the professional, the white-collar criminal, and those persons who are involved in organized crime. One other category shall be designated as "exceptional offenders" and includes the sex offender, narcotics-users, and the various other persons who violate the laws more frequently than accidental offenders.

THE CIRCUMSTANTIAL OFFENDER

Traffic law violations are classified as crimes in most instances. They are prohibited or required by law and are enforced by penal sanctions of fine and/or imprisonment. Some of the offenses listed in the traffic codes are classified as felonies. Except for such offenses as those felonies that may involve some deliberate act, the traffic violator generally falls into the circumstantial offender category. The vast majority of other criminal law violators are also classified in this category.

Although probably less than 1 percent of the entire U.S. population has a record of formal charges for nontraffic criminal violations, the number still adds up to millions. The circumstantial criminal may have been detained as a juvenile or arrested as an adult or both. He is usually a first offender, or "first arrest," and his first official *recognized criminal act* becomes a matter of record.

The circumstantial offender may have committed any of a thousand or so offenses, such as one of the following. (1) A young man is several miles from home and has just lost his bus fare. His parents will be expecting him in a few minutes and his dinner will be waiting. As he walks along—despondent and frustrated—he sees a bicycle on the sidewalk. The young man knows that stealing is wrong, but he rationalizes that he is not going to steal the bike. He's just going to ride it a few blocks and drop it, just enough to get him home on time. A criminal? He may repeat the action two or three times before his misdeeds come to the attention of the police and, subsequently, the juvenile court. (2) A young man is goaded into defending the honor of his charming female companion by striking an antagonistic "loud mouth." As the police officer arrives on the scene, he sees only the physical attack and did not witness the disturbance of the peace. (3) One of the most common of all "accidental offenders" is the shoplifter who commits a theft on impulse because of the combination of temptation and opportunity.

The circumstantial offender is one who usually commits his crime without premeditation or design prior to the act, but because of the circumstances as they occur at the time, all of the elements of the crime are present and the violator becomes another statistic. Because of the larger number of circumstantial, or accidental, offenders, they give the police the greatest problems. They often commit one offense and never repeat. Many of them do not develop patterns that lead to their identification, and they are not discovered. When they are apprehended, their cases are appropriately adjudicated. Unless they develop asocial or criminal behavior patterns, they are seldom heard from again, but there are thousands more who take their places on the court calendars and "police blotters." Their offenses are unpredictable and there seems to be little the police can do to prevent them except by maintaining a constant and vigilant patrol.

CAREER CRIMINALS

The career criminal is a failure. He spends a lifetime in and out of custody. Although the offender who falls into this category may be difficult to distinguish from the professional criminal, specialists do make the distinction on the basis of individual personalities of the violators rather than their crimes.

Crime is a way of life to the offender in this category, and it usually starts at a very early age. Exactly where and when he was indoctrinated into a life of crime varies, but it is usually during adolescence. The "street culture" or "delinquent subculture" is part of the child's environment, and if the child's activities and attitudes are not directed toward lawful and socially accepted activities and attitudes, his life of crime usually begins.

The career criminal is in the lower levels of the criminal class structure. He is a misfit in the law-abiding community. He develops and maintains social and "business" relationships that help him eke out a living in his own parasitic way and that protect him from discovery and apprehension as long as possible.

If he were to be identified by his crime specialty, the career criminal is usually found in the category of "property" offenders. Because he is not willing or able to consistently make a living by lawful means, he must make a profit out of his crimes. The individual who commits murder for a living may be classified in this category, but he is not likely to continue such employment for as long a period of time as other criminals because of his particular specialty. The career criminal is usually a

burglar, a robber, petty thief, a dealer in stolen cars, or a check man. Whatever his crime, the career criminal is a specialist and his arrest record will generally reflect a series of similar offenses.

PROFESSIONAL CRIMINAL

There are a few factors that distinguish the professional from the career criminal, the most significant of which is the comparable degrees of success. The career criminal's record usually shows a long series of arrests and delinquency since childhood; the professional criminal's record is free from such a pattern. Any arrest record that he may have will show comparatively lower frequency and—in all probability—a lower percentage of convictions for those arrests. The professional can be so classified on the basis of his comparative proficiency and success.

The professional criminal does not consider himself a criminal, and he is not likely to associate with other persons who are criminals. He is an assimilationist, blending himself into the total community in a respectable middle-class environment, and his friends and associates are respectable citizens, frequently leaders in business and government.

A police officer may refer to a frequently arrested shoplifter, pickpocket, or burglar as a professional thief. Actually, it may be largely a matter of semantics to attempt to distinguish between the two, but for the sake of keeping the two classes apart in this chapter, I suggest that you consider the professional as one who is more apt to commit the more sophisticated crimes of theft by fraud, embezzlement, and confidence games, and such burglaries as those involving the "cracking" of safes and high-value losses that require skill and planning. The professional is more difficult to identify as a criminal because he is usually prepared to register surprise or indignation when found out and will make apologies or restitution because of "this terrible mistake." He may have influential friends who make excuses for him and whom he uses—probably without their awareness of the fact that they are being used—to get him out of his troubles. The professional criminal is also prepared for his defense, and it is not unusual for him to buy witnesses and to be represented by high-priced attorneys.

White-Collar Crime

As a contrast to the professional criminal, who makes a business out of his crimes, the white-collar criminal makes a crime out of his business. This category includes the businessman and professional who violate the criminal statutes during the normal course of their business. Crimes

by employees committed against their employers may be regarded by some experts as white-collar crime, such as the bank official who is finally indicted for embezzlement of hundreds of thousands of dollars of the bank's money over a period of several years.

White-collar crimes as referred to in this chapter include such offenses as price-fixing by so-called "competing" corporations, making false statements in income tax claims, making fraudulent advertising schemes, selling food supplement and vitamin pills or energy potions that do not do what they are purported to do for the body. Other white-collar crimes include adding water to frozen food products, false labeling and packaging by butchers and grocers, and many fraudulent practices carried on by virtually every type of business and profession in existence. Some lending institutions manage to collect more than the legal interest rate; some attorneys charge for investigative services that are never performed; some doctors charge their patients for drugs that are not actually administered; and some politicians keep their well-oiled machines running on their constituents' gasoline. Most of these crimes are not detected, and relatively little punitive action is taken.

How is it that in this society the white-collar criminals can get away with their offenses, sometimes flaunting violations with what appears to be absolute impunity, and get fat off the naiveté of the public? To put this problem in its true perspective, it is first essential to point out that the number of observers who would ask this question are obviously in the minority. It is simply a matter of fact that a generally accepted attitude with regard to white-collar crimes is one of detached passivity. The phrase *caveat emptor* (translated as "let the buyer beware") has been applied in the attitudes of many agencies, including the courts, toward the victims of white-collar crimes. Although they are in the statutes as crimes, the white-collar crimes are not prosecuted or otherwise handled in the same manner as those of burglars and robbers.

Although there have been some notable exceptions, the president of a law-breaking corporation is not likely to be sent to jail for a violation of the Sherman Antitrust Act. Many studies have been made of this subject, and the consensus of the criminologists who have studied white-collar crime is that a preponderance of the larger corporations in the United States in nearly every category, including banking, manufacturing, mining, securities, mercantile, and numerous others have not only been guilty of criminal offenses and sustained little or no punitive action, but they have been constant repeaters over a period of several years.

White-collar criminality is deleterious for the entire community. It enriches the pocketbooks of the people who commit the offenses, but common knowledge throughout the community that such a situation exists and that the violator is not impugned or punished in any manner because of his political or monetary power or because of a lack of sufficient evidence to prove the offense or for any other reason causes the people in the community to develop their own standards and ethical values accordingly. The "guy who cheats a little bit" is really not too bad when he has the biggest house, the biggest cars, the most money, and the greatest social prestige in town. The white-collar law violator, people rationalize, is not *really* committing a *serious* crime. Nobody is getting hurt. The man is a good citizen otherwise and, therefore, is not a criminal but a shrewd businessman. Other side effects of "turning the other way" when it comes to white-collar crimes are that it reduces respect for the law ("laws are only for fools" or "laws are made to be broken") and for the entire system of the administration of justice.

One example of the general attitude of the lawmakers toward one type of white-collar crime is the Sherman Antitrust Act. Offenders may reap millions of dollars in profits while their punishment—if handled as a crime—is merely for a misdemeanor. Three methods for enforcement of that particular law are (1) criminal prosecution (the last resort although the first alternative), (2) cease and desist orders by the courts upon appeal by the U.S. Attorney General or a state district attorney, or (3) the victims may sue in civil court for damages. Although the offense is a criminal matter, it is most frequently handled as a tort with no penal sanctions involved.

Career criminals, professional criminals, and white-collar criminals are strange bedfellows—who all, for their own peculiar reasons, express contempt for the laws, for government, and for government "bureaucrats." They are all criminals who pose a menace to the peaceful pursuit of happiness in any community.

Organized Crime

Prostitution, gambling, illicit liquor production and distribution, and narcotics trafficking are all "big money" to the underworld. Whenever any of these vice enterprises extends beyond a "single agent" operation, it takes on the characteristics of organization. But it may not be as simple as it appears. Organized crime has its tentacles sunken deeply into virtually every type of criminal operation in the United States. It uses many legitimate businesses as a "cover" to explain the wealth of the organized crime operators and their presence in locations where they can get "a piece of the action" in vice operations.

In his book *Police Administration*, 2nd ed., O. W. Wilson defines organized crime as the combination of two or more persons for the purpose of establishing, in a geographic area, a monopoly or virtual monopoly in a criminal activity of a type that provides a continuing financial profit, using gangster techniques and corruption to accomplish their aim.[44]

In the summer of 1963 a small unobtrusive-looking man of Sicilian descent made a television debut. His name was Joseph Valachi. His act was neither music nor sleight of hand; it was more of a monologue. The storyteller's tale was an awesome one that he presented before the television audience via a U.S. Senate subcommittee hearing. It was all about the machinations of an evil subculture in the United States and other countries that he called "Cosa Nostra," or "our thing," more commonly known as the Mafia.

The Mafia had its early beginning in 1282 in Sicily, when the townspeople of Palermo formed a vigilante group that roamed the countryside killing French soldiers to avenge the rape-slaying of a young bride. The cry of the people was *Morte alla Francia Italia Anela* or "MAFIA," which translated means "Death to the French is Italy's cry." Since that time the Mafia has continued to exist under a variety of conditions. For hundreds of years the predatory band of renegades consisted of heroes to the people of Sicily in the form of an "underground," who harassed the French oppressors. As it exists now, the organization was formed in the eighteenth century as an underground organization to combat the French oppression of the Sicilian people. The Mafia very effectively plundered, robbed, and kidnapped for ransom, and the movement's members and leaders were respected by the citizens as the Robin Hoods of Sicily. After the island was unified as a part of Italy, there was no longer a need for the Mafia underground and they were out of a job. But the band of pirates on the highways and the mountains continued to operate. Their method was the same, but their victims became their own countrymen. The champions became, as a result of political transformation, an organization of notorious criminals.

Many distinguished experts on organized crime in the United States have known of the Mafia in the United States and of its insidious purpose. It was first exposed in this country by New Orleans' Chief of Police, David Hennesey, in 1890, and it is still in existence. Joseph Valachi's testimony concerning the existence of the Mafia, or Cosa Nostra, as he called it, was not as spectacular in its content as it was in its character. The revelation by Valachi was a breach of the code of silence, or "Omerta," by one of the organization's own members.

Although the details of an organization can be carefully laid out

[44] O. W. Wilson, *Police Administration*, 2nd ed. (New York: McGraw-Hill Book Co., Inc., 1963), p. 299.

in orderly fashion, and committee reports and documents prepared by eminent specialists can provide incontrovertible proof that organized crime exists, the direct testimony of one of the co-conspirators had a greater impact and was a more convincing type of proof. Whatever Mr. Valachi's accomplishments may have been in his lifetime, they were eclipsed by his testimony about the Cosa Nostra. It was a most dramatically convincing vehicle, one that provided the millions of television viewers a glimpse at the true story of the Mafia and organized crime.

Dr. Donald R. Cressey wrote the following introduction to the consultant paper he presented to the President's Crime Commission that succinctly outlines the problem of organized crime in the United States:

> In the United States, criminals have managed to organize a nation-wide illicit cartel and confederation. This organization is dedicated to amassing millions of dollars from usury and the illicit sale of lottery tickets, chances on the outcome of horse races and athletic events, and the same on manipulation of sexual intercourse, narcotics, and liquor. Its presence in our society is morally reprehensible because any citizen purchasing illicit goods and services from organized criminals contributes to an underground culture of fraud, corruption, violence, and murder. Nevertheless, criminal organizations dealing only in illicit goods and services are no great threat to the nation. The danger of organized crime arises because the vast profits acquired from the sale of illicit goods and services are being invested in licit enterprises, in both the business sphere and the governmental sphere. It is when criminal syndicates start to undermine basic economic and political traditions and institutions that the real trouble begins. And the real trouble has begun in the United States.[45]

Organized crime has a bureaucratic structure, and in many respects is similar to a large corporation with a franchise system. Two significant differences are the types of businesses involved and the manner in which the business is conducted and the company rules enforced. There is considerable involvement of organized crime in legitimate business, but its principal moneymaking ventures are gambling, narcotics, prostitution, business and labor racketeering, boxing, bootlegging of liquor, and murder. In each of the major metropolitan areas where organized crime flourishes, there is a leader who rules by force and fear. There are no formal organizational manuals or charts, but the members know what areas "belong" to whom and which of the many operators is in charge. The organization is secret, and the secrets are carefully guarded, with death a punishment for their revelation.

[45] Donald R. Cressey, *The Functions and Structure of Criminal Syndicates*, consultant paper to the Task Force on Organized Crime (Washington, D.C.: Government Printing Office, 1967), p. 25.

A capsule look at organized crime may provide some insight into the scope of the problem. Heroin traffic is estimated to cost users in the United States more than $300 million each year. "Lucky" Luciano is alleged to have made a profit of approximately $10 million per year from prostitution and narcotics smuggling prior to his imprisonment and eventual deportation to Italy, from which he continued to operate as a worldwide Mafia leader. Al Capone, a small-time procurer from New York, moved to Chicago and failed to gain admittance into the Mafia but did manage to muscle his way to the top of an organization that yielded for him an annual estimated income of $20 million. In the ten years from 1920 to 1930, one estimate of Capone's earnings showed that he had amassed at least $25 million from gambling, $10 million from prostitution, $10 million in narcotics, and $50 million from the illicit liquor and beer industry that thrived during prohibition. In 1950 Malcolm Johnson wrote of "scarface Al Capone":

> Of all the gangsters who flourished during prohibition, none attained such power and wealth as Scarface Al Capone. This deceptively mild-looking little man with soft brown eyes migrated from Brooklyn to build an empire of crime in Chicago with influential underworld connections throughout the country. It was one of the ironies of the times that Capone enjoyed complete immunity from the law for the reign of terror he invoked. He was never brought to trial for any of his major crimes including the numerable murders committed by his paid gunmen on orders from himself. When the law finally nailed Capone it was for income-tax evasion. He was convicted in 1931, served seven years in prison, then retired to a life of luxury in Florida until his death, or paresis, in January, 1947. Capone's gang lieutenants carried on his organization, which is still active in Chicago.[46]

The Eighteenth Amendment to the U.S. Constitution provided fertile ground for organized crime and its principals. Prohibition was an attempt to change human behavior by legislation, and the people who wished to partake of alcoholic beverages were forced to violate the law to satisfy their wants. Organized crime readily, willingly, and capably provided for the needs of those people who were willing to violate the law to avoid changing their behavior patterns. Organized crime thrived because of the need for a powerful organization that could sustain such an illicit operation in defiance of the law. Organized crime exists when the following factors are present: (1) There is a need for a product or service by a large number of people; (2) society is failing to provide such a

---

[46] Quoted by Gus Tyler, *Organized Crime In America* (Ann Arbor Paperback, University of Michigan Press, 1967).

product or service by lawful means; and (3) there is an organized group ready and willing to provide the product or service.

There have been many investigating teams and committees established and sustained for the purpose of studying the problem of organized crime. Local, regional, and nationwide intelligence units investigate and disseminate to other agencies information concerning organized crime and the many people who comprise its ranks. Varying degrees of success are met in combating organized crime, but it continues to thrive in our society.

During an extensive Senate investigation in 1951, Senator Estes Kefauver and his committee in their *Third Interim Report* reported to an apathetic nation:

> There is a sinister criminal organization known as the Mafia operating throughout the country with ties in other nations, in the opinion of the committee. The Mafia is the direct descendant of a criminal organization of the same name originating in the island of Sicily. In this country, the Mafia has also been known as the Black Hand and the Unione Siciliano. The membership of the Mafia today is not confined to persons of Sicilian origin. The Mafia is a loose-knit organization specializing in the sale and distribution of narcotics, the conduct of various gambling enterprises, prostitution, and other rackets based on extortion and violence. The Mafia is the binder which ties together the two major criminal syndicates as well as numerous other criminal groups throughout the country.[47]
>
> The power of the Mafia is based on a ruthless enforcement of its edicts and its own law of vengeance, to which have been creditably attributed literally hundreds of murders throughout the country.

In their final report, the committee concluded:

> The most shocking revelations of the testimony before the committee is the extent of official corruption and connivance in facilitating and promoting organized crime. Nevertheless, it should not be assumed that our revelations cast doubt as to the integrity of the great preponderance of law enforcement and other officials. On the contrary, our findings and conclusions relate only to a small but disturbing minority of such officials. The committee found evidence of corruption and connivance at all levels of government—Federal, State, and local. . . . The evidence of corruption and connivance with government officials on the state and local levels with organized crime is present in four different forms:
>
> 1. Direct bribe or protection payments (juice) are made to law enforcement officials, so that they will not interfere with specific criminal activities.

[47] Special Committee to Investigate Organized Crime in Interstate Commerce, *Third Interim Report* (Washington, D.C.: Government Printing Office, 1951).

2. Political influence and pressure of important officials or political leaders is used to protect criminal activities or further the interests of criminal gangs.
3. Law enforcement officials are found in possession of unusual and unexplained wealth.
4. Law enforcement officials participate directly in the business of organized crime.[48]

Why does our society allow organized crime in all of its ugliness and with its Saroyan-like characters with the "funny" monickers (Bugsy, Scarface, Two Fingers, Fats, Ducks, Lucky, Trigger, Little Augy, Big John) to continue to thrive like a leech sucking the life blood from a society that cannot spare the blood? It is apparently accepted in a society as a "not-so-ugly" and "not-so-unwanted" syndicated service that has permanently ingratiated itself to a large enough segment of society that it is a necessary part of society—necessary, that is, to those who avail themselves of the goods and services that organized crime provides for them.

The organized crime leaders do not resemble the "common criminal." Cressey explained the difference between the "common" criminal and the organized crime principal for the President's Crime Commission Task Force on Organized Crime:

The basic distinction between ordinary criminals and organized criminals in the United States turns on the fact that the ordinary criminal is wholly predatory, while the man participating in crime on a rational, systematic basis offers a return to the respectable members of society. If all burglars were miraculously abolished, they would be missed by only a few persons to whose income of employment they contribute directly—burglary insurance companies, manufacturers of locks and other security devices, police, prison personnel, and a few others. But if the confederation of men employed in illicit businesses were suddenly abolished, it would be sorely missed because it performs services for which there is a great public demand. The organized criminal, by definition, occupies a position in a social system, an "organization," which has been rationally designed to maximize profits by performing illegal services and providing legally forbidden products demanded by the members of the broader society in which he lives. Just as society has made a place for the confederation by demanding illicit gambling, alcohol and narcotics, usurious loans, prostitution, and cheap supply of labor, the confederation makes places, in an integrated set of positions, for the use of skills in a wide variety of specialists.[49]

[48] Special Committee to Investigate Organized Crime in Interstate Commerce (A Senate Investigating Committee), (Washington, D.C.: Government Printing Office, 1951).

[49] Cressey, *Criminal Syndicates*, p. 29.

Congressional Record, Tuesday, March 11, 1969:

U.S. Senator John McClellan, Chairman of the Subcommittee on Criminal Laws and Procedures in a speech before the U.S. Senate stated:

"Legitimate business is another area into which organized crime has begun most recently and widely to extend its influence. In most cities, it now dominates the fields of juke box and vending machine distribution. Laundry services, liquor and beer distribution, nightclubs, food wholesaling, record manufacturing, the garment industry, and a host of other legitimate lines of endeavor have been invaded and taken over. The Special Senate Committee to Investigate Organized Crime in Interstate Commerce, under the leadership of Senator Estes Kefauver, noted in 1952 that the following industries had been invaded: advertising, amusement, appliances, automobile, baking, ballrooms, bowling alleys, banking, basketball, boxing, cigarette distribution, coal, communications, construction, drug stores, electrical equipment, florists, food, football, garment, gas, hotels, import-export, insurance, jukebox, laundry, liquor, loan, news services, newspapers, oil, paper products, radio, real estate, restaurants, scrap shipping, steel surplus, television, theaters, and transportation." [50]

"Victimless Crimes"

During recent years, considerable discussion and legislative debates have taken place involving crime categories that have been called "crimes without victims," or "victimless crimes." Although laws may be enacted and enforced for what the courts have described as essential for the public health, welfare, and morals, among other considerations, some individuals have assumed the posture that there are certain activities that involve personal habits and private morals. In line with the personal nature of the acts involved, the argument usually evolves around the question as to whether personal choice of consenting adults in their own privacy should be free from legal restraints or whether there should be laws in existence.

The criminal statutes that are usually discussed in this "victimless crime" category usually include prostitution, homosexual and other sexual practices generally described as perverse, obscenity in publication and in exhibitions, gambling, and the abuse of narcotics and dangerous drugs. Depending on the speaker, this list may vary somewhat, but they usually involve a question of private versus public morals. Two of the many views expressed are presented here for your consideration with a view to your own exploration and evaluation.

[50] John McClellan in a speech given before the U.S. Senate, March 11, 1969, as reported in the *Congressional Record*, CXV, No. 43, p. 3.

An American Bar Association committee report presented one view:

> The burdens imposed on the criminal justice system by overcriminalization must be significantly reduced and, where possible, eliminated completely.
>
> a. Legislative reform commissions should be established to consider repeal of laws which define victimless conduct as criminal and which divert the resources needed by the criminal justice system to combat urban crimes.
>
> b. Repeal of such laws should be given top priority by the nation's legislatures.
>
> c. Where appropriate, repeal of laws governing victimless crimes should be accompanied by a strengthening of social agencies most qualified to provide necessary services to those whose conduct is now controlled only by criminal law.[51]

Los Angeles' police chief, Edward M. Davis, had this to say about the matter:

> There have been demands that these so-called "victimless" crimes be legitimized by legislation. This course of action, it is argued, would enable the police to deploy manpower against seemingly more serious crimes—those involving complaining victims. Assertedly, this re-allocation of police resources would result in reduced levels of crime. Supporters of this concept maintain that these offenses should be accepted as manifestations of an enlightened public morality, and that police control must be viewed as an unwarranted abridgement of individual freedoms. However, such a point of view displays a dangerous naivete which does not consider the pernicious nature of "victimless crimes."
>
> . . . Crimes of the "victimless" character attack the individuality which is so highly valued by Americans for they have an eroding effect upon our principles and values, and particularly of those persons directly involved.[52]

Summary

In this chapter we have explored, although somewhat cursorily, many of the explanations of the causes and effects of crime, several categories of

[51] American Bar Association Special Committee on Crime Prevention and Control, *New Perspectives on Urban Crime* (Chicago: American Bar Association, 1972), p. 1.

[52] Edward M. Davis, "Victimless Crimes—The Case for Continued Enforcement," *Journal of Police Science and Administration*, I, No. 1, March 1973, p. 11.

criminal offenses and the people who commit them, and a discussion of some of the problems that face the criminal justice system in our modern society. Crimes and the people who commit them should not be classified or graded as one labels fruits or vegetables for canning and the market. Although paragraph headings and names we have attached to some of the subjects covered in this chapter for the sake of discussion may encourage such categorization, may we hasten to add that the study of criminology is not an exact science, but a searching inquiry into the vagaries of man and his environment.

Exercises and Study Questions

1. In what ways may human needs be used to explain the causes of crime?

2. What was Maslow's heirarchy of needs and how did he describe it?

3. Describe Beccaria's "pain avoidance" theory.

4. What are psychological needs? Physiological needs? Social needs?

5. Who was Lombroso, and what did he have to say about criminal characteristics in individuals.

6. How did Sheldon explain the endomorphic, ectomorphic, and mesomorphic body shapes and their relationship to crime?

7. Describe the phenomenon known as the "Myth of Melbourne" and the current position of the XYY syndrome in relationship to the predictability of crime.

8. List and discuss at least three of the current theories on crime cause.

9. In his Chicago study, what did Shaw show with his pin maps.

10. Shaw's study involved several minority groups. Of those listed, which race or ethnic group showed the greatest propensity for crime?

11. Define Social Ecology.

12. Describe Sutherland's theory of differential association.

13. How does Haskell's reference group theory differ from Sutherland's explanation of crime.

14. Describe the circumstantial offender and give at least three examples of types of crimes most likely to fall into this category.

15. Distinguish a career criminal from a professional criminal as described in this chapter, and give examples of types of crimes likely to be committed by each.

16. What types of criminal activity are most frequently associated with the phenomenon known as organized crime?

17. Recommended semester project: Write a one paragraph definition of "victimless crime" and prepare an argument representing your views as to whether they should be abolished or strictly enforced.

Suggested for Additional Study

BLOCH, HERBERT A. AND GILBERT GEIS, *Man, Crime, and Society,* (2nd Ed.). New York: Random House, 1970.

————, *Psychology Today, An Introduction.* Del Mar, Calif.: CRM, Inc., 1970.

CRESSEY, DONALD R., *Theft of the Nation: The Structure and Operations of Organized Crime in America.* New York: Harper & Row, Publishers, 1960.

KEFAUVER, ESTES, *Crime in America.* New York: Doubleday and Company, Inc., 1951.

————, President's Commission on Law Enforcement and Administration of Justice, *Task Force Report: Organized Crime.* Washington, D.C.: Government Printing Office, 1967.

QUINNEY, RICHARD, *The Problem of Crime.* New York: Dodd, Mead, & Co., 1970.

SUTHERLAND, EDWIN H. AND DONALD R. CRESSEY, *Principles of Criminology* (6th Ed.). Philadelphia: J. B. Lippincott Company, 1960.

TAFT, DONALD R. AND RALPH W. ENGLAND, JR., *Criminology* (4th Ed.). New York: Macmillan Co., 1964.

3

Scope of the Crime Challenge

Introduction

What is criminal law? What is a crime? How do we measure the incidence of crime? Each of these questions stimulates a series of responses that we shall attempt to explain in this chapter. In the United States we are constantly reading and hearing about the phenomenal growth of crime and the increased crime problem. Statistical reports are either alluded to or are directly quoted to confirm this growth in crime. The most widely used source of general crime statistics is the Federal Bureau of Investigation's Uniform Crime Reports, which reports on a variety of statistical breakdowns, particularly in the Crime Index. That document has reported to us consistently since 1930, with only minor relief during a short period of time in one year or another, that crime in America has reached "epidemic" proportions and each year the "disease" worsens. In view of these alarming facts, perhaps the next logical step for us to take in the study of the problem of crime is to analyze the specifics of *crime*.

Origin of Criminal Law

What is criminal law? Although a legal dictionary will go into much greater detail, a working definition of criminal law is: A rule regarding human conduct that requires or prohibits a specific act, that has been enacted by political authority, that applies to all persons to whom the rule refers, and that is enforced by punishment prescribed and administered by the local, state, or federal government that has legal jurisdiction. No matter how reprehensible or amoral the act or omission may seem, there are certain factors that must exist before the rule can legally classify an act or omission as a crime: (1) It must be specific; (2) it shall have been enacted by a political authority; (3) it must be uniform in its application; and (4) it must be accompanied by penal sanction.

Criminal law is a system of rules that one must obey because of their structure. Although at one time under common law an act might be held punishable by some form of governmental sanction, the primary requirement of criminal law is that the law must be written. It may have had its origin in religious beliefs, social customs, or merely popular demand by influential lobbyists, but the act only becomes unlawful as a result of official action of government.

To continue our discussion, we must now define crime itself. Edwin H. Sutherland defined it in this manner:

> The essential characteristic of crime is that it is behavior which is prohibited by the State as an injury to the State and against which the State may react, at least as a last resort, by punishment. The two abstract criteria generally regarded by legal scholars as necessary elements in a definition of crime are legal description of an act as socially harmful and legal provision of a penalty for the act.[1]

Criminologists Taft and England succinctly explain their definition of crime in this manner:

> Before any act or omission can be officially labeled a crime, four principles have to be established: (1) that the conduct actually occurred, (2) that the conduct was in violation of the criminal law, (3) that the conduct was committed with intent, and (4) that the alleged violator was capable of the conduct.[2]

The United States is a nation of laws. The entire system is regulated by laws, all of which must be specifically written. The student errs enormously, however, when he seeks to determine what is—and what is not—law by seeking his answers only in the legal code books. The legal code is the basic document and the principal source of the law, but there is another source of the law that cannot be overlooked: the courts.

---

[1] Edwin H. Sutherland, *White Collar Crime* (New York: Holt, Rinehart and Winston, 1949), p. 31.

[2] Donald R. Taft and Ralph W. England, Jr., *Criminology*, 4th ed. (New York: Macmillan Co., 1964), p. 21.

Although the legislative branch of government is charged with the responsibility of introducing and passing the laws, the final determination of how they shall be applied—if at all—is made by the courts. The law may remain the same as originally written, but it is subject to human interpretation that may change with the general public opinion and the personal philosophies of the judges and Supreme Court Justices. The courts hear the testimony, examine the evidence, then hear the attorneys' arguments, and study the precedents set by the previous cases of similar nature. The process of determining what is law with regard for prior cases with identical sets of circumstances is known as *stare decisis*, or "adhere to the decisions."

Criminal jurisprudence in the United States is fashioned after the English system, with a few exceptions. Notable among those exceptions is the difference in the basic law of each system. The codified law as enacted by legislature is the basic law in the United States, and it is modified and changed by a series of court decisions. The British basic law has been the Common Law, or the decisions of the courts themselves. The laws were made as each case was adjudicated and were court-made laws. When each case came to court, the Common Law was researched for a similar case upon which to base the current situation. If there was no precedent, the case at hand became the precedent for subsequent cases. This was the origin of *stare decisis*.

Specificity is very essential to our legal system. The law must be clearly understood—it must specifically state what it is intended that it state. For example, auto theft involves the taking of an automobile with the *specific intent* to deprive the owner of his property. The uniformity principle is also very important in our legal system. In theory this principle means that the law is applied to all its violators on an impartial and equal basis. The uniformity principle is, however, applied somewhat at variance with theory, as may be witnessed by the student of jurisprudence or the casual observer.

Punishment must be prescribed in order for the law to meet all the "legal" requirements. To merely require or prohibit a certain act is not sufficient. What to do if the law is violated must be planned and written into the law. The punishment distinguishes between the felony and misdemeanor. A felony is punishable by a sentence of death or imprisonment in the state prison, and a misdemeanor is punishable in some lesser manner. The threat of punishment as described in the law may serve as a deterrent to the would-be offender. This attitude is based upon the classical theory. By prescribing the punishment in the code, there is greater likelihood that it will be more uniformly applied.

About punishment, Taft and England state:

From the societal viewpoint the purpose of punishment is not to balance accounts or to take vengeance upon a criminal but to assure that he will not repeat his crimes. Punishment will be used when it is the only way to prevent repetition or when it will deter others from committing crimes. . . . The public still relies principally upon deterrent punishment. Moreover, the typical criminal himself accepts the traditional view and defines justice as equal treatment of men for the same acts, rather than in terms of an estimate of their future needs and behavior.[3]

The exact origin of criminal laws vary from law to law. There are basically two types of crimes: *mala in se* and *mala prohibita*. The former is interpreted as including those crimes that are "evil in themselves," and the latter is made "evil by law." The *mala in se* crimes are those against the person and certain property offenses that violate the rules of common decency, the various religious tenets, and those that pose a threat to the health and safety of the community. The *mala prohibita* crimes are those that the legislative representatives of the society make illegal, and they include such offenses as overtime parking or other minor vehicle code laws, gambling, betting on horse races off the track when betting at the track is legal, and a variety of others.

Some criminal laws originated with personal wrongs. Before our modern criminal justice system evolved, acts of personal violence, ravishment, or theft of another person's property were a personal matter and called for the victim or a member of his or her family to seek retribution. The original theory was "an eye for an eye and a tooth for a tooth" or similar attitudes. However, the avenger was not always capable of taking action with the desired results. He sometimes suffered additional injuries of person or loss of property. He was forced to seek aid, sometimes from "vigilante" groups of his peers who organized for their own self-protection. At other times the avenger was obliged to employ professional soldiers of fortune or other professionals to handle his job with dispatch.

The next step in the evolving process was for the people to call upon the government to provide law enforcement and protective services. Today, the professional government law enforcement agents are trained and capable, and they investigate the alleged violations, identify and apprehend the offenders, and hail them before the courts for appropriate punitive action.

Retribution through the criminal courts is in the form of fines or imprisonment or both. The fine money goes into the public funds because a violation of criminal law is a wrong against the state or the people as

[3] Taft and England, *Criminology,* pp. 8–9.

a whole. If the victim wishes to seek personal financial recompense, he must then go to the civil courts and institute a tort action, a personal matter. The goal in a tort action is to receive financial retribution or for the court to order the wrongdoers to perform, or to refrain from performing, a specific act.

Some criminal laws have been created because of an emotional reaction to indignities foisted upon helpless and unsuspecting victims. Other criminal laws had their origins in the religious and social mores of the community. These offenses are largely those that would be found in the *mala in se* category. Similar rules or laws are found listed among the basic doctrines of the many religions, such as the Ten Commandments. They include such offenses as criminal homicide, child molestation and similar sex offenses, burglary and theft, and criminal assault.

Another category of offenses are those that arose out of a conflict of interest among different special interest groups, or those that are legislated to fulfill a basic need to aid in expediting the smoother functioning of government rules and regulations. These laws most frequently fall into the *mala prohibita* type of offenses. Tax and licensing regulations, reporting requirements, import and export laws, some traffic laws, and similar laws establish certain acts as crimes by stating that they are crimes.

Law as a Social Force

The law itself may be utilized by society as a social force, a regulatory device. Bloch and Geis discuss this phenomenon in *Man, Crime, and Society.*

> Criminal law is the crucial element in the specification of human behavior. In many ways, individuals learn, though not always in detail, what the law expects of them and what they may and may not do. Recognition of the sanctions contained within the law may affect their behavior and personality in a variety of ways. This does not necessarily indicate, in the classic philosophical view of Thomas Hobbes, that all individuals function because of fear of the law. It does suggest, however, that an awareness of the law provides restraints and incentives to perform in a specified manner, even if, for some reason, the law may be distasteful. How law makes its impact depends upon given individuals and the particular qualities, but that the law operates as a significant social force can hardly be questioned.[4]

[4] Herbert A. Bloch and Gilbert Geis, *Man, Crime, and Society,* 2d ed. (New York: Random House, 1970), pp. 21–22.

The imminence of crime and criminal behavior in the United States or in any other country has been explained quite fluently by Emile Durkheim in his *Rules of Sociological Methods*. He states:

> There is no phenomenon that presents more indisputably all the symptoms of normality, since it appears closely connected with the conditions of all collective life. . . . What is normal, simply, is the existence of criminality, provided that it attains and does not exceed, for each social type, a certain level, which it is perhaps not impossible to fix in conformity with the preceding rules. . . . To classify crime among the phenomena of normal sociology . . . is to affirm that it is a factor in public health, an integral part of all healthy societies.[5]

Whether to accept or reject Durkheim's point of view is a matter of personal choice. The fact is that his statement has been borne out for at least four thousand years to date, and at the time of this writing there appears to be no spectacular change in sight.

Consider, also, Quinney's statement on the existence of crime in society:

> Crime is such an essential part of society that a society without crime is inconceivable. As long as men make laws, there will be crime. The forms of crime, to be certain, will change as human values change. But as long as men continue to value and preserve, condone and condemn, behavior will be labeled as criminal. And as long as a society includes as one of its cherished values some measure of individual freedom, there will be violations of the criminal law. A crimeless society could only be one that is static and unchanging, one in which persons cease to value and to aspire, and a society more totalitarian in control than we would want to imagine.[6]

Implications of Criminal Statistics

The student, the academician, the police practitioner, and the concerned private citizen are all impressed in some way by statistics on crimes and criminals. Statistical reports are intrinsic to virtually every discussion and study of the problem of crime. Statistical indices reflect trends, identify specific problems, report tabulated facts about crimes and the people who commit them. It is extremely important that any set of statistics, no matter how valid or reliable, be considered with certain

[5] Emile Durkheim, *Rules of Sociological Methods* (Glencoe, Ill.: The Free Press, 1950), p. 68.

[6] Richard Quinney, *The Problem of Crime* (New York: Dodd, Mead, & Co., 1970), p. 202.

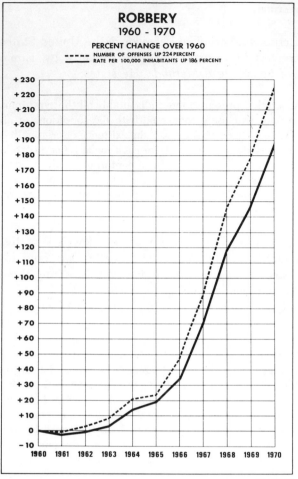

ROBBERY
1960 - 1970

PERCENT CHANGE OVER 1960
- - - - - NUMBER OF OFFENSES UP 224 PERCENT
———— RATE PER 100,000 INHABITANTS UP 186 PERCENT

FBI CHART

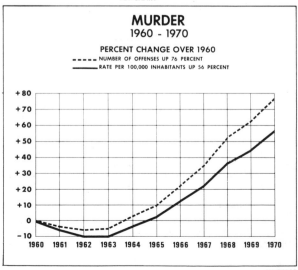

MURDER
1960 - 1970

PERCENT CHANGE OVER 1960
- - - - - NUMBER OF OFFENSES UP 76 PERCENT
———— RATE PER 100,000 INHABITANTS UP 56 PERCENT

FBI CHART

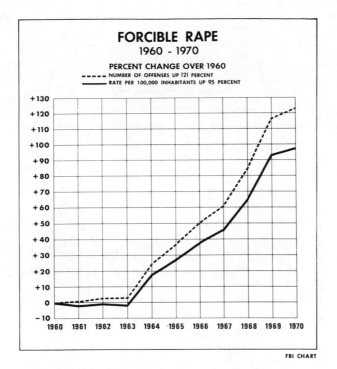

FBI CHART

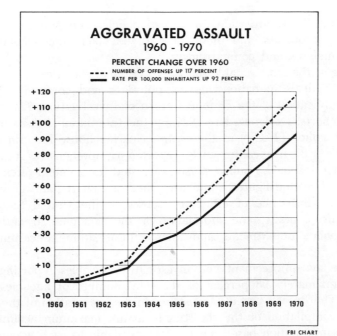

FBI CHART

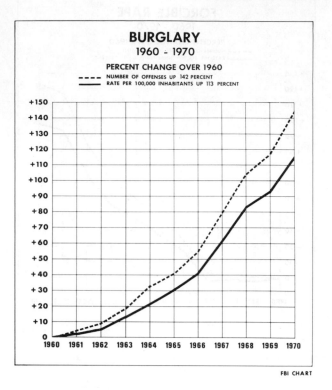

FBI CHART

reservations. There are wide varieties of policies and practices involved in the input process, and these must all be taken into account when making analyses and comparisons.

One of the most reliable sources of criminal statistics in the United States that deals in nationwide computations and comparisons is the annual publication of the Federal Bureau of Investigation, *The Uniform Crime Reports*. Designated in 1929 by the International Association of Chiefs of Police (IACP) as the central clearing house for criminal statistics, the FBI has continuously reported comprehensive statistics of crimes reported to the police, persons arrested for criminal offenses, and a variety of related figures, summaries, analyses, charts, and graphs concerning the incidence of criminal offenses in the United States. The *Reports* also contain some information on the personnel strength of the various police departments and related information concerning their activities.

The law enforcement and investigative agencies reporting represent approximately 96 percent of the total number of agencies in the country. The Bureau provides assistance in the preparation of the reports and the compilation of the statistics to assure maximum accuracy and complete information based on the data available to each agency.

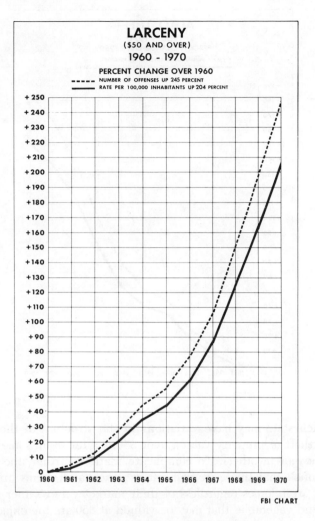

LARCENY
(\$50 AND OVER)
1960 - 1970

PERCENT CHANGE OVER 1960
- - - - NUMBER OF OFFENSES UP 245 PERCENT
———— RATE PER 100,000 INHABITANTS UP 204 PERCENT

FBI CHART

The principal data report in this publication is known as the Crime Index. The Crime Index consists of seven types of offenses, which do not necessarily represent the crimes that one might consider the most serious in the legal or moral sense. The criteria for selecting this list of offenses were their likelihood of being reported to the police and the consistency and accuracy with which they would be reported. The Crime Index represents those crimes that are most likely to be reported to the police. They are: (1) criminal homicide, (2) forcible rape, (3) robbery, (4) aggravated assault, (5) burglary or breaking and entering, (6) theft of property valued \$50 and over, and (7) auto theft.

A closer examination of the Crime Index offenses requires some definition of terms, principally because each state and local jurisdictions

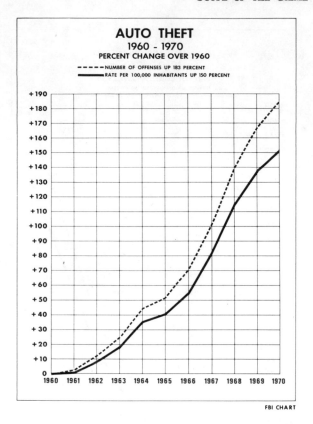

AUTO THEFT
1960 - 1970
PERCENT CHANGE OVER 1960
- - - - NUMBER OF OFFENSES UP 183 PERCENT
——— RATE PER 100,000 INHABITANTS UP 150 PERCENT

FBI CHART

within each state may have variations in the structure of the laws. For example, theft of property valued over $50 is a felony in some states and a misdemeanor in others. To complicate matters further, the theft laws vary so much that there are some items such as firearms and automobiles that are felonies regardless of their market value. Other items such as fruits and vegetables that may be valued at $50 are the object of grand theft when stolen, while $50 worth of lumber might be considered petty theft, a misdemeanor. The FBI lists are paraphrased here.

Criminal Homicide. These are murder and nonnegligent homicides that include willful, unlawful killing of a human as distinguished from negligent causes of death. They exclude accidental or justifiable homicides.

Forcible Rape. Forcible rape includes rape by force, assault to rape, and attempted rape. Excluded from this category are those acts classified as rape when the female is under a specific age and the act of sexual intercourse occurs, in this case usually by consent of both participants.

Robbery. Taking of something of value from another person or from the immediate presence of that person through means of force or fear is robbery. A weapon may or may not be used. The element of fear for imminent loss of life or safety must be present.

Aggravated Assault. An assault may be classified as aggravated whether or not a weapon is used. This classification of assault may be determined by the very nature of the weapon used, such as a loaded gun or knife capable of causing harm; or the method in which an object not normally considered a weapon is used, such as a chair leg wielded as a club. The assault may also be classified as aggravated by the nature and extent of injury that is inflicted during the assault, such as a blow with a fist to the head of the victim who sustains a fractured skull.

Burglary. Burglary generally involves breaking and entering or at least a surreptitious entry by means of a tool or nonauthorized key. But this classification also includes an entry of specified buildings and places without force when, at the moment of entry, the perpetrator entertains the *intent* to steal something or to commit some felony.

Theft, $50 and Over. Market value is used to determine which items fall into this category. Excluded from this classification are embezzlement (committed by a trusted relative or employee and not always reported to the police) and theft by means of fraudulent checks and credit cards.

Auto Theft. Auto theft includes the temporary or permanent taking of an automobile. Certain unauthorized use of a vehicle in unusual situations may be excluded.

When you examine the *Uniform Crime Report* for any given year, you will find that offenses are also broken down into Parts I and II. The Part I classification is based on offenses reported to the police. It includes the Crime Index offenses plus the balance of *thefts* including those of items valued at less than $50. The Part II classification, although reported in sequence to Part I and along with the Crime Index, has a distinct difference from the other two. The Crime Index and Part I are computed on the basis of the offenses actually *reported* to the police, whether or not the cases are solved and/or arrests are made. The Part II classification is a compilation of *persons arrested* for the listed offenses. There is no attempt to report those offenses that occur but for which no arrests are made in Part II offenses in the Uniform Crime Reports. An increase or decrease in the number of any category of crime in this classification is just a reflection in the change in the number of arrests, nothing more.

The Part II crimes include: arson, forgery and counterfeiting;

fraud; embezzlement; stolen property (buying, receiving, and possessing); vandalism; weapons (carrying and possessing); prostitution; commercialized vice; sex offenses; narcotic and drug offenses; gambling;
offenses against the family, or children; driving while under the influence
(alcohol or drugs); liquor law violations; drunkenness; disorderly conduct; vagrancy; other state and local laws not covered elsewhere; and
the juvenile detentions (or detention and release) for violation of curfew or loitering and runaway.

When examining the Part II offenses, it becomes immediately apparent why it would be more difficult to use many of the categories in
such a manner as we use the Crime Index. Departmental policies, community standards, and discretionary practices of the officers are just
three of the variable factors to consider. The number of arrests for
drunkenness has no direct relationship to the number of alcoholics in
the city, nor does the volume of vice arrests directly reflect the true
facts about the nature and extent of vice activities in any given location.
Many sex crimes committed by consenting adults in private never come
to the attention of the police—child molesting is frequently committed
by friends or members of the family—and criminal offenders of all types
seldom tell the police about their crimes. What the Part II statistics do
tell us, then, is the *number of persons arrested and/or charged with
those offenses.*

Integrity of Reports

At best, the statistics reflected in the *Uniform Crime Report* and any
other collection of indices represent only those numbers that are reported to the FBI, which acts as the clearing house. The user of the
Report is entitled to expect each reporting agency to report with integrity and consistency. However, not all of the crimes committed are reported *to* the police, and there is always the possibility that not all of
the known offenses are reported *by* that same police agency. It is pretty
much like the situation in which you tell someone to stand at a street
corner and report to *y* on how many automobiles pass that corner during
a specified time span. The report you receive depends on many variables, and what you receive may be an exact count of the number of
automobiles that passed. If you assign the same individual to perform
the same task daily and give you a similar report at the end of each
period of surveillance, you could reasonably assume that the method of
counting and reporting would at least be consistent, and that any gross
changes in the statistics would be a reasonably reliable reflection of the
actual changes in the traffic flow. Audits are made and a variety of tech-

niques are utilized by the FBI in an advisory capacity, and the agencies themselves are dependent upon the same statistics for a variety of purposes. All of these factors serve to assure the integrity of the report.

What purposes do the Crime Index and various components of the Uniform Crime Reports actually serve? They show trends and, sometimes, significant changes in patterns in certain offenses and arrests in specific cities or counties or portions of the country. The system of reporting has been in use for over forty years; therefore, it may be considered consistent and reliable. Increases or decreases in crime occurrences may reflect social changes, variations in criminal activity, and possibly the effectiveness of the police.

Various circumstances in a police department may change substantially and have such a distorting effect on a reporting system that it may be difficult to assess the true situation. For example, a new police chief may drastically change policies and investigative priorities to such an extent that an unusual emphasis on burglaries might lead to a greater number of arrests and more stolen property returned to the victims. Publicity for phenomenal success in the clearance and recovery rate might cause citizen groups to focus on that specific crime, perhaps even to the solicitation of reports to the police. Following his successful operation for a few months, the chief might be alarmed to find that the number of reported burglaries per month has tripled. Does this reflect a greater incidence of crime in our chief's city? Your guess is as valid as mine.

Other variables in the Uniform Crime Reporting system may be a change in the efficiency of the statistician, a follow-through system to verify that crimes investigated by the officers are reported to the department, an improvement in the system of preparing reports, and the enforcement policies of the department and the individual officers. With all of these variables in mind, it can generally be expected that there is even some constancy to the variables, and the statistics in the Uniform Crime Reports may be used with confidence, although not blind faith.

Some observers express more serious concern for the reliability of the Uniform Crime Reports. Taft and England list "several reasons for the unreliability of criminal statistics in the United States":

1. Diversity of definitions of the crimes within the fifty states, the federal government, and the District of Columbia.
2. Diversity of sources, consisting of some eight thousand reporting agencies.
3. Undiscovered crime. Exactly how many crimes occur is impossible to determine.
4. Unreported crime, although it has been discovered.
5. Reported crime that is unreported by the police.[7]

7 Taft and England, *Criminology*, pp. 46–48.

Taft and England also observed in their discussion of the Uniform Crime Reports that the statistics carry with them no guarantee of accuracy; in fact, the report itself makes that point clear in its introductory remarks. Another admonition to the reader of the Reports is that comparisons of crime rates between cities can be misleading. According to Taft and England, "The configurational nature of criminal activities is not apparent in published statistics (many crimes are committed concurrently, such as assault and robberies, burglaries and thefts that are reported as only one crime)." They also state:

> The real significance of crime in American culture cannot be shown from FBI statistics. Labor racketeering, organized traffic in illicit liquor, prostitution, gambling, narcotics, and stolen goods, and the intricate inroads of crooked commercial and financial practices in legitimate business are far more costly in time, money, and social well-being than the piddling amounts stolen by honest thieves and robbers.[8]

Richard Quinney's opinion of crime reporting and its validity appears in his publication *The Problem of Crime.*

> Any given violation of the criminal law likely carries with it a certain probability that it will come to the attention of law enforcement agencies. The probability that an offense will not be reported or recorded is related to a number of factors: (1) Some offenses are known only to the offender and, thus, are not likely to be reported by the offender. (2) Because of a lack of knowledge of the criminal law, victims and witnesses will not report criminal violations. (3) Witnesses to an offense may not want to report the offense because of inconvenience, embarrassment, fear or lack of interest in law enforcement. (4) The victim or witness may fear the possibility of being implicated in the violation or other violations if investigated. (5) The victim or witness may fear reprisal if the criminal offense is reported. (6) Friends and relatives may try to protect the offender and, therefore, not report the offense. (7) The victim may fear unfavorable publicity and embarrassment. (8) Social values and public opinion do not favor the full enforcement of certain laws. (9) Some criminal offenses because of their nature are not readily visible to the general public or law enforcement agencies. (10) Law enforcement agencies may wish to conceal some criminal offenses.[9]

The Justice System and Its Relationship to the Crime Problem

The three major components of the system of criminal justice have an extensive repertoire of relationships to the problem of crime in the na-

---

[8] Taft and England, *Criminology,* p. 58.
[9] Quinney, *The Problem of Crime,* p. 116.

tion and within the individual jurisdictions of the various agencies. Although they will be discussed in depth in later chapters, perhaps a brief review of the responsibilities of some of those agencies will provide a base from which the study may be carried forward.

Law Enforcement and the Crime Problem.   The law enforcement component has a responsibility to make every effort to (1) prevent crime, (2) repress the incidence of criminal activities, (3) identify and apprehend the individuals who violate the laws, and (4) to assist in the presentation of testimony and evidence to assure the accused a fair trial with conviction of the guilty as a goal. The activities of the average police officer are by no means limited to these responsibilities, but these are the most closely related to the problem of crime, our topic for this chapter.

Crime prevention involves direct contact with criminal law violators and potential violators, and an attempt to divert them into lawful activities. The likelihood of success in crime prevention is greater with the young child who has not yet developed static behavior patterns or attitudes favorable to criminal activities. Field contacts by the patrol or community relations officer provide many opportunities for the officers to discuss the disadvantages of a life of crime, the likelihood of apprehension, and negative effects of criminal conduct on one's self-image. Because acts committed by juveniles do not constitute criminal acts, dealing positively with juvenile delinquents and near-delinquents and diverting them into law-abiding behavior patterns constitute crime prevention.

Repression of crime is accomplished by reducing the opportunity for persons to commit crimes. Aiding private home occupants and businessmen in rendering their residences and places of business burglary and theft resistant is one method of reducing crime opportunities. Vigilant patrol and creation of a feeling of police omnipresence is essential to alter the plans of some persons who are intent upon committing crimes. Field interviews of individuals whose presence and activities on the streets indicate to the officer the need to ascertain the lawful nature of their activities are a regular crime repressive police function.

Along with the diligent patrol and frequent contact with the people in his district on a continuous basis to prevent and repress the incidence of crime, a third function must likewise be conscientiously performed: that of identification and apprehension of those individuals who do commit crimes. Exercising his professional prerogatives of using his discretion in making decisions as to priorities and other matters of judgment, the law officer must enforce the law as intended by the legislature. It is the police officer or investigator of other agencies of the law enforcement sector of the criminal justice system who is responsible for introducing the individual into the system once he has been identified as the person responsible for a criminal act. Careful inquiry and skillful collection of evidence often leads to the identification of the persons responsible for a crime. In order that the person be assured of his constitutionally guaranteed rights to a speedy and fair trial, he should be brought before the court and *proven* guilty.

The fourth item listed above—that of assisting the court—is a continuation of the law enforcement or investigative agency responsibility for the arrest. The case is by no means closed until a disposition has been made on the charges. Although the courts component now has the responsibility for processing the case through certain procedural steps, it is still up to the investigating and arresting officers to present their evidence and testimony and to assist the court in assuring the accused a fair trial with the conviction as a goal.

The Courts and the Crime Problem.   As the processing component of the system of justice administration, the courts have as their primary objective the fair and objective adjudication of the allegations. In accordance with the Constitution of the United States and the respective states of the nation, along with laws prescribing correct procedure, this component is actually involved much earlier than the time of arrest.

As an officer of the court, the prosecuting attorney advises and assists the law enforcement agency in the investigative process and development of the evidence. He is a police legal advisor in most cases, but in some instances he may actually direct the investigation, such as in major fraud situations involving many local jurisdictions.

In his role as prosecutor, it is the responsibility of the district attorney to present affidavits and witnesses to the judge who sits as a magistrate and makes a determination as to whether there is sufficient cause for the issuance of a search or arrest warrant or a complaint charging an individual with an alleged crime. Because of his unique position as an officer of the court, it is the prosecutor's responsibility to evaluate the case and make his own decision whether to bring the matter before the magistrate in the first place. Once he initiates the action and an individual is to be processed through the courts, the prosecutor assumes the burden of proving guilt of the accused beyond all reasonable doubt. He is also charged with keeping a timetable to assure the accused a speedy trial, the right to be faced by his accuser, and all of the other rights of the accused, who is innocent until he is *proven* guilty.

The court has a responsibility for maintaining schedules that will efficiently keep the cases moving along as required within specific time constraints. The presiding judge must handle the calendar and schedule hearings and trials in the various divisions of the court to assure a minimum delay. He must supervise counsel to the extent that there is no manipulation of the court for an illegal or improper advantage to one side or the other in the adversary system. As a magistrate, the judge determines whether there is sufficient cause for issuance of a warrant, then later in his role as judge, the same man or woman sits on the bench and determines whether the warrant was acted upon within the law and if the evidence or testimony is to be admitted at all.

Efficient court administrators have emerged as a relatively new profession. The judge has a full-time responsibility in the courtroom and must rely upon professional assistance to handle the ministerial and routine matters of the court, which include the scheduling of trials and hearings, handling of fines and forfeitures, personnel assignments and management, records-keeping, and generally keeping the court functioning smoothly.

In 1967, the President's Commission on Law Enforcement and the Administration of Justice reported on its findings during an appraisal of the courts in our nation:

> The Commission has been shocked by what it has seen in some lower courts. It has seen cramped and noisy courtrooms, undignified and perfunctory procedures, and badly trained personnel. It has seen dedicated people who are frustrated by huge caseloads, by the lack of opportunity to examine cases carefully, and by the impossibility of devising constructive solutions to the problems of defendants. It has seen assembly-line justice.[10]

In the opening address at the National Conference on the Judiciary, on March 11, 1971 at Williamsburg, President Richard M. Nixon unveiled what might be a workable device to improve our court system. He stated:

> Today I am endorsing the concept of a suggestion that I understand Chief Justice Burger will make to you tomorrow: the establishment of a National Center for State Courts.
>
> This will make it possible for State courts to conduct research into problems of procedure, administration and training for State and local judges and their administrative personnel; it could serve as a clearing house for the exchange of information about State court problems and reforms.[11]

[10] President's Commission on Law Enforcement and the Administration of Justice, *Challenge of Crime in a Free Society* (Washington, D.C.: Government Printing Office, 1967), p. 128.

[11] "Justice in the States," from *Addresses and Papers of the National Conference on the Judiciary, March 11–14, 1971 at Williamsburg, Virginia* (Washington, D.C.: Government Printing Office, 1971), pp. 8–9.

Chief Justice Burger later addressed the same conference. His topic was "Deferred Maintenance." He stated that today the American system of criminal justice

> in every phase—the police function, the prosecution and defense, the courts and the correctional machinery—is suffering from a severe case of deferred maintenance. By and large, this is true at the state, local and federal levels. The failure of our machinery is now a matter of common knowledge, fully documented by innumerable studies and surveys.
>
> As a consequence of this deferred maintenance we see
> First, that the perpetrators of most criminal acts are not detested, arrested and brought to trial;
> Second, those who are apprehended, arrested and charged are not tried promptly because we allow unconscionable delays that pervert both the right of the defendant and the public to a speedy trial of every criminal charge; and
> Third, the convicted persons are not punished promptly after conviction because of delay in the appellate process.
> Finally, even after the end of litigation, those who are sentenced to confinement are not corrected or rehabilitated, and the majority of them return to commit new crimes. The primary responsibility of judges, of course, is for the operation of the judicial machinery but this does not mean we can ignore the police function of the shortcomings of the correctional systems.[12]

In his call for reform and a review of existing procedures in the court component of the criminal justice system, Chief Justice Burger also addressed the problem or economics as affected by court delays:

> Someone must remind the bar and the public of the enormous cost of a trial. Reliable estimates have been made indicating that the cost is in the neighborhood of $250 per working hour in some courts, not including plant and equipment cost—or lawyers.[13]

Edward Bennett Williams, Chairman of the American Bar Association Committee on Crime Prevention, stated the following:

> I submit the time has come to take a long agonizing look at our criminal courts. The criminal courts of troubled urban America are failing wretchedly. Like scarecrows put in the fields to frighten the birds of lawlessness, tattered and unmasked from neglect, frightening to no one, they have become roosting places for the crows. To the innocent, to the victims of

---

[12] "Justice in the States," pp. 10–11.
[13] "Justice in the States," p. 16.

crime, to the witnesses of crime, to the illiterate, the uneducated, and the poor, many of our big city criminal courts are a sham and a broken promise.[14]

In his presentation, Mr. Williams presented specific proposals for change in the urban criminal justice system with an emphasis on the courts component. Those proposals included the following:

1. Recognize mandatory use of the grand jury as outmoded and no longer necessary.

2. Use the bail system with more imagination. Money bail for the poor is meaningless. Bail can be used as a means to enforce drug-free periods by lifting bail in cases of drug abuse.

3. At arraignment judges should make liberal use of the discovery procedure (allowing the defendant to have access to evidence and testimony that will be used against him in a trial) so that more persons will enter pleas.

4. Dispense with the written motions, provide for oral motions ten days after the arraignment, and provide that the case may be set no later than sixty days from the time the case is instituted.

5. Modernize the preparation of transcripts through computerization.

6. Take no more than one day in jury selection.

7. The trial judge should order a background report on each defendant at the time the case gets into the court. In the event the defendant is found guilty, sentencing can be handled immediately without delay.

8. The case should be set for appeal immediately after sentencing, and there should be a ten day maximum for filing the record with the appellate court.

9. Argue cases without the now-required briefs.

10. The appellate process should be unsigned, short, and concise.[15]

In the Bar Association's report on the Committee on Crime Prevention several months later, that committee presented their list of recommendations for improvement of the court process, which included those presented at Williamsburg in 1971, as well as the following:

1. Transfer nonserious offenses, such as traffic and housing code violations, to specialized bodies, and transfer to nonjudicial bodies certain types of conduct that "harm no one other than those involved." (The list

[14] Edward Bennett Williams, Chairman of American Bar Association Committee on Crime Prevention, "Crime, Punishment, Violence: The Crisis in Law Enforcement," from *Addresses and Papers of the National Conference on the Judiciary, March 11–14, 1971 at Williamsburg, Virginia* (Washington, D.C.: Government Printing Office, 1971), pp. 36–37.

[15] Paraphrased from "Crime, Punishment, Violence: The Crisis in Law Enforcement," pp. 36–38.

included public drunkenness, narcotics addiction, vagrancy, and deviant sexual behavior).

2. Divert some cases before trial into a period of probation without conviction, which would involve prosecutorial discretion.

3. Provide more funds to probation officers to "permit careful screening of defendants to determine those meriting pretrial release, to provide close supervision for those who are released, and to assure the early preparation of preventive reports."

4. "Computers should be utilized to assist the court in scheduling, doing routine paperwork, avoiding conflicts, equalizing work loads, analyzing backlogs, and providing various types of judicial statistics needed for effective court operation and planning."

5. Cut down on the "intervals between the time when a defendant is arrested or charged and the time his trial commences. . . ."

6. Provide trained court administrators to provide specialized management skills to the courts and to allow the judges to concentrate on the facets of their responsibilities for which they are best prepared: hearing and deciding cases.

7. Call upon bar associations and law schools to provide such trained management specialists.

8. Develop an individual calendar system so that individual judges are responsible for cases all the way through and there is an accountability for any "inordinate delays in particular cases." [16]

In the same report of the Bar Association's Committee on Crime Prevention and Control, the committee reported:

To function efficiently, any large and complex institution needs skilled administration, a fact that the courts have been terribly slow to recognize. Unlike hospitals, which in the last quarter century have increasingly entrusted their administration to management experts rather than practicing physicians, the courts have left the supervision of their business in the hands of the judges whose principal responsibility is—and should be—to hear and decide cases. As case loads continue to swell, the need to utilize trained court administrators becomes increasingly acute. Not only can they free judges to concentrate on their judicial responsibilities, but they can bring to the judiciary the type of management expertise rarely found in courts at the present time.[17]

Defense attorneys are officers of the court as well as the prosecutors, and they have the same responsibility to do what they can to cut down on time delays and to make every effort to expedite the

---

[16] American Bar Association Special Committee on Crime Prevention and Control, *New Perspectives on Urban Crime* (Chicago: American Bar Association, 1972), pp. iv, v.

[17] American Bar Association Special Committee, *New Perspectives on Urban Crime*, p. 95.

process while at the same time assuring their clients of a fair trial and their constitutionally guaranteed rights as related to the case from before arrest until after release. The publicly employed public defender serves the court as a regular body of defense attorneys for the indigent, but there is also a need for supplementary assistance when the court will appoint a private attorney to perform the service at the expense of the county.

The Bartered Plea. The clogged and extremely overburdened courts in our system could be brought to an immediate and dramatic halt if all of the persons charged with any kind of a law violation from a minor traffic violation to the most serious felonies were simply to plead not-guilty and ask for a trial. To ask for a jury trial would further compound the impossible situation. The courts place heavy reliance upon the process known as *plea bargaining* which treats conviction and the guilty plea as negotiable items that can be traded off as one would handle merchandise in a flea market. The process has been going on for many years and is as essential to the courts as a steam valve in a pressure cooker. Time and load factors add to the concern of the courts as well as legal time requirements between the various steps in the process of taking a case to court. Unless each case is disposed of in some manner as quickly as possible, a dozen more cases are stacked up in line waiting for a "speedy trial," as provided by the Constitution.

The ABA's Special Committee on Crime Prevention and Control made this observation on the bartered plea:

> Guilty pleas serve as the safety valve which enables many overburdened courts to hold their own against the flood tide of cases confronting them. The high incidence of pleas to a lesser charge is disturbing, however. Too often it represents a beleaguered court's willingness to be more lenient than it would ordinarily be solely to save court time—a practice known in court parlance as "giving away the court house for the sake of the calendar."
>
> . . . The problem is that the fundamental goal of dispensing justice fairly and evenly through the judicial process is jeopardized when increasing numbers of guilty pleas become essential for the courts to avert paralysis and collapse.[18]

The responsibility of the judge and the other officers of the court—both prosecution and defense—is to make judicious use of the device as a means of expediting the process truly "in the interest of justice" and in accordance with the laws. They must constantly guard against the

[18] American Bar Association Special Committee, *New Perspectives on Urban Crime,* p. 69.

bartered plea being used by unscrupulous persons to manipulate the system and render it ineffective. Above all, particular emphasis must be made on the importance of eliciting guilty pleas only from those who are—in fact—guilty. If the courts are so overburdened that innocent persons find it more to their advantage to plead guilty and to get their time in jail awaiting trial declared by the judge to be their punishment, while the innocent persons who hold out for a trial languish in jail for greater periods of time, then the ends of justice have certainly not been met.

Corrections and the Crime Problem. Once an individual has been found guilty of some criminal offense and is moved on to the next step in the sequence, he enters the corrections area of influence. Probation officers are involved in the judicial process and perform presentence investigations along with recommendations to the court as to what they believe will be a most appropriate method for dealing with the punishment and rehabilitation of the persons convicted of crimes. The authority for actually imposing the sentence is that of the judge, but he strongly weighs the recommendations of the probation officer. Once the judge has prescribed the sentence, the corrections component of the system assumes authority and responsibility.

The model penal code drafted by the American Law Institute has yet to be adopted in its entirety by any state, according to Project Director Charles L. Newman at the Center for Law Enforcement and Corrections at Pennsylvania State University. Sentencing and treatment provisions of that model code include the following:

a. To prevent the commission of offenses

b. To promote the correction and rehabilitation of offenders

c. To safeguard offenders against excessive, disproportionate, or arbitrary punishments

d. To give fair warning of the nature of the sentences that may be imposed upon conviction of offense.

e. To differentiate among offenders with a view to a just individualization in their treatment

f. To define, coordinate, and harmonize the powers, duties, and functions of the courts and of administrative officers and agencies responsible for dealing with offenders.

g. To advance the use of generally accepted scientific methods and knowledge in the sentencing and treatment of offenders.[19]

The process of probation involves casework with individuals who have been determined by the courts as guilty of some criminal act. With

---

[19] Center for Law Enforcement and Corrections, *Probation, Parole and Pardons: A Basic Course,* Training Module 6913 (University Park, Pa.: Pennsylvania State University, 1969), p. 9.

the juvenile offender, the language is different because of the difference in juvenile court and probation procedures, but many of the techniques are similar. Essentially, the role of the probation officer is that of a change agent: to work with the offender to effect some change in the offender's habits and attitudes so that there is less likelihood that he will repeat his criminal or asocial activities. The individual is placed at liberty under the supervision of a caseworker, the probation officer.

Parole is quite similar to probation in working style and the objectives are similar. The principal difference is that the individual who is on probation may have served some time in a local or county jail but he has not been incarcerated for extended periods of time, as has the parolee. The process of parole is a conditional release from a correctional institution following a protracted period of imprisonment, from several months to several years. Both probation and parole are alternatives to imprisonment in an institution and the objective is to assist the convicted offender in adjusting to the socialized community life. Failure to successfully adjust to the environment may have been a contributing factor to the individual's commission of his crime, and the caseworker is charged with the responsibility of working with the individual to help him learn to cope with community living.

"But does it work?" one may ask. Complete success (whatever that is) is certainly unattainable, but the goal of the caseworker is to strive for maximization of results. Consider this statement in response to that question:

1. In spite of the fact probation and parole services have generally been poorly staffed and supported, about 75% of those placed on probation have not had their probation revoked.

2. In the case of adult parolees, out of 35% to 40% of those who have had their parole revoked, only one third return for the commission of new offenses.

3. According to usual estimates, the revokation rate on juvenile aftercare is somewhat higher than for adult parolees.

4. The above figures should be seen only as indicants of probable success.

5. Probation and parole have not been given a fair trial for the level of professional personnel and support for optimum programming has never been available.[20]

An alternate title for probation and parole may be *community-based treatment*. By using that title, the process may have greater significance. The Corrections Task Force of the President's Commission on

---

[20] Center for Law Enforcement and Corrections, *Probation, Parole and Pardons: A Basic Course*, p. 13.

Law Enforcement and the Administration of Justice made this observation:

> A key element . . . is to deal with problems in their social context, which means in the interaction of the offender and the community. It also means avoiding as much as possible the isolating and labeling effects of commitment to an institution. There is little doubt the goals of reintegration are furthered much more readily by working with an offender in the community than by incarceration.[21]

In 1963, the California legislature financed the State Board of Corrections in a study of probation services. As a result of that study, the State of California has been involved in a probation subsidy program since 1966. The basis for this program is the assumption that the most effective of professional services should be offered at the local level by community-based correctional services. In addition, it was felt that: (1) Crime and delinquency are products of the community and, therefore, resolution of the problems must be in the community; (2) local treatment has an advantage because the offender remains close to his family and social ties that bind him to conformity; and (3) local treatment is less expensive because it permits the offender to maintain financial self-sufficiency for himself and his family.[22]

The subsidy program costs one-sixth the expense of institutional treatment at the state level, according to Gerald Buck and Don Hallstrom. The state pays participating county probation departments a standard fee for each juvenile or adult who is retained at the local level instead of being committed to state institutions. A prerequisite for granting of funds is that the agency must be using techniques other than routine supervision, which may include the following: (1) employment of only the highest quality personnel, (2) reduction of the supervisor-caseworker ratio, (3) reduction of the caseload to fifty maximum, (4) diagnostic classification of cases and application of differential treatment based on individual needs, (5) more clerical assistance to free professionals from nonprofessional responsibilities, and (6) improved support services, such as training, research, psychological services, and volunteer services.

---

[21] President's Commission on Law Enforcement and the Administration of Justice, *Task Force Report: Corrections* (Washington, D.C.: Government Printing Office, 1967), p. 28.

[22] Information concerning the subsidy program and community-based treatment was compiled by two colleagues, Don Hallstrom and Gerald Buck of the Orange County Probation Department, who are co-authors with me on *Criminal Justice Organization and Management,* 1974 (in press, Goodyear Publishing Company, Pacific Palisades, California).

The main gate at the California Institute for men, Chino.
Courtesy California Dept. of Corrections.

Institutional Corrections. Most traditional of the institutions are the local city or county jails and the penitentiaries, or prisons. More recently the system has utilized smaller residential units, such as halfway houses, camps, and open units. The institutional directors are equally concerned with the two principal responsibilities of corrections—rehabilitation of the offender and safety to the community—and their responsibilities are multifaceted. The institution must maintain custody and control of the prisoners during their incarceration and must also provide educational, training, and counseling services to make a maximum effort toward their rehabilitation with a goal of a redirected crimefree mode of living.

The jails house a great many people who are innocent. They are being housed pending posting of bail or the final adjudication of their cases in court. Only after they have been proven guilty in court, or they have entered a plea of guilty, can they be considered convicted offenders. Their period of custody lasts from several days to several months, seldom longer than a year except in the case of consecutive sentences.

The residential treatment centers are halfway between the probation mode and that of incarceration. As a condition of probation or parole, depending on the individual's history, the offender is required to live at the center and to participate in the various individualized treatment programs. Such centers, which are located in the heart of the city rather than in some isolated spot miles out of town, serve as a base from which the residents may accomplish their reintegration into the community and at the same time receive the intensive treatment and counseling that may be prescribed in their individual programs.

The purpose for correctional institutions include the following:

1. To seek to limit confinement to persons actually requiring it, for only as long as they require it, and under conditions that are lawful and humane.

2. To afford both the community and the offender temporary and partial respite from each other in order to facilitate resolution of the crisis which led to commitment.

3. To make the confinement experience constructive and relevant to the ultimate goal of reintegrating the offender into the community and of preventing recidivism.

4. To educate the community and its agencies about the problems of reintegrating offenders in order to elicit their collaboration in carrying out specific rehabilitative efforts and in improving conditions which militate against such efforts.

5. To seek continual improvement in the system's capacity to achieve these ends.[23]

For the juvenile, generally persons under the age of eighteen, there are principally two basic types of institutions: detention and shelter. The detention facility is for temporary care and custody of a child who has committed a delinquent act in a physically restricting facility pending court disposition or the child's referral to another agency. The second type of juvenile facility is for dependent and neglected children and provides physical restricted custody pending return home or placement for care in another location, such as a foster home. The methods for redirection and reintegration of juveniles place a major emphasis on environmental modification, changes in peer influences, greater involvement with family and community, and individual casework.

The institution serves as a warehouse to store convicted criminals in a location that protects society from those individuals who are housed therein, and it meets the needs of those prescribed punishments that call for isolation from society for specified periods of time. Except for local jails, where little more than short-term physically restricting custody is possible, the longer-term institutions are responsible for reducing crime and delinquency through programs that provide for rehabilitation

---

[23] Joint Commission on Correctional Manpower and Training, *Manpower and Training in Correctional Institutions* (Washington, D.C.: American Correctional Association, 1969), p. 36.

of the offenders. The task is monumental, and the risks for failure are great, but the most promising method of reducing the rate of recidivism—or repeat offenders—is through aggressive efforts to rehabilitate the offender.

Diversion from the Criminal Justice System. Professionals in every component of the system frequently make discretionary decisions to divert the delinquent or criminal law violator away from the formality of the system as an alternative to introducing him to the system by arrest, or they may divert him into some program of treatment in lieu of punishment. The diversion practice takes place frequently with the juvenile offender encountered by the police officer. Estimates have been made that approximately one half of all juveniles who have committed delinquent acts are warned and released without further action. The officer or investigator who chooses to issue a warning instead of making an arrest is employing the diversion alternative.

The prosecutor and defense may stipulate with the consent of the court the provision that the accused person will seek psychiatric or medical help for his problem, which is considered a causative factor for his criminal behavior. The court may initiate the action and suspend or delay a sentence pending the defendent's referral and treatment by a detoxification or narcotics center, or an institution for mentally disordered sex offenders. Sometimes a referral is made by the court to a private organization, such as Alcoholics Anonymous, or to the care of a private physician or some other individual. All of these diversions from the criminal justice system serve to relieve some of the load that burdens the system to the point of negative returns. Eleanor Harlan, Robert Weber, and Fred Cohen have this to say about diversion:

> The diversion of persons from the criminal justice system has long been practised in the United States, largely because the system allows—in fact, requires—considerable discretion on the part of the police, with regard to decisions to arrest or dismiss and court referral or informal disposition, and on the part of the prosecutor or intake worker, with regard to official or unofficial processing.
>
> . . . Arguments against informal prejudicial processing are: (1) that broad powers of discretion may be abused; (2) that enlarged discretionary power results in inconsistent law enforcement and disrespect for law; (3) that discretionary power may be used to further staff convenience at the expense of other goals of crime prevention and control.
>
> . . . The proponents of diversion, however, are advocating that prejudicial disposition be made a conscious and clearly defined policy, that the processes of diversion be given some procedural regularity, and that decisions be made on the basis of explicit and predetermined criteria.

Assuming that alternate resources are made available and that nonjudicial procedures are defined, the extended use of unofficial or informal disposition need not necessarily result in an increase in "invisible" decision-making by individuals with great discretionary authority.[24]

Although diversion from criminal conviction and a possible term of imprisonment in a correctional institution may seem appealing, particularly to the individual who is about to be convicted, the "break" they are about to receive may not be so great after all. A civil commitment may be for a period of time until the patient is "cured," which may be for a considerably longer period of time than if the person were convicted and sentenced to serve a specific number of days or months. This is another argument for a more uniform application in diversionary alternatives.

Summary

This chapter actually consists of two major parts. The first part addresses the awesome problem of the extent and wide-ranging scope of the occurrence of crime in the United States, beginning with a definition of crime and some of the background of our modern legal system. Law originated from the need of civilized society to have some form of ordered liberty to assure survival. From a matter that required personal retribution for an act of theft or personal violence, the idea that such acts were—in fact—wrongs against the entire society emerged as the prevailing philosophy as it is today. It made more sense to have specially employed policemen, prosecutors, judges, and corrections personnel handle the problems of crime. Along with the refinement of the law as a social force came the need for a more sophisticated system of crime definition and reporting, statistics and record-keeping. Crime Indexes are explained to an appreciable extent in the first part of this chapter.

In the second part of the chapter, we examine the problem of crime and its relationship to the various components of the criminal justice system. Crime prevention and protection of the people are the goals of all components of the system, and each of the many separate agencies within the components have interrelated objectives developed for the purpose of accomplishment of those goals. Law enforcement has prevention and repression of crime, identification and arrest of law violators, and provision of assistance to the courts to assure a fair trial and success-

---

[24] Eleanor Harlan, J. Robert Weber, and Fred Cohen, *Diversion from the Criminal Justice System* (Washington, D.C.: Government Printing Office, 1971), pp. 1–2.

ful conviction of the guilty as its principal objectives regarding its role in the criminal law enforcement aspects of its responsibilities. The courts and the officers attached to the court as prosecutors, defense attorneys, as well as the judges themselves are pledged to uphold the laws and the constitutions of the federal and state governments. The principal thrust of corrections programs is toward the eventual rehabilitation of criminal law violators. As a system—however loosely affiliated many of these agencies may be—all of the agencies function surprisingly well. Many criticisms have been offered regarding the system, but so many have been supported both financially and politically that as a result, we have witnessed considerable improvement in the system.

Exercises and Study Questions

1. What, specifically, are the elements necessary to classify an act as criminal?

2. How did Taft and England define crime? How do the two definitions of crime presented differ?

3. What is the difference between *mala in se* and *mala ad prohibita* crimes?

4. List and discuss: factors that underwrite the credibility of the Uniform Crime Reports; factors that adversely affect their credibility.

5. What is the meaning of *stare decisis?*

6. How would you describe law as a social force if you were asked?

7. What is Durkheim's theory regarding crime? Do you agree?

8. List the seven offenses that comprise the Crime Index. Why were those specific offenses chosen for the Index?

9. List some of the factors that might explain why the Crime Index report may not be completely accurate.

10. What may happen to the crime statistics in a city if there is a change in the public's support and confidence in their police department?

11. List and discuss each of the following:
    a. Law enforcement objectives regarding the crime problems.
    b. The role of the courts in relationship to the number of people who are arrested for criminal law violations and the likelihood that they will repeat their crimes some time in the future.
    c. The role played by probation and parole in behavior modification.
    d. Recent trends in correctional philosophy to reduce crime.

12. Describe at least five of the recommendations by the American Bar Association's Committee on Crime Prevention and Control. State whether you agree or disagree with each recommendation you list, and justify your argument.

13. What is the "bartered plea" and how does it work?

14. Recommended semester project: Prepare a series of charts and graphs that show the crime patterns for the city or county in which you live, covering the most recent five-year period, then prepare a press release as if it were to be distributed to your local newspaper. Be sure to explain any sharp increases or decreases as well as general trends.

Suggested for Additional Study

FBI Uniform Crime Reports for the previous five years.
Taft, Donald R. and Ralph W. England, Jr., *Criminology* (4th ed.). New York: Macmillan Co., 1964.

4

Evolution
of the System of
Administration of Justice

Introduction

Modern criminal justice has its roots in the history of modern civilization. As with any other system in our society, the evolution process involves modification, improvement, renewal, refinement, a series of trials and errors, and the eclectic development of newly acquired skills and bits of knowledge. Some of the earliest methods and institutions in the administration of justice have survived for centuries and are still considered effective. Some of those methods and institutions have similarly survived but have been considered archaic and ineffective. Laws and their enforcement have been utilized as control devices for at least four thousand years. The heavier the population per land space, the more regulated are the people. It is a matter of survival that there are laws and regulations.

Examples of some of the vestiges of early civilization that are still evident in modern society are the grand jury and the jury trial (1166 A.D.), the town marshal (1655), capital punishment (2000 B.C.), the public defender (1913), juvenile court (1899), the penitentiary (1790), probation (1841), and many more. The purpose of this chapter is to briefly scan some of the highlights in the evolution of the system of administration of justice in the United States. An understanding of the historical developments of the system may lend to an enrichment of the experiences in learning about the system as it is today, how it might have been, how it should be, and—possibly—how it will be in time to come.

Development of Law Enforcement

The history of civilization reflects a parallel history of various forms of social controls, laws and regulations, and some type of enforcement body to carry out the will of those who govern as the enforcement arm of the executive authority of the government, as prescribed by the laws promulgated by the legislature, and as interpreted by the judicial body within the governmental structure. The mode of law enforcement has depended largely upon the type of government in existence, ranging along the entire spectrum of political and philosophical thought.

Law enforcement in the United States is generally modeled after the English system of law enforcement, as is the court system and some of the correctional concepts in current practice. But law enforcement did not originate in England. Historical data record that laws and law enforcement existed in ancient Egypt, Rome, China, Greece, and all of the civilizations that have been documented by recorded data.

Ancient History

Some historians have written that there were laws and some sort of police enforcement as long ago as 4000 B.C. in China and Egypt. It is only logical to assume this if there was any form of civilization. The first permanent record of any sort concerning law enforcement to which we can refer with any authority are the Codes of Hammurabi, the Babylonian ruler who lived about 2000 B.C. His codes were inscribed on stones of black diorite, found by modern archaeologists, and are still legible. They prescribe and proscribe rules of conduct and provide for specific methods of punishment for the violators. They have been called one of the greatest contributions to mankind.

Other evidence of ancient law enforcement is the ephori of Greece, a body of five ephors elected each year at Sparta and given almost limitless powers. They possessed the highest executive power in the country, and there were no controls over their personal conduct except the influence and authority of the other members. They were a combination of investigator, judge, jury, and executioner. An ephor presided over the Senate and Assembly, carried out its decrees, supervised education, levied fines, inflicted other forms of punishment, arrested and tried other ephori for suspected transgressions, and performed all other types of regulation. This type of law enforcement naturally spawned the corrupt enforcer and enriched the greedy because there was no control over them by the people, except to vote against them at election time, if they dared.

The English Background of Our U.S. Police System

The police role as we know it in the United States is to serve as the enforcement arm of the executive branch of government. The powers and limitations are established by law and are generally limited to the protection of life and property and the enforcement of written laws only. The judging and punishing of offenders is the responsibility of other branches of our government. Although the origins of the many peoples in this country are in almost every part of the world, the U.S. police system is principally based upon the English system. Federal, state, and local law enforcement agencies operate independently within their own spheres of jurisdiction without any semblance of hierarchy. As we discuss the historical evolution of English law enforcement, the similarities will be readily apparent.

During the latter part of the Anglo-Saxon period in the ninth century, King Alfred established what was to be one of the most significant police roles in English history. Recognizing the need for stricter adherence to the rules of society by the people, Alfred established a "tithing system" in each county, or "shire." The chief judicial and law enforcement officer in each shire was the "shire-reeve," an appointee of the crown. In the language of the Saxons, the reeve had been known as the *gerefa.* This individual was the local government, representing the state in all matters of nationwide or local importance. He served at the pleasure of the king, and his tenure was dependent upon order within his own jurisdiction as well as profits to the king.

Law enforcement under the broad, general control of the shire-reeve was accomplished by means of the tithing system. Each head of a household would be responsible for his own family's conduct, as well as that of the other tithings, or members within his group of ten families. These ten families would be under the direction of one of their number designated as chief tithingman. The philosophy of this method was to make neighbors responsible for each other, compelling them to bring the wrongdoer to trial or else suffer the consequences themselves. It was an honor system on a national scale. The tithings were grouped into larger units known as "hundreds"; the hundreds in the shire, or county, comprised the major structure of the political organization within the shire. All able-bodied men in the shires were usually armed, and were always ready to form the *posse comitatus,* or "power of the county," wherever and whenever the "hue and cry" was sounded by the shire-reeve or one of his lieutenants—the chief tithingman—announcing that a wrongful act had been committed by someone within the shire. The shire-reeve and his posse would seek out the violator and bring him to trial and punishment. Everyone within this system was involved in the enforcement of the laws and edicts of the land under the guidance of the shire-reeve.

The Norman king, William the Conqueror (1027–1087), kept the tithing and shire system during his reign, but reinforced its strength by giving the shire-reeve a military rank in addition to his already powerful civil position. He was usually selected from the landlord baronage, and the position was frequently passed along from father to son for several generations. The shire-reeve served at the pleasure—or displeasure—of the king and usually retained a firm grip on that office as long as he was instrumental in gaining a profit or advantage for the crown.

The prototype of our American county sheriff maintained his role as chief law enforcement officer in the shire for several hundred years. Sometime early in the Norman period (1066–1285) the *Comes Stabuli* (constable) appeared on the scene. Constables were hired on a full-time basis to aid the shire-reeve in carrying out his duties, thereby giving some continuity to the task of law enforcement. The *Comes Stabuli* were not much unlike the modern American town constable or chief of police.

In 1072, the *Vicecomes,* or traveling (circuit court) judges, were introduced to the English scene, and the law enforcement powers of the sheriff and constables were separated from their judicial powers.

Prior to the year 1166, there were many different types of private policemen hired by the citizens and merchants to protect their persons, their homes, and their shops. The shire-reeves and the assistants, the *Comes Stabuli,* were more concerned with the more important matters of the crown, such as land and tax problems, and crimes against the populace as a whole rather than crimes against individual victims, such as burglary or assault. But during the year of 1166—a significant one for the history of law enforcement—King Henry the Law-Giver issued his *Legas Henrici,* which made criminal law enforcement a public matter. He separated offenses into felonies and misdemeanors by defining the felonies and leaving all other offenses in the category of misdemeanors. His decree stated: "There will be certain offenses against the King's peace, arson, robbery, murder, false coinage, and crimes of violence. These we deem to be felonious."

Magna Carta was signed under protest by King John in 1215 and was an agreement that the people would be provided "due process of the laws," protecting the individual against unnecessary infringement upon his rights and liberty by the crown. Governmental organization was changed so that there was more local control with a separation of state and local governments. Article 13 of Magna Carta stated in part, ". . . the city of London shall have all its ancient liberties and free customs . . . and all other cities and villages shall have their liberties and customs." Another article in that wonderful document concerned due process read: "No freeman shall be taken or imprisoned or disposed or outlawed or banished or in any way destroyed except by the legal judgment of his peers or the laws of the land."

In Westminster, then capital of England, King Edward I established a curfew in 1285 by ordering that the city's gates be closed so that the undesirables would be locked out of the city at nighttime, and the residents and other occupants be locked in. In order to enforce the curfew, a night watch was created. The night watchmen were called bailiffs. Their duties included guarding the gates to the city between sunset and sunrise, checking on the security of all places within the city, and keeping track of all "persons and lodgers." Members of the night watch were selected from the ranks of able-bodied men in the community on a compulsory basis and were paid for their services. They carried lanterns and staffs while on patrol and were virtually ineffective, according to historians. One branch of the night watch of that time was the *Police Desmour,* charged with the responsibility of regulating street-walkers and prostitutes and keeping them in their designated areas.

In his Edict of Winchester in 1285, Edward charged local property owners, in groups of one hundred each, with responsibility for keeping the peace in their respective districts. Thus, the tithing system was reinforced by this edict. The edict laid down the principle of local rather than central government responsibility for law enforcement.[1]

It was not until about the fourteenth century that policemen were actually trained for their jobs. The office of justice of the peace was created to replace the shire-reeve, and to more efficiently handle the duties of his office. Each shire, or county, was provided three or four men "learned in the law" with full authority to "pursue, arrest, chastise, and imprison." They were assisted by the constables, who had previously been under the control of the shire-reeves. The justice of the peace retained his role of policeman and judge for about seventy-five years, when the office evolved into a strictly judicial role.

The years 1500 to 1800 are called the Period of Watch and Ward. Several different police systems were inaugurated during these years in England. There were basically three new systems: the merchant police

---

[1] Donald R. Taft and Ralph W. England, Jr., *Criminology,* 4th ed. (New York: Macmillan Co., 1964), p. 319.

or Ward and Watch, the parochial police, and the military police. The merchant police were private watchmen employed by the bankers and merchants to protect their property. They guarded the places at night-time and also worked as private detectives for the purpose of locating and recovering stolen goods. One of those detective forces was the Bow Street Runners, a colorful cutthroat group of bounty hunters for criminals and their booty. They carried on their operations initially for Magistrates John and Henry Fielding in the early 1800s.[2]

The second type of police force to appear during the Watch and Ward period was the parochial police, who were employed by the religious parishioners for the protection of their members and their property. The third police force was the government-operated military police under the direction of the provost marshal and the crown.

In 1655 Oliver Cromwell divided England and Wales into twelve police, or military, precincts. He placed a marshal in charge of each precinct and maintained control of the people by means of this system during his reign. The rule was military and the law was Martial Rule, which superseded all forms of local government control. Magna Carta and the Bill of Rights were disregarded under the guise of military expediency.

By 1792 the population of London had grown to nearly 1 million. In that year the Middlesex Justices Act provided for a police force of only 126 constables, which was hardly conducive to crime control. Regarding that era, Taft and England reported:

> The inadequacy of so small a number in London . . . (of one million people) . . . soon became evident. Crime and disorder went unchecked, the latter becoming particularly threatening after the turn of the nineteenth century, when riots against the corn laws and against machines put the English government in fear for its very existence.[3]

In 1829, Sir Robert Peel, a Member of Parliament, introduced a bill to found a centrally controlled system of law enforcement in the Greater London Metropolitan area. He based his conclusions as to the need for a new police system upon a study completed by Dr. Patrick Colquhoun. The various police agencies, both public and private, were ineffective. Peel labeled the Ward and Watch the "shiver and shake watch." He stated that the men comprising the watch spent half the night shaking from the cold and the other half shaking from fear. Sir Robert's bill was passed, and the entire world watched the creation of one of the first truly professional police agencies. The police departments in the United States

[2] Henry Goddard, *Memories of a Bow Street Runner* (New York: William Morrow, 1957).

[3] Taft and England, *Criminology*, p. 320.

were patterned after the London Metropolitan Police, as we shall see in this and succeeding chapters in this book.

Sir Robert first divided the London Metropolitan area (not the City of London, which is a small and separate entity) into sectors, or districts, and replaced the existing police systems with his new organization, one sector at a time. He personally interviewed and selected all candidates for the new department, and out of 12,000 who applied, he put together a force of 3,314 men. Tenure was dependent upon the ability and production of the men, and candidates served a probationary period. Turnover during the first few years of operation was enormous, and Sir Robert stated: "The securing and training of proper persons is at the root of efficiency." By 1835 the entire department was organized and operational, with headquarters at Scotland Yard. The exact origin of the name Scotland Yard is subject to debate, but the ancient buildings and grounds bore the name until 1890, when the department moved to New Scotland Yard.

The force was organized along military lines, although their uniforms were nonmilitary in appearance and they were allowed to carry only truncheons, or short nightsticks. Police agencies have since been considered parliamentary in nature. Numbered police badges were issued to identify the men as individuals as well as officers of the law. The salaries of these new officers were dependent upon their effectiveness in reducing crime, and they were assigned to shifts that rotated around the clock. The reporting system was improved so as to provide statistics on the crime picture in the area as well as to provide modus operandi information to assist in the identification and apprehension of offenders. A detective bureau was established for the purpose of conducting investigations under circumstances in which the appearance of the uniform would hinder investigation.

Twelve principles of modern law enforcement emerged at the time of the Peelian Reform and the establishment of the new London Metropolitan Police Department. As you read them here, compare them to the requirements of law enforcement today in the United States nearly a century and a half later.

1. The police must be stable, efficient, and organized along military lines.
2. The police must be under government control.
3. The absence of crime will best prove the efficiency of the police.
4. The distribution of crime news is essential.
5. The deployment of police strength, both by time and area, is essential.
6. No quality is more indispensable to a policeman than a perfect

command of temper. A quiet, determined manner has more effect than violent action.

7. Good appearance commands respect.

8. The selection and training of proper persons are at the root of efficient law enforcement.

9. Public security demands that every police officer be given an identifying number.

10. Police headquarters should be centrally located and easily accessible to the people.

11. Policemen should be hired on a probationary basis before permanent assignment.

12. Police crime records are necessary to the best distribution of police strength.

We have devoted a great deal of space to the English police system because it is apparent that the American "system" (actually, an absence of a system is more descriptive of the potpourri of police agencies in the United States) developed along the same general lines in techniques and traditions. The various law enforcement officers who appeared in England have their American equivalents, as we will see in subsequent chapters. These include the modern American sheriff, marshal, constable, justice of the peace, jury, grand jury, and the many other police officials who comprise the American law enforcement segment of the criminal justice system.

The Evolution of Law Enforcement in the United States

In 1833, the City of New York was so impressed with the efficiency of the Metropolitan Police Department in London that a delegation was sent to that city to study the department with a view toward adopting some of their ideas. The result was the formation of the New York City Police Department in 1844 along the general lines of Scotland Yard. The department in New York was the first of its kind in the United States, followed by Boston in 1850, and many other cities since then. The major difference between the two systems is the form of control. The American police forces are comparatively free from any federal or central control; each autonomous community is responsible for the establishment, maintenance, and administration of its own police department.

But let's go back to the earlier beginnings of law enforcement in the United States. When the settlers came to this country, they brought with them their various traditions and customs. As a body, the new residents of this country were suspicious and contemptuous of a strong central government; local autonomy was fiercely defended. The law enforcement bodies were no exception in this trend toward local control. Although the systems of the Old and New World were similar, the controls were diametrically opposed. The control of the local police in most European countries was by strong central governments. The English customs had the greatest amount of influence on our police systems, so the offices of the shire-reeve and constable in England became the sheriff and constable in the populated areas of this country, and the U.S. marshal was the law enforcement officer in the territories and unpopulated areas. The local sheriffs and constables were elected for short terms by the people whom they served instead of being appointed by any central authority. This was, of course, after the settlers had emancipated themselves from English rule and formed an independent government.

New England became a land of settlements and villages centering around industry and commerce. The municipal type of government was formed, and the municipal police officer—the constable or "watch and ward" type of patrolman—was elected into office. In the South, agricultural and rural, the county form of government and the county sheriff were adopted as most suitable to fill the needs of the people.

It appears that when the first counties were established in Virginia in 1634, the office of *sheriff* was introduced to the United States. Maryland followed, and in both states the sheriff was delegated the same powers of the office held in England.[4]

Many other types of law enforcement were tried in various parts of the New World. These various systems were usually holdovers from the native countries of the residents of the different communities. For example, in New Amsterdam, later New York, the police patrol officers of the night watch for many years were called the "rattle watch" because they carried with them larger versions of the rattles now used as party toys with which to warn would-be offenders of their presence. Boston had an organized night watch as early as 1636, whose purpose it was to patrol the streets to combat larceny. Philadelphia had a similar night watch, and other cities of any size had some semblance of night patrols. Most of them were vigilante, or volunteer, groups that poorly supplemented the sheriffs and constables and their few assistants.

A day watch, organized to combat crime when the night watch was not operating, was created about 1800 in New York. This was the first daytime, paid police force to appear in America, and the two separate watches—night and day—continued to operate independently for many years. Other communities followed the lead of New York by hiring full-time, paid policemen, but there is no record of there ever having been a round-the-clock police force in the United States until 1844, when New York City combined the day and night watches into a single police force

[4] Larry A. Giddings, Mark Frustenberg, and Henry J. Noble, *Manual on Training for Sheriffs*, LEAA Grant No. 268 (Washington, D.C.: Government Printing Office, 1968), p. viii.

The signal bell was used by many police departments to summon their officers to headquarters.
Courtesy Police Department, Lawton, Oklahoma.

fashioned after the London Metropolitan Police Department. Boston followed in 1850, and the modern noncivilian police force as we know it today made its appearance on the American scene. It is interesting to note that it was not until the year 1855 that the police were allowed to wear uniforms. Prior to that time, it was considered un-American for civilian police officers to wear any clothing that would give them a military, or "uncivilian" appearance.

The people in Chicago were confronted by "policemen" with a very definite military appearance; law enforcement duties were performed by soldiers from Fort Dearborn until about 1855, at which time the city's population had reached 100,000.[5]

Since 1844 the police service in the United States has remained pretty much the same in some respects and has changed drastically in other respects. Let's take a look at some of the landmarks in the progress of law enforcement in the cities and counties of the United States. Many systems that originated many years ago appealed to the residents and became so much a part of the communities that they are still in existence today throughout the country.

[5] Taft and England, *Criminology*, p. 320.

The sheriff and constable are constitutionally elected officers and are usually designated as the chief law enforcement officers in their respective areas of jurisdiction. The sheriff is generally the title assigned to the officer for the county, and the constable is usually responsible for a smaller area, such as an unincorporated township. Their terms of office are usually for two to four years, and in many states they cannot succeed themselves in office. The philosophy behind this law is that within a short period of time in office an individual cannot gain too much control over the people who elect him. The office of constable is slowly fading into oblivion, but the sheriff is pretty well ensconced in county government in many parts of the country with little likelihood that he will disappear from the scene for many years to come. We will discuss the duties of the office of sheriff later in this book, but a cursory glance at the comparative roles of the sheriff of the past and present will show that there is actually little difference.

Election of municipal chiefs of police was quite common when local departments were first established. Public suspicion of government officials was prevalent, based upon actual experience with the corrupt officials who served for life at the pleasure of the king. Short terms assured the people that their police administrators were new to the job and would not have time to become corrupt or too powerful in office. This system was found to be an illusory concept, however. Not only were the chiefs not able to gain control of the community, but they hardly had sufficient time to gain control of their own officers or to acquire sufficient experience to perform their jobs efficiently. Their terms were so short that they did not give up their civilian occupations while in office. The artisans, shopkeepers, and businessmen had their futures to consider, so they were policemen on a part-time basis only and seldom devoted their full energies and resources to the important task of running a police department.

Because of this lack of professionalism that resulted in election of politicians as police administrators, the trend has been for many years to permanent appointments of administrators qualified by experience and ability instead of by popularity at the polls. Tenure is based upon continued good performance and substantial results in the reduction of crimes and traffic collisions, and clearance of crimes. The elected police chief system remains in only a few cities.

In the mid-1800s, administrative police boards were established. The chief of police was a professional and retained his job on a continuous basis, but the theory of the board system was to maintain civilian control over the police department to assure responsiveness to community needs. The boards were composed of judges, mayors, and private citizens, and the police chiefs served at their pleasure. This system lasted many years, but it was found that there were many major disadvantages, including the prevalence of political corruption. At best the board members often proved themselves bungling, inexperienced, meddling amateurs.

The next step in the evolution of police administration was state control of the local agencies. This system was a reaction to the politically corrupt local boards, and the theory was that the new system would be free from local partisanship and that the citizens throughout the state would be assured of adequate and uniform law enforcement. After all, they argued, the state laws were promulgated for the entire state, and the state could best determine how those laws should be enforced. Except for several cities that still operate within the framework of this type of administration, most states and cities found that this system was not the answer to the problem. Control reverted to the local governments. The reasons for failure were that the laws were *not* uniformly applied. They were completely disregarded in some areas and overenforced in others. Fiscal support and police protection in some sections of the state were disproportionate. There was too much absentee administration and a lack of responsiveness to local demands and needs.

The next system of police administration to appear was the commission government charter. The elected commissioners were charged with operating various branches of city government, and the public safety commission (police, fire, and sometimes health and sanitation departments) was one of those commissions. This system was found inadequate as was the administrative police board comprised of amateurs. It, too, is on the decline.

The mayor-council and council-city manager types of municipal government are now more prevalent and efficient as local systems. The former type of government is quite efficient when the mayor is a full-time official and a capable administrator. The latter type assures more continuity in the business administration and executive control of the overall operations because a professional nonpolitical administrator is managing the affairs of the community. Under either system, the chief of police is usually selected on the basis of education, experience, and demonstrated ability, and he continues to serve as administrator of the police department as long as he continues to perform the job efficiently and effectively.

Development of the Judicial System

The judicial system in the United States operated on a very localized level for many years, and much of the system that migrated with the people from England still remains quite similar in many respects to today's small-unit court—the justice of the peace and his justice court. According to a 1971 report of the Advisory Commission on Intergovernmental Relations:

> In the colonial period, the lower courts were justice of the peace courts. By the 19th century, there was an increasing tendency to replace the JPs with magistrates or local inferior courts with somewhat increased or specialized jurisdiction. In some cases, the county courts were given jurisdiction concurrent with the justices of the peace.[6]

Although the report states that many jurisdictions abandoned the justice of the peace, that report indicates that in 1971 only seventeen states had abolished the justice court statewide, and that at least four more had replaced that court in selected cities. More than half of the states apparently have justice courts to this date, a court that originated in fourteenth-century England.

The jury by the peers of the accused, or persons selected from the same community occupied by the accused, and the grand jury originated in the year 1166 during the reign of King Henry of England. The jury heard testimony and passed judgment on guilt or innocence. The grand jury was charged with the responsibility to make inquisitions into facts of crime and render *Vere Dictums,* or verdicts, which were called indictments. The modern grand jury is utilized today in various ways. Some states utilize the grand jury for all felony prosecutions,[7] which is a duplication of the process of pretrial investigative procedures and parallels or duplicates the process of initiating felony prosecutions in the municipal court by means of a preliminary hearing. Current recommendations are that the grand jury be either discontinued entirely or that it be used at the discretion of the prosecutor as a means of expediting a case by avoiding the delays of court and the extension of information secrecy until the actual time of the trial in the higher court.[8]

The system of federal courts was established by the Judiciary Act of 1789, which also established the office of the Attorney General and the federal marshal, who serves as the court bailiff for the thirteen federal districts.[9]

---

[6] Advisory Commission on Intergovernmental Relations, *State-Local Relations in the Criminal Justice System* (Washington, D.C.: Government Printing Office, 1971), p. 89.

[7] Advisory Commission, *State-Local Relations in the Criminal Justice System,* p. 51.

[8] The grand jury proceedings are secret, which means that the identity of witnesses and disclosure of evidence may be held in confidence during continued investigations that may involve a series of indictments.

[9] Rita W. Cooly, "The Office of the U.S. Marshal," *Western Political Quarterly,* XII, No. 1, Part 1, March 1959, pp. 123–40.

The court systems in existence today are little different in basic structure from the times when they were established in their respective states by constitutional proclamation. The court of last resort, or the highest appeal court, is the state supreme court. The next level of court is the intermediate appellate court, which exists in approximately one-half of the states, and which hears appeals from the trial courts. The third level court is the court of original or general jurisdiction, which usually hears criminal felonies and civil cases of greater significance (usually determined by the amount of money sought as reparation), with the designation superior court, and with countywide jurisdiction. The fourth level consists of the courts of limited jurisdiction, which handle misdemeanors, most traffic cases, small claims, police courts, and civil cases of lesser significance. These lower courts are found in the smallest subdivision within the state, and usually serve court districts of rural areas and/or one or more smaller cities. In some states the size of the court district has determined which court is to be installed, such as in California where the justice court serves a district with a population less than 40,000 and the municipal court serves a district with a population of 40,000 or more.

The historical development of the state has a bearing on the courts as well as the evolution of law enforcement. For example, California as a Province still felt the Mexican influence. According to Elizabeth Pedrotti,[10] "There were the *avuntamientos* (town councils), the *alcaldes* (magistrates or mayors), the *jueces de paz* (justices of the peace), the *regidores* (councilmen) and the *sindicas* (clerks)."

Pedrotti quotes Paul Mason in his *Constitutional History of California:*

> The judicial system provided for the provinces of Mexico corresponds very closely with the present judicial system of California; the tribunal and courts of *segunda instancia* correspond with our supreme and appellate courts; the courts of *primera instancia,* with our superior courts; the *alcaldes* courts, with our municipal courts and the justices' courts with our own justice courts. The judicial system adopted by the first constitution was the system already established under the laws of Mexico.[11]

Juvenile Court. The first juvenile court in the world was established in Illinois in 1899. According to Saleem A. Shah:

> When Illinois established the first juvenile court in the world in 1899, expectations for its performance were high. It gave to juvenile delinquency

---

[10] Elizabeth Pedrotti, *The California Court System* (Sacramento, Calif.: State Printing Office, 1967), p. 1.

[11] Paul Mason, *Constitutional History of California,* n.d., n.p.

a status of something less than crime. Youthful deviance defined as delinquency was to be treated correctively, not by punishment.[12]

Jeffrey E. Glen and J. Robert Weber reported that the court was to deal with children who had violated the criminal law, or children who had been brought to the attention of the court as neglected, homeless, or otherwise disreputable.[13] They reported that by the 1920s virtually every state in the United States had passed some special legal provisions for delinquent and neglected youth. There were benefits from the change.

In removing children from the jurisdiction of the criminal court by establishing the juvenile court the intent was to do away with both the punitive philosophy of the criminal court as well as the method of trial and punishment. A new philosophy was developed. The child was regarded as immature and thus not wholly responsible for his acts. The child was entitled to protection, rehabilitation, or retraining. The juvenile court was to act as a wise parent who would plan for the total welfare of the child rather than punish the child for a specific act.[14]

In 1938 the federal government passed a Juvenile Court Act, which provided for handling juvenile federal law offenders in special juvenile courts, and by 1945 every state in the union had enacted legislation providing for such courts.[15] The courts have not necessarily been totally separate from the regular court system, however. Glen and Weber report:

At the outset of the juvenile court movement, the "court" itself was conceived of as nothing more than a different set of procedures for dealing with youths. Thus, there were no "juvenile courts" as separate judicial entities.

In recent years, several alternative schemes for juvenile court organization have been tried. Some states, such as Connecticut and Utah, have established statewide juvenile courts, with their own judiciary, completely separate from the civil and criminal courts of the State. Other states, including California, Washington, and Ohio, have established separate divisions of their highest courts of general trial jurisdiction to deal solely with juvenile cases.[16]

[12] Edwin M. Lemert, *Instead of Court/Diversion in Juvenile Justice* (Washington, D.C.: Government Printing Office, 1971), from the introduction by Saleem A. Shah of the National Institute of Mental Health, p. iii.

[13] Jeffery E. Glen and J. Robert Weber, *The Juvenile Court—A Status Report*, Department of Health, Education and Welfare Publication No. (HSM) 72-9115 (Washington, D.C.: Government Printing Office, 1972), p. 1.

[14] Glen and Weber, *The Juvenile Court—A Status Report*, p. 2.

[15] Lemert, *Instead of Court/Diversion in Juvenile Justice*, p. iii.

[16] Glen and Weber, *The Juvenile Court—A Status Report*, p. 3.

Development of the Correctional System

Traditional methods of punishment for many centuries were capital punishment, physical torture, and banishment. Such methods were decisive and permanent; the punishment of death served the needs of the group by eliminating the wrongdoer and satisfying a desire for revenge. Torture was an extension of the "eye for eye and tooth for tooth" philosophy, and included such things as crucifixion, exile into starvation, maiming, drawing and quartering, branding, dragging through the streets, and cutting off or out the offending part. Methods of taking the offenders' lives were demonstrative and served as a public spectacle to deter others from committing similar crimes. Stoning, hanging, beheading, poisoning, and being thrown from a convenient cliff constituted the different types of capital punishment.

During the eighteenth and nineteenth centuries, although still emphasizing corporal punishment, torture and banishment, the penal system was making some subtle changes. According to one source,[17] the Quakers in 1682 "initiated a century and a half of experimentation with new penal concepts." A long list of capital crimes were abolished, and the various types of torture were replaced by imprisonment at hard labor. The prisoners were intended to reflect in solitude as repentance.

During the time of reformation, penologists began to recognize criminals as persons who had committed crime as a matter of free will because it gave them pleasure or profit. The correctional tool of imprisonment was implemented to penalize lawbreakers to the extent that the pleasure or profit gained by commission of the crime was negated by the punishment. The Walnut Street Jail was opened in Philadelphia in 1790 by a Quaker organization under the leadership of Dr. Benjamin Rush.[18] Harry E. Barnes and Negley E. K. Teeters reported that although the place was merely a converted jail, it was, in practice, a penitentiary for the Commonwealth of Pennsylvania and received commitments from throughout the state. A block of small cells was constructed with a small exercise yard attached. The prisoners were placed in solitary confinement where they were forced to meditate and serve penitence.[19]

---

[17] Center for Law Enforcement and Corrections, *Jails and Prisons,* Training Module 6908 (University Park, Pa.: Pennsylvania State University, 1969), p. 3.

[18] Center for Law Enforcement and Corrections, *Jails and Prisons,* p. 4.

[19] Harry E. Barnes and Negley E. K. Teeters, *New Horizons in Criminology,* 2nd Ed. (Englewood Cliffs, N.J.: Prentice-Hall, Inc., 1972), p. 12.

Known as the Auburn Plan, the silent system was established in 1815 at the New York State prison at Auburn.[20] Both the Auburn method and the Walnut Street jail system were copied throughout the United States, and there are vestiges of the Auburn method still in evidence today in many of our large penitentiaries.[21] Under this method, prisoners were required to keep silent while working in workshops and factories during the daytime and while confined in cells at night. Punishment was severe and attempts at rehabilitation were minimal. Gradually since then, there have been progressive developments toward prison reform fashioned after the Elmira Reformatory at Elmira, New York, which was opened about 1865. Recent trends lean toward individualized treatment and attempts at various rehabilitative methods.

Probation. The practice of conditional release on the individual's own recognizance and the suspended sentence originated in Anglo-Saxon times and was brought to the colonies as a part of the common law that was later codified in the United States.[22] Probation as practiced today, which involves a period of supervised freedom during which time the probationer is expected to develop acceptable life-style and behavior patterns and to divert his energy and desires from criminal activities, originated in Boston in 1841. John Augustus, a local craftsman, volunteered his services to the court to screen and place in the community those children that were considered worth the risk, then provided some supervision while they were out on probation.[23] That same source reports that this voluntary probation service was given official recognition in 1869, when the state of Massachusetts assigned a state agent to the Board of Charities in Boston, who attended court hearings, made arrangements for placement of juveniles on probation to friends of the court.[24]

The first law that made probation a legal service was passed in Boston in 1878. At first the probation officer was appointed by the mayor, then this responsibility was later passed on to the courts. By the late 1890s a statewide probation system had been adopted in the state of Massachusetts. Since that time probation has extended throughout the

[20] Vernon Fox, *Introduction to Corrections* (Englewood Cliffs, N.J.: Prentice-Hall, Inc., 1972), p. 12.

[21] Fox, *Introduction to Corrections,* p. 12.

[22] Center for Law Enforcement and Corrections, *Probation and Parole,* Training Module 6907 (University Park, Pa.: Pennsylvania State University, 1969), p. 2.

[23] Center for Law Enforcement and Corrections, *Probation, Parole, and Pardons: A Basic Course,* Training Module 6913 (Universiay Park, Pa.: Pennsylvania State University, 1969), p. 8.

[24] Center for Law Enforcement and Corrections, *Probation, Parole, and Pardons,* p. 8.

United States, including juvenile probation (about 1900), and federal probation, which was established in 1925.[25]

Parole. Although involving casework and other techniques quite similar to those of probation, parole has been separate and distinct in origin and development. The program involves "aftercare" type casework with convicted offenders following a period of imprisonment, and the principal thrust of parole is reintegration and socialization. Parole and pardon are related in some respects. They both follow a period of imprisonment. The pardon is a form of executive clemency action in which the individual may be granted a pardon on condition that he be transferred to the colonies or to some place in bondage to work out an indebtedness to the crown or to some other person. A pardon may have involved a reduction in sentence in return for some favor or for good conduct. Parole is structured as a conditional release from imprisonment. The individual is provided the opportunity to "make it" on the outside under supervision prior to being released completely on his own at the conclusion of the prescribed time for him to be under the control of the corrections agency.

Indentured service was a form of conditional release, or parole, which originated in England in 1717. The prisoner was purchased from the Crown and was taken to the colonies for a prescribed period of mandatory service. Another form of parole was a conditional release from prison for certain reasons such as good behavior known as the *ticket of leave*. Used in England and Australia in the eighteenth century, the leave was granted to persons who were allowed to seek employment in certain districts under specified conditions. "Until 1811 tickets of leave were freely given to prisoners for good conduct, meritorious service, or the purpose of marriage." [26]

The indeterminate sentence and an early form of parole appeared in 1837. It was known as the Mark System, or the Irish System. Created in England and adopted in Ireland, the conditions were these: (1) Imprisonment was with training and employment, (2) employment was on public works, and (3) eventual release from prison was made conditional on good behavior and monthly reports.[27] The first working system of parole is attributed to Alexander Maconochie in the penal colony on Norfolk Island in New South Wales in 1840.

The Elmira Reformatory Plan of 1876 featured the indeterminate

[25] Center for Law Enforcement and Corrections, *Probation, Parole, and Pardons,* p. 8.

[26] Center for Law Enforcement and Corrections, *Probation, Parole, and Pardons,* p. 7.

[27] Center for Law Enforcement and Corrections, *Probation, Parole, and Pardons,* pp. 8–10.

sentence and parole concepts, as reported by the Center for Law Enforcement and Corrections.[28] Education in Elmira was compulsory, prisoners were granted privileges on the basis of capacity and behavior, and they were selected for parole according to the following provisions: (1) required to maintain a good record for one year, (2) had to submit suitable plans for employment, (3) required to report to guardian upon release and the first day of each month, and (4) the guardian submitted regular reports on the inmate's progress to the Elmira Reformatory.

Summary

The history of the system of administration of justice is quite extensive, and this chapter is in no way intended to detract from some serious in-depth study of the matter. In this chapter we have merely touched upon some of the highlights in history. We have missed in our discussions more than we have included, obviously, and the serious student interested in the historical progress of the justice system should continue his research. Law enforcement had its origins in symphony with the development of civilizations, and there has yet to be any evidence to the contrary. The courts and the police—law enforcement—in the United States are principally based upon English common law that later migrated to the colonies with the people, and which have evolved into a somewhat sophisticated series of agencies with similar and interrelated responsibilities. Corrections systems have had more recent beginnings, or so the historical chronologue has indicated. Actually, modern corrections—or penology as it was called for some time—has developed principally during the last century.

Exercises and Study Questions

1. What country had the greatest influence on our modern system of law enforcement in the United States?

2. According to the text, what was Hammurabi's contribution to the criminal justice system?

3. What are the similarities between the shire-reeve of early England and the sheriff of the county where you live?

4. At what time in history were the crime classifications of felonies and misdemeanors defined?

[28] Center for Law Enforcement and Corrections, *Probation, Parole, and Pardons*, pp. 7–8.

5. What was Magna Carta, and what influence did it have in relationship to modern law enforcement?

6. What was the purpose for curfew when it was established, and how does it compare with curfew as we know it today?

7. What was the contribution of Sir Robert Peel to law enforcement?

8. Discuss the principles of the Peelian Reform and explain how each of the principles relates to modern law enforcement in your state.

9. What is the major difference between the municipal police forces in the United States and the local forces in England, if any?

10. In what major city of the United States did the army provide police services for a period of time.

11. What were the lower courts in colonial times?

12. What are the lower courts in modern times? How does this compare with colonial times?

13. Describe the function of the grand jury.

14. What is the court of last resort?

15. In which court in your state are felony trials held?

16. When and where was the first juvenile court established?

17. What is the Auburn Plan?

18. What was the contribution of John Augustus to criminal justice?

19. Recommended semester project: Select one component of the criminal justice system (police-court-corrections) and write a detailed history of the evolution of that component for a certain period of time, such as "prior to U.S. independence," or "Civil War to 1900," or "since 1945."

Suggested for Additional Study

GIDDINGS, LARRY A., MARK FURSTENBERG, and HENRY J. NOBLE, *Manual on Training for Sheriffs,* LEAA Grant No. 268. Washington, D.C.: Government Printing Office, 1968.

GODDARD, HENRY, *Memories of a Bow Street Runner.* New York: William Morrow, 1957.

PRINGLE, PATRICK, *Hue and Cry: The Story of Henry and John Fielding and Their Bow Street Runners.* New York: William Morrow, 1955.

TAFT, DONALD R. and RALPH W. ENGLAND, JR., *Criminology* (4th ed.). New York: The Macmillan Co., 1964.

5

Law Enforcement

Introduction

Each type of law enforcement agency had a different origin. Of all the types of police organizations, the municipal police force is the most common and one of the most essential branches of local government intrinsic to an orderly civilization. Some police forces or investigative agencies have been created to fill a specific need as you will see as you read of the various agencies in this chapter. Law enforcement agencies have been created at the state and federal levels for the purpose of enforcing taxation, licensing, and other revenue laws. Others have been formed to meet particular needs on a statewide or national basis because of the lack of efficiency of the local police or the dilemma caused by the inability of local police departments to carry out certain duties beyond restrictive jurisdictional boundaries. Such organizations as the narcotics bureaus and alcoholic beverage control departments, highway patrols, and similar departments have statewide jurisdiction. Federal agencies are able to cross state lines and cooperate with the police of foreign countries because of their nationwide jurisdiction. Still other agencies, found at all levels of government, have been created and perpetuated because they serve as convenient instrumentalities of special interest groups. These little "empires" may convince their supporters that only they are capable of performing the specific investigations required of them and that any other arrangement would be catastrophic. Other special enforcement bureaus or divisions of various government agencies have arisen as a result of distrust of certain local police agencies due to the real or imagined inefficiency of those agencies. Except for the local city and county police agencies, the majority of police forces, particularly federal and state forces, are of relatively recent origin. The first state police agency—the Texas Rangers—was not created until 1835. The first federal police agency was the Postal Inspection Service, which was founded in 1775. The Secret Service followed in 1865.

Another type of police agency that should be included in a discussion of the police system is the private police department. Private police forces are generally formed by large corporations because of their need for more concentrated protective services than can be provided by the government police. Many private police agencies are very capable and efficient. An example of a very organized and efficient private police force is the railroad police of the United States and Canada, the largest privately supported police agency in the world. The force is composed of several thousand agents stationed throughout the two countries, supported by approximately four hundred separate railroads.

Many other very efficient private police agencies exist to perform all types of protective and investigative duties. As a matter of fact, industrial policing is a highly specialized police function that requires a great variety of skills. There are other organizations, however, that have been composed of hoodlums and troublemakers. A vivid example of such a force was the Coal and Iron Police in Pennsylvania, created by several mine operators for the purpose of forcibly breaking up labor strikes. That particular organization was outlawed by the Pennsylvania State Legislature in 1835.

When studying the police system, consider first the various local police forces, each responsible for policing its own respective political subdivision of the state: the cities protected by the city police, and the unincorporated and rural areas policed by the constable, the marshal, or the sheriff. Each jurisdiction could be related to the other jurisdictions as interlocking pieces in a jigsaw puzzle. The many state and federal agencies have similar jurisdictional relationships with the emphasis placed on division of responsibility as opposed to geographic allocation of jurisdictional boundaries. There are overlapping pieces in the system's jigsaw puzzle, however, and there are jurisdictional disputes and conflicts. The conflicts are probably more evident in the federal jurisdictions because they all have no geographic boundaries within the United States, whereas the local departments are separated by city limits and county lines.

There is considerable overlapping of federal police and investigative responsibilities, and also to a lesser extent of state agencies. Rivalry, distrust, and intrigue have been the products of jurisdictional conflicts, although the trend during recent years has been toward a greater amount of cooperation and more professional attitudes. Three alternatives to the existing interforce conflicts of federal agencies with overlapping jurisdictions have been advanced by observers of the problem. One alternative is to retain all of the existing agencies, but to redefine their respective jurisdictions systematically to assure a minimum of conflict. The second alternative is to establish a central bureau by consolidating all of the existing agencies. The third alternative is to retain the present system, or "nonsystem," and to establish an interdepartmental committee as a single coordinator to direct the efforts of the many agencies with a minimum of duplication and conflict. Similar proposals could be applied to the many agencies of the states. At the local levels, there should be no displacement of the existing arrangement of having police departments in each separate political subdivision that are directly accountable to the people of that jurisdiction. The first proposal of the preceding three that were presented with respect to the federal agencies—retention of the existing agency but redefining the jurisdiction—already applies to local police agencies. The second proposal—consolidation of all agencies—is not practicable nor desirable at the local police level. The third proposal —that of coordination of several agencies—is feasible. Coordination of such operations as records keeping, training, laboratory, and similar functions placed at strategically located positions in the state and operated jointly by the many contributing and participating agencies would result in a greater amount of uniformity in procedures, greater efficiency, and would assist the progress of police service toward eventual professionalization.

There are nearly one-half million officers and agents working for approximately forty thousand separate agencies in the United States with law enforcement and/or investivative responsibility. Such a nonsystem of cooperating agencies has room for improvement, but a great deal of credit must be accorded to the many thousands who perform their duties as capability as they do. Such is the police nonsystem.

The Local Police

THE MUNICIPAL POLICE DEPARTMENT

The entire police and policing picture centers around the city or township police department. They are charged with crime prevention and repression, traffic law enforcement, protective patrol services, arbitration in neighborhood and family disputes, apprehension and arrest (or citation or warning) of criminal law violators, and recovery of stolen property. The local police officers also perform a multitude of nonenforcement tasks, such as providing information and assistance to visitors and tourists, as well as residents, vehicular and pedestrian traffic control, safety education, crowd control at sporting events and other public gatherings, and the general task of maintaining order and peace in their respective jurisdictions.

The city police departments comprise a large portion of the more than forty thousand law enforcement agencies that employ nearly one-half million men and women in the United States to provide for the protection, comfort, assistance, and maintenance of a moral conscience for the nearly 200 million people in their jurisdictions. The organization of the municipal police department will be outlined in the next chapter. The entire Part IV of this book is devoted to the primary police functions that are performed by the local law enforcement agency. The local agencies—although not specifically mentioned in those chapters—include the municipal police departments, town constabulary, township and borough police, and county law enforcement agencies.

The federal and state law enforcement and investigative agencies have limitations on their scope of authority, which usually restrict their officers and agents to the investigation and enforcement of only those laws and other matters that specifically relate to their specialties. The municipal police department is charged with the responsibility for taking an active part in both investigation and enforcement of federal and state laws as well as the ordinances of their own specific political subdivisions. The extent to which they become involved varies with the nature of the offenses and their working relationship with the various other agencies.

The city policeman may arrest a common thief and uncover a cache of smuggled tax-unpaid liquor and a kilo (roughly two pounds as packaged by smugglers) of marijuana. The jurisdictions involved in these violations include the local department, of course, but also a few other agencies. The Bureau of Alcohol and Tobacco Tax Division of the Treasury Department is responsible for "bootleg" alcoholic beverages, and the Bureau of Customs also has a jurisdictional interest in the liquor if it came across a border. The illegal narcotics in such a case may involve still additional agencies. The Bureau of Customs would have a legal interest because of the smuggling violation, although there is no legal means for the smugglers to possess the marijuana because it has been outlawed in the United States since 1937. In addition to the local police department's legal interest in effecting the arrest for the state law violations for possession of the illicit drugs, the state agents would be concerned because of the significance of the drug's presence and the state-wide narcotics problem, and the federal agents would be concerned because of the violation of a tax law involving marijuana and also the nationwide implications of smuggling the drug. The agency that would handle the case initially would be the local police department.

In the hypothetical case at hand, the local department would take custody of the evidence and properly preserve it for later presentation in court, the concerned agencies would be notified, and the appropriate reports prepared and disseminated. The suspect would be interviewed by representatives of all involved agencies and follow-up investigations initiated as a result of those interviews. But what of the initial arrest and prosecution? The local agency would, in all probability, be the one that would make the formal charges for the state violations of theft and unlawful possession of marijuana. Any additional charges would be initiated by the agencies having specific jurisdiction, and separate trials for those offenses would be held later.

In some situations there are offenses that are subject to concurrent jurisdiction, such as bank robbery, interstate transportation of a stolen vehicle, taking a kidnapped victim across state lines, and hundreds of others. Those offenses are likewise investigated and enforced by agents of more than one agency. They cooperate effectively to their mutual advantage. The prosecution is usually at the initiative of the agency in whose jurisdiction the original violation occurred, and the products of the efforts of the other agencies are added to the weight of the prosecution.

THE COUNTY SHERIFF

In the majority of counties in the United States, the sheriff is the principal law enforcement officer with his jurisdiction primarily limited to the unincorporated areas of that county. In his duties as officer of the court and in the execution of his nonenforcement duties, his jurisdiction includes the entire county. In the state of Louisiana the political subdivision in which the sheriff performs his duties is called the parish, but in nearly all other respects his roles are the same.

The sheriff fills his office by popular election in nearly all jurisdictions of the United States, and his term of office is for two, three, or four years. Rotation of the office is almost universal because legislation either limits the tenure of most sheriffs to a single term or a limited number of terms. The theory behind such a limitation on tenure is to prevent the man in office from acquiring too much power while holding that office, an atavistic attitude of early Americans who suspected the motives of anyone in public offices.

Throughout the United States the multifaceted responsibilities and duties of the sheriff vary from state to state and from county to county within the individual states. In virtually all areas, the sheriff is responsible for the service of civil processes and maintenance of the county jail and custody of county prisoners. In some jurisdictions the sheriff is "overseer of the highways." The positions of sheriff and coroner are often combined.

In parts of the South and Southwest, the sheriff serves as tax collector and as public administrator for the property of persons who die intestate. In the state of California, the county is the principal political subdivision of the state and the sheriff is the principal law enforcement official in each county. He is so designated because he maintains the county jail, serves as bailiff to the superior court, and in times of an insurrection or major disaster involving more than one city and parts of the county, he may act as the coordinator of all of the concerned police agencies as designated in mutual aid agreements between the various communities. There is no hierarchy of command in this arrangement (except during special emergencies and by prior agreement), and during normal times and conditions, the various law enforcement agencies are completely autonomous and are under the direction of their respective chiefs of police.

The sheriff and his deputies have a variety of duties, some of which are listed as follows:

1. Execute civil and criminal processes throughout the county, including various writs of execution and attachment and warrants of arrest.
2. Keep the county jail and its prisoners.
3. Keep the peace in the unincorporated areas of the county. In order that he may accomplish this objective, the sheriff and his deputies may take whatever preventive and enforcement action that he deems necessary, including arresting and taking before the magistrate people who have committed or have attempted to commit public offenses.
4. Attend superior court and obey and carry out all lawful orders of the court, and also act as court crier and bailiff.
5. Attend all meetings of the Board of Supervisors (the governing body in California) to preserve order and serve notices, subpoenas, or other processes directed by the board.
6. Investigate public offenses that have been committed and cause those who have been identified as violators of the law to be prosecuted.

The sheriff is the county officer who is charged with the authority to command as many able-bodied male inhabitants of the county to assist him in carrying out his duty to preserve the peace and to maintain order. This power is called the "power of the county," or *posse comitatus*. In some jurisdictions, the sheriff may also fill the role and the office of marshal, as described in the next paragraph.

THE MARSHAL

The role of the marshal is similar to that of the sheriff in that he serves as an officer of the court, but the marshal serves in the municipal court while the sheriff serves the superior court. The marshall serves subpoenas and civil papers, warrants of arrest, and may serve as escort for the prisoners who must be taken from the jail to the court for trials and hearings. The marshal is elected in some jurisdictions and appointed in others. Except where the marshal's office is incorporated by the local jurisdiction to include the duties of the chief of police as town marshal, his duties are usually restricted to those enumerated in this paragraph. It is no small task, but it is comparatively limited in scope.

THE CONSTABLE

The constable is recognized by the constitutions in approximately twenty states, particularly in New England, the South, and the West. Selection of the constable is usually by popular election. He serves a township, and his duties are primarily to maintain the peace and serve processes for the local justice court. He may also serve as a tax collector or poundmaster, and whatever other duties as may be described by the government in his own state and county. Constables collect fees and mileages for execution of arrest warrants, search warrants, and transportation of prisoners. In some jurisdictions, the constable may be under the direction of the sheriff.

MISCELLANEOUS LOCAL POLICE FORCES

At various times in history, and for various purposes, different types of policing organizations have been formed. Some of those organizations were formed for specific purposes and then disbanded when the need no longer continued to exist; some of the organizations continue to exist at the present time.

Vigilante committes have been formed at various locations, usually at times when the residents found that the local police were ineffective either because they were overwhelmed by the incidence of crime, or they were inefficient. Cattle rustling in the West during the 1800s was a sizeable problem that the people attempted to solve by vigilant procedures. During the late 1920s, prior to the FBI involvement in protection of banks against bank robbery and other crimes, a bankers' vigilante group was formed in the Midwest for the purpose of apprehending bank robbers. Law enforcement today calls for greater efficiency than can be accomplished by a vigilante group, and without proper guidance and training, an organization of this type could promote anarchy.

Park police have been created by some of the larger cities to provide protection and informational services to the visitors to their parks. Parkway police may be found on the parkways and boulevards in some states and have the specific purpose of guarding public buildings or monuments.

Examples of two local police forces that serve local needs but which were developed for special purposes include the New York City Housing Authority and New York City Transit Authority Police Departments. The Housing Police patrol the grounds, cellars, roofs, stairwells, and elevators of the public housing projects. The Transit Authority, including 483 subway stations,[1] provides police services on the public transportation vehicles and terminals throughout the city.

Reserves. Developed during times of extreme emergency, particularly during and following the World War II years of the early and mid-forties, the auxiliary or reserve police forces appeared on the American scene. When adequately trained and equipped, these men and women serve as the extra strength that is so direly needed at certain times of disaster or other emergency but which is otherwise unavailable. Selected from the community, some reserves are young potentials for the regular service who are screened for full-time service through assessment of their performance while on duty. Other reserves are gainfully occupied in other professions or businesses and choose the police reserves as a form of community service, often performing as officers with full peace officer authority. Under normal circumstances the reserves accompany full-time officers as the second man in the patrol unit, as public relations contacts with the community, as dispatchers, relief jailers, and they fill virtually every position in the department at one time or another in some departments.

The Coroner

With a background similar to the history of the sheriff, the coroner comes to modern enforcement from ancient times. Today he is an officer of the county and may be found in virtually all parts of the country either as coroner or medical examiner. The coroner's ancestor was called the coronator, and he represented the King of England at public hearings.

---

[1] James S. Kakalik and Sorrel Wildhorn, *Special Purpose Public Police* (Washington, D.C.: Government Printing Office, 1971), pp. 14–15.

In the United States, his principal jurisdiction involves the determination of causes of death and care and custody of the remains and personal effects of deceased persons.

The office of coroner or medical examiner may be combined with that of sheriff, tax collector, public administrator, or any other public office that may be combined with his office by law. The coroner is a county officer, and in California he fills the office of the sheriff when it is left vacant. The coroner need not be a medical doctor or have any legal knowledge to be elected, but the coroner in some jurisdictions has been replaced by a medical examiner who is a doctor, and in many others the people have elected doctors to the office.

The coroner is required by law to investigate and sign the death certificate in all of the following circumstances in California according to the Government Code, Sections 27491.1:

> . . . all violent, sudden or unusual deaths; unattended deaths; deaths wherein the deceased has not been attended by a physician in the ten days before death; deaths related to or following known or suspected self-induced or criminal abortion; known or suspected homicide, suicide, or accidental poisoning; deaths known or suspected as resulting in whole or in part from or related to accident or injury either old or recent; deaths due to drowning, fire, hanging, gunshot, stabbing, cutting, exposure, starvation, alcoholism, drug addiction, strangulation, or aspiration; death in whole or in part occasioned by criminal means; deaths associated with a known or alleged rape or crime against nature; deaths in prison or while under sentence; deaths known or suspected as due to contagious disease and constituting a public hazard; deaths under such circumstances as to afford a reasonable ground to suspect that the death was caused by the criminal act of another, or any deaths reported by physicians having knowledge of death for inquiry by the coroner.

The coroner may examine the body at the place of death and take custody of the remains for the purpose of identification or determination of the cause of death and may exhume a body, cause a post-mortem examination or autopsy to be made, or hold an inquest to inquire into the cause of death. After determining the cause of death, the coroner signs the death certificate. If an inquest jury finds that the death was caused as a result of a criminal act of another person, he shall properly notify the appropriate law enforcement agency, and the prosecuting attorney in accordance with state law. In cases when the identity of the killer is known and he is not in custody, the coroner may issue a warrant of arrest.

The purpose of an inquest is to determine cause of death and the relevant facts attendant to the death. When the inquest jury finds that the death was caused by criminal means and they accuse an individual of the crime, it is merely that—an accusation. Any criminal charges and conviction or acquittal must be brought before the courts in the same manner as any other criminal charge.

State Justice Department

The attorney general is the chief law officer and ministerial officer of the state court system, the chief counsel in all litigation involving the state, and the chief administrative officer of the state justice department. The attorney general prepares and disseminates opinions relating to the interpretations by his office of the criminal law, and in the absence of written or case law, the attorney general's opinion has the same force and effect as law.

In addition to providing assistance in the investigation and prosecution of criminal cases in the state, the attorney general represents the state on appeals from the lower courts to the appellate jurisdictions at state and federal levels, and his office processes extradition and interstate rendition proceedings for persons who have fled from the state—or have left the state—to avoid prosecution.

Some states have agencies under the supervision of the attorney general and the justice department that are created for the primary purpose of assisting local law enforcement agencies in the state in the (1) identification of criminals, (2) control and supervision of certain types of offenders, (3) location of missing persons, and (4) technical and scientific analysis of evidence.

State laws usually require that chiefs of police, sheriffs, and other law enforcement agencies forward daily the fingerprints and other arrest data to the state agency responsible for maintenance of records and statistics. The data required usually includes copies of investigation reports on felonies of all types, sex offenses, narcotics and dangerous drug violations, and certain cases of statewide significance, along with a detailed description of stolen property. It is the responsibility of this agency, which is usually a part of the attorney general's office, to coordinate and correlate this information, to attempt to identify the responsible criminals by their modus operandi (method of operation), and to promptly forward to the contributing agency any information that may assist it in identifying and apprehending the responsible parties.

A bureau of statistics may be a part of the justice department or similar state agency. If such a state agency exists, its general responsibilities should include the compilation and analysis of information relating

State police officers perform a variety of functions: top, in undercover narcotics investigations; middle, traffic enforcement; and bottom, giving roadside assistance. Courtesy Kentucky State Police.

to criminal activity in the state, crime trends, achievements of law enforcement, and the results of prosecution. The data is often correlated with that of the statistics section of the FBI for the compilation of the Uniform Crime Reports.

State Police Agencies

At the state government level in the police "nonsystem" most law enforcement and investigation agencies are specialized in nature. Their jurisdictions vary with their specific functions, but they usually have statewide authority to perform those police duties—however limited in scope they may be. Highway patrols, for example, uniformly enforce state traffic laws on the highways, and alcoholic beverage control agents enforce licensing and other liquor laws in the entire state.

Each state is different from all the others with respect to its state police agencies, depending upon its history and evolution of policing needs. Starting with the Texas Rangers in 1835 and continuing to the present, new agencies are being formed and old agencies reorganized to meet the changing requirements of the evolving community. Massachusetts employed state constables in 1865 for the purpose of suppressing commercialized vice. The Arizona Rangers were created in 1901, and New Mexico founded its state police in 1905. Both of these agencies had local police powers at their inception. The former organization is still active.

Connecticut organized a state police agency in 1903 with a primary objective of investigating and suppressing commercialized liquor and gambling violations. They now examine operators' license applicants and are involved in arson investigations. The Pennsylvania, New York, West Virginia, and New Jersey state police also double as fire, fish, and game wardens. The New York state police officers serve as court officers for justices of the peace on Indian reservations.

California's state police are limited in jurisdiction to state buildings and grounds throughout the state, including the state college and university campuses. In addition to the state police, there are many other investigative and law enforcement agencies, each with a specific agency or bureau to which it reports and a specific list of laws and rules with which it is to be concerned.

There is no uniformity in state police and investigative agencies, but there is some similarity. With that premise in mind, let's look at some of those agencies.

State Adjutant General

The National Guard and Air National Guard, or State Military Department, provide a military force with dual federal and state status, and they are available to both the federal government and the state in the event of a national or state emergency. Their organizations are set up in accordance with the laws of the states and the regulations of the Army and Air Force. The governor is the commander-in-chief. Under his direction, and in his name, the adjutant general is the chief-of-staff and commander of all state military forces.

Military control is the initial force of government and the ultimate power of government. It is defined as the "initial force" because it overcame the enemy and established the government in the beginning. It is the "ultimate force" in that the state militia is the governing authority when all other powers are ineffective to protect the state against invasion, insurrecion, disaster, or unlawful disturbances.

Some form of military control is a traditional and obviously essential part of every government. Under normal conditions this control is exercised by the local law enforcement agencies and the control is basically exerted in subtle form by the presence of the officers throughout the community, who take whatever enforcement action is necessary as the need arises. When the military force in the form of the police is ineffective, it becomes necessary to invoke the more powerful force of the government, the National Guard.

The problem of when to call upon the services of the National Guard is serious, and the responsibility for making the decision should not be underestimated in a free country such as the United States. The entire judicial system is suspended under martial rule. The habeas corpus and due process provisions of the Constitution and the Bill of Rights are suspended. Martial rule is proclaimed by the governor, and it is in existence only when the state militia supersedes one or more local police agencies by his proclamation. It is a form of executive control that arises in self-defense of the state. There must be a very real need for such martial rule before the governor may proclaim its existence. Its objective is to preserve the public safety and good order of the community. The governor has the responsibility and authority to determine the need for martial rule and to supend it at the earliest possible moment when its need no longer exists.

Under all but exceptional circumstances, the state militia will act "in aid of the civil authority." While acting in such a capacity, the militia's aid to local law enforcement agencies is limited. There is no suspension of local control or any of the judicial or legal processes. Objectives and missions are assigned by the local civil authority, and the military power shall be subordinate to civil authority. A military situation justifies the use of military force equal to the situation. This attitude toward martial rule provides the military force with more power than that of a peace officer.

The greatest difference between martial rule and civil rule is in the arrest and detention process. Ringleaders of a mob may be detained without formal booking procedures and held throughout the entire disturbance, then later released without trial. Such a detention is considered *preventive* and not *punitive*. In some cases when the military assists local police and when martial rule has not been proclaimed but when the public safety demands that such processes as preventive custody be used, the courts have ruled that such action was necessary and have refused writs of habeas corpus and denied claims of false imprisonment. In such cases the condition is defined as "preventive" or "qualified" martial rule.

The governor activates the militia, as mentioned earlier, and, if necessary, declares martial rule whenever the need for such action is called to his attention in any acceptable manner. Normal channels usually provide for such notifications to be made by the chief executive officer of any city or county, any justice of the state supreme court, judge of the superior court, or any sheriff. The request shows cause for action and a statement to the effect that the civil power is not sufficient to cope with the problem. Some states provide that martial rule may be utilized in any situation of great need, except when any such condition results from a labor controversy.

Highway Patrol

Highway patrol organizations are charged with the enforcement of state traffic laws and all laws governing the operation of vehicles on the public highways throughout the state. The primary purpose for these organizations is to provide for the safety of all motorists. Although a state highway patrol usually has principal enforcement jurisdiction on the highways in the unincorporated areas of the state, some states provide that the highway patrol officers have full peace officer authority, and they may enforce traffic laws upon any public highway in the state. In times of civil disturbance or disaster it is the responsibility of the highway patrol to keep traffic lanes moving and open.

Because of the large area to be covered, the state highway patrol is divided into geographical districts, with a ranking staff officer in charge of each district. The districts may be further divided into squads or other smaller units, depending on the needs of the agency and the size of the state. Enforcement activities are accomplished by patrol officers in uniform and distinctively marked patrol cars and motorcycles to (1) enforce the laws regulating the use of vehicles, (2) maintain preventive patrols on the highways, (3) regulate traffic movements and relieve congestion, (4) investigate traffic accidents, and (5) make surveys and studies of accidents and enforcement practices for the purpose of improving traffic safety.

Some state highway patrol organizations maintain a traffic safety section that coordinates traffic safety programs throughout the state to assure uniformity in adherence to the many traffic laws. They assist all organizations, both public and private, in planning and operating effective safety programs. They may assist local agencies by providing intensive enforcement training for traffic personnel. Auto theft records may be maintained more efficiently by a state agency such as a highway patrol because of their statewide jurisdiction, and they may provide laboratory and investigative personnel to assist local agencies in the investigation of hit-and-run cases and auto theft.

In addition to those functions listed in the preceding paragraphs, some highway patrol agencies coordinate the activity of and maintain records on commercial vehicle enforcement, maintain public scales on the highways, inspect all school buses, and investigate accidents involving school buses throughout the state. Licensing or registration of official smog control devices or headlights, or other safety equipment installation, and inspection stations may also be functions of the state highway patrol, as they are in California.

Department of Motor Vehicles

A state motor vehicle department is a service agency that has three major functions: (1) registration of motor vehicles, collection of fees, and maintaining registration records, (2) licensing drivers, collecting fees, and maintaining files on licenses, and (3) administration of financial responsibility laws. Investigators assigned to this type of agency are involved in investigation of thefts and unlawful transfer of ownership of vehicles. Other investigators will include cases of altered license plates; forged or counterfeit auto registration certificates or drivers' licenses; and a variety of suspected law violations by auto dealerships and auto wreckers.

State Bureau of Narcotics

State narcotics agents are responsible for the investigation and enforcement of violations of the state narcotics laws. Their involvement with the lone users of narcotics and the peddlers of the drugs on the streets is usually through their cooperation with the many local law enforcement agencies and their vice officers. They are pricipally engaged in the investigation of alleged infractions of the law by persons who are in lawful possession of the drugs but may unlawfully or negligently dispense them. They investigate pharmacies, hospitals, and the offices of doctors, dentists, and veterinary surgeons for illegal sale and use of narcotics. State narcotics agents also seek out manufacturers and distributors of illicit drugs, and generally enforce the legitimate use and dispensation of the drugs. This bureau is also responsible for the seizure of vehicles used in narcotic traffic and the abatement of properties used for the purpose of housing traffickers and users of drugs.

Alcoholic Beverage Control Agencies

The state department of alcoholic beverage control in many states has licensing authority concerning the manufacture, importation, and sale of intoxicating liquors. The agency has statewide jurisdiction over the administration and enforcement of the state alcoholic beverage control laws that provide for the licensing and regulation of the alcoholic beverage industry in the state. In some states such an agency may also be given the responsibility to assess and collect excise taxes on the manufacture, importation, and sale of alcoholic beverages. The latter responsibility, however, may be handled by a taxing agency instead of by the department of alcoholic beverage control.

The agents assigned to control state liquor laws are primarily involved in the investigation of applicants for licenses to sell alcoholic beverages and to report on the moral character and fitness of the applicants and the suitability of the premises where the sales are to be conducted.

Violations of the laws that are most frequently encountered by the investigators of an agency of this type are sales to minors, consumption and possession by minors, sales after hours, conduct of the premises as disorderly houses, sales to obviously intoxicated persons, and failure to "fair trade" or post prices. Investigators of the alcoholic beverage control are peace officers in most states, and they have the authority to make arrests at any place in the state. They confiscate evidence, prepare reports, and testify in court in the prosecution of criminal law violators. Because all dealers in alcoholic beverages are licensees, the department handles many disciplinary matters of licensees administratively. Punishment may consist of a written notice to comply with the regulations or a permanent or temporary suspension of the license and forfeiture of the license fees.

Fish and Game Wardens

Game wardens enforce and prevent violations of laws and other regulations that relate to the conservation and protection of fish and wildlife. The duties of a warden include effecting arrests and issuing citations and warnings to the violators. They investigate wildlife crop damage com-

Wardens Tom Meagher (left) and Art Bryarly of the California Dept. of Fish and Game check tuna delivery to a cannery at San Pedro. Cannery workers are cleaning tuna on assembly line from ship's hold.
Department of Fish and Game photo.

plaints, advise landowners on the control of wildlife, and issue kill permits. Other duties include the feeding of game birds and animals during unusual weather conditions, assisting in the planning of controlled hunts, and operating checking stations in controlled hunting areas. The Department of Fish and Game and its agents are responsible for assisting in safety programs for hunters and fishermen, for securing assistance from various organizations in planting of fish and rescue operations, and generally assisting in the maintenance of hunting and fishing areas in the state to assure both wildlife conservation and perpetuation of the outdoor sports.

Labor Law Enforcement

The division of labor law enforcement of a state's department of industrial relations or similar agency is particularly responsible for enforcing regulations assuring ideal working conditions for the workers in the state. The laws enforced by such an agency include those that relate to the payment of wages, employment of women and children, private employment agencies, ventilation and sanitary conditions of places of employment, weekly day of rest, hours of work, and general conditions of work. Agents assigned to a labor law enforcement division or bureau are responsible for the additional duties of assuring compliance with the law in labor disputes, investigating industrial accidents and industrial safety, and maintaining labor statistics.

State Fire Marshal

The state fire marshal is a peace officer in most states. He has the primary responsibility of preventing fires by performing the following functions:

1. Elimination of fire hazards on state-owned and tax-deeded property.
2. Establishment and enforcement of fire and panic safety regulations in all state institutions.
3. Investigation of fires vaulting from crime or where crime has been committed in connection with any fire.
4. The development of uniform fire and panic safety regulations and the enforcement of such regulations in areas outside of corporate cities and fire protection districts.
5. Administration of a continuous educational fire prevention program.
6. Aid and assistance to local fire officials in the enforcement of fire safety laws, ordinances, and regulations.

7. The establishment of minimum safety requirements governing the manufacture and sale of flammable clothing, the operation of circuses and tent shows, and the flame-retardent treatment of drapes and curtains used in schools or places of public assemblage.

8. Regulation of fire safety in the dry cleaning industry.

9. Regulation of the sale, discharge, and public display of fireworks.

10. Issuance of fire clearances to private institutions such as sanitariums licensed by the State Department of Mental Hygiene, Social Welfare, or Public Health.

11. The approval of fire safety plans of new institutions or additions to existing institutions before they are constructed.

Horse-Racing Board

In states where there is parimutuel betting, the horse-racing board or a similar agency administers laws governing horse racing and supervises the conduct of racing at all race tracks in the state. It allots dates for racing, supervises parimutuel betting, and licenses associations conducting the meetings and persons connected with the meetings.

Investigators assigned to the horse-racing enforcement agency are responsible for routine enforcement of the horse-racing laws and rules, and for inspectional duties around the tracks. They watch for violations in the stable area, such as tampering with the horses, or the presence of unauthorized and unlicensed persons. In the public areas, such as the grandstand and the clubhouses, the investigators look for and take appropriate action against (consisting of arrest or ejection) bookmakers, pickpockets, and other undesirables. Away from the tracks the investigators check out rumors and information concerning "fixes" of races; they search for lost parimutuel tickets and investigate license applicants and the various people who frequent the race tracks.

"Generalist" Agencies

Various licensing commissions and boards, usually at the state level, establish and administer the many laws related to their respective professions and services. The board members are usually appointed from the ranks of their own professions and serve for specific periods of time. They act to maintain ethical standards of their professions. They employ staffs of investigators, or they may make use of an investigative "pool" that provides investigators when the need arises. Investigation is the primary role of the agents assigned, but they may be designated as peace officers for specific law enforcement responsibilities. Just a few of the boards and commissions involved with this type of investigative responsibility are insurance agents, investment specialists, real estate brokers, chiropractors, medical doctors, pharmacists, dentists, athletes, accountants, engineers, beauticians, private detectives, funeral directors, nurses, social workers, and barbers.

Disaster Services

Disasters acts enacted during World War II and the years following provided legislation for the provision of mutual aid among the various political subdivisions in times of major disasters and civil disturbances. According to the laws of many states, the mutual aid is voluntary when the emergency is not extreme and mandatory when the emergency is extreme. When he determines the need for assistance in accordance with this act, the chief of police or sheriff may request assistance under these conditions: natural disaster, riot, or similar occurrence that taxes the capabilities of the police agency beyond its ability to effectively handle the situation. Mutual aid is voluntary under most conditions but mandatory during times of extreme emergency.

The State Disaster Office is usually responsible for the following:

a. Development and maintenance of the master emergency plans and programs of the state.

b. Recommendation for assignment by the Governor of appropriate emergency roles to the other agencies of state government and to the local governments.

c. Provision of assistance to agencies and local governments of the state in planning, programming, organizing, equipping, and training for necessary emergency organizations.

d. Coordination between federal, state, and local agencies of emergency plans.

e. Assistance for all agencies and local governments in obtaining federal funds and equipment to implement approved emergency plans and programs.

f. Coordination of planning activities pertaining to past attack management of resources and economic stabilization functions that might have to be performed by state agencies due to disruption of normal procedure on a national basis.

Federal Police and Investigative Agencies

The federal government has no single law enforcement or investigative agency that has unlimited jurisdiction. As pointed out in the first part of this chapter, the various city and county police agencies are responsible for enforcement of the basic state and local laws that provide for the public health, safety, and morals. The federal agencies have been created for the purpose of investigating and/or enforcing specific laws and to cope with specific problems that extend beyond the jurisdictional boundaries of state and local forces. One agency was created to protect the currency (Secret Service) and another for the purpose of enforcing federal tax regulations (Alcohol, Tobacco, and Firearms Division of the Treasury Department). These are just two of the many agencies. In the next few pages let us look at some of the police and investigative agencies of the federal government. When reading of these agencies, keep in mind the fact that there is no rank order, no hierarchy of command or responsibility. Each operates within its own sphere of responsibility and authority and reports to a specific department or bureau to which it is responsible.

DEPARTMENT OF THE TREASURY

The Secret Service. The Secret Service has been in continuous service since July 5, 1865.

> It was currency counterfeiting problems during the Civil War that established a need for a law enforcement branch of the U.S. Treasury Department. Shortly after onset of the war it was estimated that about one-third of the currency then in circulation was counterfeit. . . . The unit was instructed to launch war on counterfeiters and restore the public's confidence in the nation's currency.[2]

It took the new unit five years to round up a substantial number of the counterfeiters, reduce the amount of counterfeit currency in circulation, and establish the integrity of the "greenback."

In 1894 a small detail of the Secret Service provided some protection on a part-time basis to President Cleveland following threats to his life. It was not until after the assassination of President McKinley in 1901 that Congress officially extended the duties of the Secret Service to full-time protection of the president. In 1913 protection extended to the president-elect, in 1917 to the president's immediate family, in 1951 to the vice-president. Following the assassination of President Kennedy in 1963, protection extended to his widow and children. White House detail has primary responsibility for those protection services.

The Internal Revenue Service. The intelligence unit of the Internal Revenue Service is concerned with the enforcement of laws concerning

---

[2] "A Salute to the U.S. Secret Service," *Police Chief*, XXXII, No. 9, Sept. 1965, 8–9.

internal revenue and income taxes. It is authorized to examine bank accounts, and inquire into income matters and business transactions. The Alcohol, Tobacco, and Firearms Division has primary responsibility for the tax law enforcement relative to alcoholic beverage production and certain weapons. The enforcement agents of this unit enforce the National Firearms Act, which regulates the possession of automatic weapons and defines certain firearms that are illegal to possess.

The Bureau of Customs. Customs agents are responsible for enforcement of the laws involving illegal importing and exporting, customs, and navigation. Customs enforcement men and women guard baggage enclosures, ships, motor vehicles, aircraft, railroad cars, and patrol docks and airfields. They prevent unlawful loading or unloading or delivery of merchandise, smuggling, or other acts against the laws of the United States. Customs agents assess and collect duties and taxes on imported merchandise. The bureau is decentralized and most of its personnel are stationed throughout the country, principally at the 289 ports of entry.

DEPARTMENT OF JUSTICE

The Attorney General. The U.S. Attorney General is the chief law enforcement officer of the federal government, and his office is responsible for criminal prosecution of all violators of federal laws throughout the country. The Justice Department, under the direction of the Attorney General, has several primary operating units with responsibility for the investigation and enforcement of certain federal laws including the Immigration and Naturalization Service, the Federal Bureau of Investigation, and the Bureau of Narcotics and Dangerous Drugs.

Federal Drug Enforcement Administration. Narcotics agents have principal jurisdiction over enforcement of federal laws regulating the legal traffic in narcotics in the United States and in monitoring such traffic at both international and national levels. The Federal Drug Enforcement Administration is responsible for enforcing the federal laws regulating the production, sale, and transportation of narcotic drugs. The agents of this bureau work very closely with state and local law enforcement agents because of the need to work as a team to cope with the problems of the unbelievably efficient underworld organization of narcotics traffickers, which nets fantastic profits throughout the world. They work both undercover assignments to identify and prosecute the criminal drug trafficker and routine inspection assignments to assure adherence to the legal narcotics and drug traffic. Two of the objectives of BNDD are to reach the highest level of sources of supply and to apprehend the greatest quantity of illicit drugs before they reach the street.[3] Formerly a part of the Treasury Department, this agency now operates under the jurisdiction of the Attorney General in the Department of Justice.

The Federal Bureau of Investigation. The Federal Bureau of Investigation of the Department of Justice is not a police agency but an investigative agency with jurisdiction over all matters in which the United States is or may be a party in interest. The late John Edgar Hoover assumed the leadership of this agency in 1924 and set about the task of making it the professional organization that it is today.

The FBI has broad investigative jurisdiction encompassing all federal law violations but limits its scope to about 160 federal laws, including all of those federal statutes not specifically assigned to another agency. Among those matters that are within the primary jurisdiction of the FBI to which its investigators direct the major portion of their attention are the following: administrative investigations, admiralty matters, antitrust laws, civil rights violations, Atomic Energy Act investigations, bankruptcy violations, bribery, copyright violations, crimes on the high seas involving U.S. vessels, crimes on Indian or government reservations, espionage, Federal Kidnapping Act, Federal Reserve Bank Act, frauds against the government, illegal wearing of service uniforms, interstate transportation of stolen vehicles or stolen property, killing and assaulting federal officers, location of escaped federal prisoners, mail fraud, National Bankruptcy Act, passports and visas, patent violations, robbery and burglary of National FDIC-insured and Federal Reserve System banks, unlwaful flight to avoid prosecution or confinement, White Slave Traffic, and others. The principal investigative responsibility for protection of the national security has been placed in the hands of the FBI.

In addition to the investigative functions of the agents of the Federal Bureau of Investigation, that agency provides assistance to local law enforcement agencies with training of its officers at the National Academy and maintains a criminal laboratory that is available for assistance in local investigative matters. Since 1930 the FBI has been the central clearing house for the most complete files on fingerprint and arrest files, and the agency serves the majority of all the country's law enforcement agencies by maintaining criminal statistics and by disseminating the information on a regular basis in its Uniform Crime Reports.

Immigration and Naturalization Service. This branch of the Justice Department was created by authority of an immigration law of 1891 (26 Stat. 1085) and enforces and investigates laws related to the admission, exclusion, and deportation of aliens, as well as the naturalization

[3] Kakalik and Wildhorn, *Special Purpose Public Police,* p. 7.

of aliens lawfully residing in the United States. Its border patrol covers the borders and points of entry into the United States to prevent the illegal entry of aliens. The Immigration and Naturalization Service supervises the naturalization of aliens in the courts, provides textbooks and assists in the education of aliens seeking naturalization, and registers all aliens in the United States.

U.S. Marshal. The marshals are assigned directly to the Attorney General's office and perform general federal law enforcement activities, with duties and responsibilities similar to those of the county sheriff. Major duties consist of serving processes, making arrests, attending court, seizing property, conducting sales to satisfy liens, transporting prisoners, acting as bailiffs in the federal court, and generally functioning as federal enforcement officers.

Department of Transportation. The Coast Guard, formerly a branch of the Treasury Department in peacetime and an arm of the Navy during time of war, is the seagoing law enforcement arm of the Department of Transportation. The Coast Guard, which changed to its current name in 1915, was previously the *Revenue Cutter Service*. Duties of the Coast Guard include patrolling the coast lines of the United States to prevent smuggling of contraband and aliens, enforcing laws related to navigable waters, maintaining port security, providing sea rescue services, and the preservation of fish, animals, and birds along the coasts and islands.

The Office of Civil Aviation Security was established in 1971, in part as a response to a tremendous need for coordinated enforcement and protective services to the aviation transportation industry attributed to the phenomenal increase in the rate of hijackings. Augmented by officers of the several agencies of the Treasury, Justice, Defense, and State Departments, this agency has primary responsibility for civil aviation security, cargo security, and program development.[4]

Postal Inspection Service. The "silent investigators," or postal investigators have been in business in an almost anonymous role (hence, the silent investigators title) since 1775 when Postmaster General Benjamin Franklin appointed a man named Goddard to the position of surveyor. In 1801 the position title was changed to "special agent," and in 1880 the change was to "inspector."[5]

---

[4] Richard G. Kleindienst, *Attorney General's First Annual Report: Federal Law Enforcement and Criminal Justice Assistance Activities* (Washington, D.C.: Government Printing Office, 1972), pp. 7, 423.

[5] Arthur S. Aubrey, Jr., "United States Postal Inspection Service," *Police*, XIII, No. 2, Nov.–Dec. 1968.

Postal inspectors are concerned with two types of investigations: (1) criminal investigations relating to the postal service and (2) service investigations concerning the protection of postal revenues, the economic operation of the postal service, and conformity to the laws and regulations of the services.

Criminal laws involving the postal inspectors are covered in Title 18 and Title 39 of the U.S. Code. Those laws involve mail-conducted lotteries, obstruction of correspondence, theft of mail, frauds through the mails, burglary or robbery, and use of the mail to distribute obscene and crime-inciting material.

Other Federal Police Agencies

The State Department Office of Security is another of several agencies that investigates the backgrounds of critical personnel. Its principal duty is to investigate visa and passport applications.

Under the Department of Defense, the military services operate both criminal investigative and intelligence units. In the Air Force, the Office of Special Investigations (OSI) handles both types of investigative and enforcement duties.

The Department of Interior has four units charged with the investigation and enforcement of federal laws. The Fish and Wildlife Service enforces the laws involving migratory game birds, fish and wildlife restoration acts, and international agreements on interstate transportation of wildlife. The Bureau of Indian Affairs maintains order and suppresses illegal liquor and drug traffic on Indian reservations. The Bureau of Mines investigates and enforces regulations concerning mine accidents, explosions, and fires. The National Park Service maintains a staff of National Park Rangers, who perform police services in the national parks throughout the country.

The Department of Agriculture enforces more than fifty laws that protect the farmers and consumers. This agency is also responsible for national standards in weights and measures in cooperation with the local and various state agencies.

The Department of Health, Education and Welfare is involved in police type enforcement work in the areas of purity and standards of food, drugs, cosmetics, and standard labeling laws.

Within the Department of Labor is the Bureau of Labor Standards. This bureau was established in 1934 to promote industrial safety and health. Responsibilities include the development of standards in the field of labor legislation and labor law administration, and working with the various other agencies involved in implementing international labor standards.

U.S. Forest Service. Rangers of the Forest Service are principally concerned with fire prevention and control problems, and management of recreation areas. Their law enforcement activities involve theft or damage to trees, setting fires, and failure to have spark arresters on motor vehicles.

Independent Agencies with Federal Jurisdiction

In addition to those agencies that are directly related to the executive arms of government, there have been numerous quasi-government agencies that operate with the full force and effect of law enforcement agencies, except that they enforce most of their rules by means of administrative actions. A representative sampling of those agencies includes the following:

1. The National Transportation Safety Board investigates all civil aircraft accidents and regulates civilian air traffic.
2. The Civil Service Commission has an investigative division that performs the following functions:
   a. National agency checks, inquiries, and personnel investigations for nonsensitive positions.
   b. Thorough investigations beyond the scope of (a.) for sensitive positions.
   c. Investigations on matters relating to the enforcement of civil service laws and rules.
   d. Qualification investigations of applicants for high-level administrative and professional positions with the agencies of the federal government.
3. The Federal Communications Commission regulates interstate commerce by means of the many communications media. Their personnel are responsible for enforcement of the Communications Act, which provides for licensing and regulating of operators and broadcasting stations. In cooperation with an international committee, the FCC designates frequencies to various applicants and works to assure maximum compatibility among the many licensees.
4. The Federal Trade Commission is responsible for looking into—and taking appropriate action when necessary—incidents of unfair competition and deceptive and monopolistic practices in interstate commerce.
5. The Securities and Exchange Commission prosecutes malpractice cases in the securities and financial markets.
6. The Interstate Commerce Commission regulates common carriers in interstate commerce and is also involved in the investigation of railroad accidents.

Military Police and Investigative Agencies

Within the jurisdiction of the military services and the Uniform Code of Military Justice are several enforcement and investigative agencies that function similarly to their civilian counterparts. Those agencies include the military police of the several services and the Armed Services Police, which is a consolidated agency of the several services in certain metropolitan areas in which there is a concentration of military installations and personnel. Each service has a criminal investigation division that concerns itself with investigations of crimes and other violations of the Uniform Code of Military Justice and related matters that involve the military services and the military personnel and civilians who are affected by the code.

Operating along somewhat different avenues of investigation, generally with low visibility and dependent on informants and observations of certain individuals and their associates, are the intelligence or counter-intelligence units. These units are concerned with subversive activities, sabotage, treason, disaffection, and other matters of a sensitive nature that affect the services. These agencies include the Office of Special Investigations (OSI) of the Air Force, Office of Naval Intelligence (ONI), and the Counter-Intelligence Corps (CIC) of the Army.

General Intelligence Agency

Interest in this agency of the federal government is often quite high because of the glamour attributed to it by news publicity at various times of international cases. Actually, it is a correlative function as far as the criminal justice system is concerned. The Central Intelligence Agency is not an enforcement or investigative agency. In a short statement mailed to a student recently the CIA stated:

> Our agency is concerned with gathering information about foreign activities in the military, political, scientific, and economc fields.[6]

International Cooperation of Police Agencies

Reference is frequently made in popular television and motion pictures to some form of super agency of several governments that may operate

[6] Excerpted from a communication to a student from the CIA Director of Personnel.

under the director of some international organization. Actually such an organization does exist, but on a different scale and at a lower key. Such an organization is the Interpol, or the International Criminal Police Organization. In an interesting article Arnold Sogalyn explained the mission and function of Interpol.[7] Interpol is a truly international agency employing the manpower and resources of approximately 111 countries located throughout the world. Operating through the Secretariat at Paris, this organization can exchange information and assistance on criminal matters such as drug traffic, smuggling, or theft operations without having to negotiate through diplomatic channels for each new situation.

Originally represented by the FBI from 1939 to 1950, membership by the United States for many years following that decade was on an informal basis with the Bureau of Narcotics, the Bureau of Customs, and the Secret Service. In 1958 Congress amended the Enchling Act to permit the Attorney General to designate the Treasury Department as the U.S. representative to Interpol. Since 1958 the United States has continued its membership in the organization through the Treasury Department's Office of Law Enforcement Coordinator in Washington, D.C.[8]

Private Police and Investigative Agencies

In the United States in the year 1969 more than 800,000 people were employed in either the public or private sectors of security services. One out of every 250 persons in the entire population of the nation was employed as a policeman, investigator, guard, watchman, or some other capacity in security involving an expenditure of more than $40.00 per capita for those services.[9] While we have for so many years addressed ourselves to a study of the government-based security services within the criminal justice system, an equally large number of people and types of operations have been developing almost without attention—or recognition—into a massive network of private police systems. James Kakalik's and Sorrel Wildhorn's excellent report on private police in the United States was funded by an LEAA grant to study the scope and impact of the private police, and should be the subject of intensive study during the next few years just as the study of the public police has been during

---

[7] Arnold Sogalyn, "The Role of Interpol in Law Enforcement," *Police Chief*, XXXII, No. 12, Dec. 1965, pp. 57–59.

[8] Sogalyn, "The Role of Interpol in Law Enforcement," pp. 57–59.

[9] James S. Kakalik and Sorrel Wildhorn, *Private Police in the United States: Findings and Recommendations* (Washington, D.C.: Government Printing Office, 1972), p. 10.

the preceding generation. According to Kakalik and Wildhorn, the principal agencies such as Burns, Pinkerton's, and the Railway Police provided most of the professional investigative services in the United States until about 1924.[10]

The private police are employed to protect private interests and supplement—rather than compete with—the protective and enforcement activities of the public police. With powers of inquiry and arrest the same as that of any other citizen (which, incidentally, is not substantially different than the powers of the public police), the private police perform either on a contract or in-house basis the following functions:

> (1) information gathering (e.g., preemployment checks, insurance or credit application checks, insurance claim investigations, antipilferage undercover work in retail and industrial establishments, criminal investigations, martial investigations; (2) maintaining order on, and proper access to, private property (e.g., guarding sporting events, recreational events); and (3) protection of persons and property by preventing and detecting crime, reducing losses to crime, and/or apprehending suspected criminals (e.g., guarding homes and commercial, institutional, and industrial establishments, antishoplifting activities in retail establishments, armored transport of valuables, alarm systems, surveillance systems, locks, and mobile patrolling).[11]

The effectiveness of the private police depends to a great extent on their role perception: how the private police themselves see their roles and how the public perceives them. About this problem, Kakalik and Wildhorn made the following observations:

> There are two polar views of private security. One holds that private security services (provided by high-quality personnel and equipment) effectively complement the public police by providing security and other related services in areas and situations where the public police do not—either because the public police are not given adequate resources or because they are legally constrained from doing so. This view also holds that current controls and regulation are adequate, since private police seldom abuse their powers. The other view holds that the private security 'industry" feeds on fear and provides ineffective security services by untrained, low-quality personnel who are a potential danger to the public and who, in fact, abuse their limited powers. This view also holds that current controls on, and regulation of, private police are inadequate.[12]

---

[10] Kakalik and Wildhorn, *Private Police in the United States*, pp. 17–18.
[11] Kakalik and Wildhorn, *Private Police in the United States*, p. 24.
[12] Kakalik and Wildhorn, *Private Police in the United States*, p. 1.

This assessment of the effectiveness of private police prompted the following statements:

> Perhaps the relative lack of information on effectiveness stems from the greatly increased demand for contract security services over the past decade, the limited supply of such services, the fact that purchases of such services are, for various reasons, often interested in obtaining low-cost, rather than high-quality, service, and the fact that such effectiveness evaluations would require extensive and costly data collection.
>
> . . . It must be remembered that there are two dimensions to effectiveness, or benefits. First, there are the objective, or measurable, benefits; for example, the reduction in losses to crime effected by a specific security program, or the number of burglars caught after, as compared to before, a particular alarm system was installed. The other dimension is the user's or purchasers' *perceptions* about benefits. A homeowner may feel more secure when he contracts with a central alarm services firm, even though there might be few objective benefits. On balance, it must be concluded that users perceive the benefits of private security as being worth the cost, since private services are increasingly in demand.[13]

Special needs of private sectors of the community require the services of private police patrols and investigation agencies. During the professional growth and development of the governmental agencies, their private counterparts have kept pace in many respects. Representing private individuals and corporations, these private operators serve in a wide variety of roles as representatives of those who employ them.

Concentrated patrol of special areas, such as private islands or residential complexes is accomplished by private guards. Popular motion picture and television representations of the types of duties performed by these individuals is based on some fact. Internal investigations of officers and employees of corporations from banks to service station chains, from warehouse to factories are not quite so glamourous, but they do consume considerable time of private investigators. Another principal type of work conducted by these men and women is industrial espionage, which has all of the flavor of international espionage, but involves substantial fortunes instead of domestic security. Patents and formulas on toys, soaps, tools, automobiles, and virtually every type of competitive industry are extremely valuable and the subject of considerable concern to their owners or custodians.

[13] Kakalik and Wildhorn, *Private Police in the United States,* p. 25.

Summary

In spite of, or because of, the various divisions of authority and responsibility, law enforcement and criminal investigations on a nationwide, statewide, or local level somehow manage to maintain the peace and protect the lives and property of a large percentage of the population. Proponents for centralization of power may profess that efficiency would be increased by arguing that not only would the best of talents throughout the country be pooled and harnessed but the various agencies would be more inclined to work toward common objectives with consistent policies. Proponents for decentralization of power and perpetuation of the system as it is now, with the various agencies each striving to accomplish its own objectives—which may or may not be similar to another agency— agree that this "local rule" philosophy is the answer to maximum police efficiency.

Actually, it appears that local autonomy has many distinct advantages. One of those advantages is that the local police chief, who lives in or near the city where his department operates, is responsive to the needs of his own community and is directly aware of the community standards in moral and social behavior and knows his jurisdiction intimately.

Both concepts have value. Local direction of daily police operations is more directy relevant to the specific needs of the community. However, coordination of information systems, communications, training, laboratories, research, and many specialized services may be accomplished more efficiently by a central agency.

During the lifetime of the reader, "revolutionary change" has been commonplace in many facets of law enforcement and so has the lack of change in yet other facets.

The existing police system has been analyzed, discussed, evaluated, compared, studied, and inspected from within and from without. No doubt, changes will be made. At the present time the trend appears to be toward pooling of resources and facilities in information and communications systems, training programs, laboratory services, intelligence operations, and research projects. Additionally, there is some pooling of the traditional field operations by either a "joint powers" consortium or by consolidation of several agencies into one.

In this chapter we have examined the many agencies of the law enforcement component of the criminal justice system, from the local to the state and federal police departments and investigative agencies, with a recap on the private segment of the system that has previously received little attention. The private agencies are commercial profit-based service organizations designed and operated to provide specific services in the interest of those who contract their services for a fee. The public agencies are government-based agencies that provide either general or specific services in the interest of the government-defined needs of the public, and the fees are derived from taxes.

The local police departments of municipalities and the county sheriffs of the many counties and parishes throughout the country provide the basic police functions essential to the maintenance of the society of ordered liberty in this representative republic. The special purpose agencies that operate within the smaller governmental subdivisions include such units as housing authority or transit authority police who provide patrol and protective services in specific locations and on district-owned vehicles. Other local officers include the marshal and constable, who perform court-related functions in the lower courts just as the sheriff performs in the superior court in the county. The coroner has certain police responsibilities, but is principally concerned with death investigations and certain matters related to personal effects and estates of the deceased and the appropriate disposition of the remains. He does have the ultimate authority in the determination of cause of death, but usually conducts his investigations in cooperation with the county prosecutor and the police departments, who have the investigative personnel and extensive resources at their disposal to perform most effectively.

At the state level—although the term "level" should not be interpreted to imply that there is any hierarchical scale of authority-responsibility relationships—the police and investigative agencies are involved in matters of general or specific interest but with a statewide jurisdiction. The highway patrol, for example, patrols the highways and enforces traffic regulations throughout the state, but does so within city limits by invitation from the cities and in agreement with the local departments. State licensing and regulating agencies are concerned with minimum standards, ethics, and occupation-oriented laws. For example, the Department of Motor Vehicles is responsible for the licensing of motor vehicles, vehicle operators, salesmen, agencies, and administrative matters involving the automobile industry.

The federal law enforcement and investigative agencies are principally concerned with the police power of the federal government. National and international matters of significance consume the time and energies of the agencies of the federal government, such as the U.S. Marshal, the Federal Bureau of Investigation, Secret Service, Postal Inspection Service, and a long list of special needs agencies. The federal agencies have jurisdiction throughout the United States and its protectorates, and, in many cases throughout the world in matters involving the United States. Their work in the jurisdictions of other agencies involves considerable cooperation and coordinated efforts of the many agencies involved. There are many investigations that involve overlapping, or concurrent, jurisdiction. Each agency concerns itself with those matters falling within its respective jurisdiction and the efforts and the results are—hopefully—the product of a cooperative relationship. There are problems, of course, but in such a vast system involving hundreds of thousands of individuals there is a surprising degree of efficiency and effectiveness.

Exercises and Study Questions

1. What is the exact relationship of the Federal Bureau of Investigation to the police department in the city where you live?

2. List the state police and investigative agencies operated within your state.

3. What is the largest private police agency in the United States, according to the text?

4. What were the three alternate ideas that have been suggested to relieve or reduce interforce conflicts of the several federal agencies with overlapping jurisdiction?

5. What is your opinion of the autonomy of local departments with law enforcement responsibilities—should there be more or less autonomy?

6. Give at least three examples of hypothetical cases involving concurrent jurisdiction.

7. Discuss the condition known as "martial rule" and its relationship with local law enforcement agencies in the jurisdiction where it is in effect.

8. In which matters are the duties and responsibilities the same for the sheriff, the marshal, and the constable?

9. List at least four occasions when the coroner is responsible for the investigation of death.

10. If you had a case for the state fire marshal, how would you go about making contact with him?

11. Under what branch of government is the Coast Guard assigned, and what are its basic responsibilities?

12. Describe the functions of the BNDD, and explain how it would operate in cooperation with your local police department in a case of concurrent interest and jurisdiction.

13. Recommended semester project: Visit or write to a state law enforcement or investigative agency in your state and request as much information as you can about its origin, its functions, and entrance re-

quirements. Prepare a paper and present an oral report in class on how that organization operates, and whether you believe it is an effective organization as it stands.

Suggested for Additional Study

KLIENDIENST, RICHARD, *Attorney General's First Annual Report: Federal Law Enforcement and Criminal Justice Assistance Activities.* Washington, D.C.: Government Printing Office, 1972.

SMITH, BRUCE, *Police Systems in the United States* (2d ed.). New York: Harper and Brothers, 1960.

6

The Courts

Introduction

The basic structure and functions of the courts have changed little since the days when they were organized in the colonies after the English model. There is a federal court system that functions for the needs of the federal government, but the courts that serve the vast majority of cases and causes are creations of the state constitutions and serve as state systems. The courts comprise the third branch of government for the balance of power in running the affairs of the people. The court system is a loosely knit affiliation, because the courts usually operate with virtual autonomy in their everyday operations within their own spheres of authority.

In this chapter we shall review the functions and responsibilities of the courts and discuss the processes involved in taking a case to the courts for adjudication. We shall begin by reviewing the function of the judge in his role as magistrate, when he reviews affidavits and makes determinations about warrants, as opposed to when he presides at the trial in his role as judge and rules on the law and makes judicial decisions. Other officers of the court who play important roles in the drama of the courtroom are the prosecutor and the defense attorney. They are responsible to the court to assure their clients of a fair and impartial trial. The probation officer, as an extension of the court, conducts presentence investigations and makes recommendations to the judge as to which might be the appropriate disposition of the convicted offender.

The court component of the system of administration of justice is the "process" part of what could be considered a three part system, as discussed earlier in this text: law enforcement, the courts, and corrections. The law enforcement component has the responsibility for "input" of the persons to be processed through the system (and for making the discretionary decisions as to which ones not to introduce to the courts). The courts "process" individuals through this system and the corrections component acts as the "output" phase. In this three step process, the correctional institutions and probation and parole agencies have the responsibility for rehabilitation and reintegrating the individuals who have been processed back into society. The ideal model is to keep everyone out of the system, but because crime prevention is not 100 percent effective, the next ideal model is to process the individual so effectively that once he has gone through the "output" phase he will not return. Because this has not been entirely effective either, what we have in reality is a circle, with many of our citizens and guests moving within a continuous cycle within the system. Recognizing this never-ending circle in many cases as a serious problem to be addressed with incisive judgment, the judge holds the future of many people in his hands and he must make decisions that indicate the greatest likelihood of success.

The Courts and Their Relationship to Law Enforcement

The American system of criminal jurisprudence is based upon codified laws. There are criminal codes of a wide variety that cover all those acts or omissions that the elected legislators have deemed essential to rule an orderly society. New laws are added with increasing regularity, and old ones are changed or rescinded. Such a system of laws, with prescribed punishment for each offense, serves to "put people on notice" as to what their society expects of them in good conduct and what they may expect in the way of punishment should they violate the rules. It also provides the police with a set of guidelines that they must follow in their orderly process of law enforcement.

The part played in the system of jurisprudence by the courts is most important.[1] Three major premises comprise the Doctrine of Judicial Supremacy in the American system: (1) The courts, and only the courts,

---

[1] For an objective analysis of the process of judicial review by one of the country's foremost authorities on the Constitution you are invited to study: Leonard W. Levy, *Judicial Review and the Supreme Court* (New York: Harper Torchbooks, Harper and Row, 1967). Dr. Levy's introduction to this book of essays explains historical notes on judicial review and comprehensively explains the concept and controversy regarding it. The other selected essays provide a further look into the Constitution, the Supreme Court, and judicial review.

may make the final determination as to what is law and what is not; (2) the courts may require—through legal means at their disposal—adherence to lawful conduct by the administrative branch of government; and (3) the courts may invalidate a legislative action on the basis of unconstitutionality. This doctrine refers to the Supreme Court, but the general principle is carried down to the lowest court at state level. A state legislature may enact a law that a city council heartily endorses and that reflects the attitude of the community. As a result of such endorsement, the city administrator may convey the message to the police chief, who orders his officers to enforce the law "to the letter." When a defendant appears in court, a "not-guilty" decision or a suspended sentence may reflect an attitude on the part of the court that the law is either unfair of unjust. The defendant might be found guilty and sentenced, then appeal to a higher court, and on up through the various higher courts to the state or even the U.S. Supreme Court. The Supreme Court might then decide that the law is unconstitutional and, therefore, invalid. This does not mean that the law was *illegal* because it was promulgated by legal process and it is *legal*. All of the subsequent police and court action was likewise legal, but once the decision is rendered by the Supreme Court, the law is no longer enforceable.

The court hears testimony and takes an affidavit to determine whether or not to issue a warrant of arrest or a search warrant. The lower court in a felony case will hear testimony and receive evidence and decide whether to "bind the case over" or remand the defendant to the higher court for trial. In a jury trial, the jury determines fact and truth, and the judge determines what is lawful. In the absence of the jury, the judge determines both fact and law. On the basis of a violation of "due process," a technical error, or other action on the part of the prosecution —or the police—that denies to the defendant any of the constitutional safeguards, the judge may declare a mistrial and the criminal may go free because he is innocent until *proven* guilty. Ensuring "due process" is a fundamental responsibility of the court as well as determining guilt or innocence and prescribing punishment for the guilty.

Federal Courts. In the federal system of justice administration, there is a complete system of courts to serve the various needs created by the Constitution and various acts of the legislative and the executive branches of government. For the military service and adjudication of the Uniform Code of Military Justice, there is the system of Courts Martial, and the Military Court of Appeals. There are various special purpose courts in addition to the Military Courts, including the Court of Systems and Patent Appeals, the Court of Claims, and Customs Court. At the trial level, ninety-three district courts are located throughout the country.

Appeals from the district courts are remanded to the appellate courts for the resolution of issues of procedure and constitutionality.

The Supreme Court. State sovereignty is great according to the U.S. system of government as it was intended by its founders, and with respect to that sovereignty the final arbiter in a case or controversy in any state is that state's supreme court. Only under certain circumstances shall the case be studied and decided by the U.S. Supreme Court, and the primary qualifications must be that there is a diversity of citizenship of two or more states, or there must be a federal question involved.

Although the Supreme Court is involved in a few administrative and supervisory functions as head of the federal judicial system, the principal role of the court is to decide cases. "Original" cases may be taken directly to the Supreme Court, and this is the type of case that usually involves issues to test or challenge the constitutionality of a rule or law. The second type of case decided by the Supreme Court is the appeal from the lower federal or state courts. These cases involve the same type as those that are listed above, as well as suits to enforce laws or treaties of the United States, cases involving diversity of citizenship, and suits to enforce the U.S. Constitution.

The Supreme Court of the United States consists of a chief justice and eight associate justices. They are appointed by the President with the advice and consent of the Senate, and they hold office for life during their good behavior. There can be no question as to the tremendous influence that the Supreme Court has upon not only the judicial system and law enforcement but upon the entire populace of the nation. Not only must the members of the court be great jurists, but they must be master statesmen as well. The Constitution is the supreme law of the land, and the Supreme Court serves to interpret and perpetuate its principles.

The State Court System

Justice Courts. The justice court, which is still very much in evidence, is a vestige of colonial days, and usually serves the smaller and less populous judicial districts. A rural and small-town or village court, the justice court has limited jurisdiction in criminal matters. It is restricted to misdemeanors of lesser significance and handles only minor civil cases. The functions of the small claims court, a do-it-yourself court, which is concerned only with a maximum of $200 or $300 and where attorneys are excluded, may be assigned to the justice court as it is to the larger municipal court. The justice of the peace in this court may not have any legal experience, as is the case in some states, and may perform his services while operating some other business at the same time. The bailiff for the justice court is the constable, who keeps peace in the courtroom, serves subpoenas and writs, and generally carries out the directions of the court.

Municipal Courts.   This court may be called the mayor's court, the police court, or by some other name that designates it as one of the trial courts where the greatest volume of cases are tried in civil and criminal matters. The municipal court may serve one city or several. It usually consists of a court district that is one of several within a county and that serves a population greater than that of the justice court. In states that have no justice courts, the municipal court has replaced it. Jurisdiction involves civil cases in which the claimant seeks damages amounting to $5,000 or some similar amount determined by law as the maximum, with higher amounts referred to the superior court. Misdemeanors committed within the municipal court's jurisdiction are tried in this court, and preliminary hearings for felonies may be held in the municipal court to determine if there is sufficient proof that a crime has been committed and that there is reason to believe that the accused should be held to answer to the charges in superior court.

The municipal court judge sits as a magistrate with a related, but separate, role than he performs as a judge. In his role as magistrate, the judge is acting upon information and belief at the time he issues the warrant. He later examines the evidence in his judicial role and admits its introduction if it has been collected in accordance with the law and Constitution. The municipal court judge may hear pleas for dismissal on the grounds that the evidence that is about to be introduced was collected in violation of some provision of the Constitution, or through some error in procedure. The trial or hearing is held at that point; then the judge examines the evidence on a *motion to suppress evidence,* and he determines whether he will allow the evidence or testimony to be used in the trial. Evidence that is excluded may not be considered either by the judge or the jury when determining guilt of the accused. The judge has the authority to dismiss the charges and order the release of the accused, or he may order the jury to find the accused not guilty because of the absence of sufficient legal basis to sustain the charge, or the judge may actually reduce the charge of a felony to a misdemeanor before the trial. In California, this is quite common in crimes of theft, assault, drug abuse and marijuana possession.

The preliminary hearing that is held by the municipal court for the purpose of hearing testimony and examining evidence to make a determination as to whether the accused should be *bound over* to answer the felony charges in superior court leads to the judge's instructions to the prosecuting attorney that he should file an *information* in that court that initiates the felony trial. In some cases, an alternative method is used for bringing the case to the higher court. That alternative is known as the *indictment*, which emanates from the grand jury. In such a case, the prosecuting attorney may choose to avoid the open court preliminary hearing in favor of the secrecy of the grand jury proceedings, where the hearings held in secret sessions may lead to secret indictments of perhaps a number of persons accused of related crimes.

In misdeameanor cases, the municipal court judge may sentence the accused to jail and/or probation and/or a fine. Although the term of probation is not considered as punishment, violation of that probation may well lead to a period of incarceration for the violation. In a felony case, the judge may receive a guilty plea but he must *certify* the plea to the superior court along with the case, where the superior court judge will pronounce the sentence.

The bailiff for the municipal court is the marshal, whose duties and responsibilities to the court are similar to those of the constable to the justice court.

Superior Court. There is usually only one superior court per county, although there may be literally hundreds of divisions of that court as there are divisions of the municipal court. Jurisdiction of the superior court includes (1) juvenile court, a separate civil division of the court that directs the county's juvenile justice network, including guidance and direction of the juvenile probation efforts; (2) all felony trials and related hearings; (3) certain "high misdemeanors" in some states; (4) civil suits involving reparation for an amount larger than that allowed in the municipal court; (5) court of equity, in which an order to "right a wrong or injustice" is sought rather than money damages; (6) probate court, which is involved in the estates and related matters of the deceased; (7) appeals from the lower courts on matters of judicial error or constitutional issues; (8) courts of conciliation or divorce; (9) writs of habeas corpus and other types of legal actions involving property and debts; (10) reciprocal enforcement of family support laws in cooperation with other states; and (11) sanity and alcoholic commitment hearings.

Superior court judges recommend candidates for the grand jury each year, select and supervise the county probation officer, sit as an appellate court in issues appealed from justice or municipal courts, and perform a variety of other court-related services including the performance of marriages, issuance of warrants, and issuance of writs and similar court orders.

The sheriff and his deputies serve as bailiffs to the superior court. Besides serving writs and subpoenas, the sheriff may provide protection for the judges of the several courts and building security, and perform any other services required by the court.

The District Courts of Appeal

The appellate courts meet at various locations in the state. In some jurisdictions the appellate court operates on a circuit court basis and convenes for a few months in each of two or three different locations. Each appellate division serves a specified portion of the state and its various trial courts. The division is comprised of three judges who sit and decide on issues as a group, but more often they review cases on an individual basis, meet frequently and discuss their cases, and then either concur with the judge who is writing the decision, or they dissent. The majority view is the binding one, as it is with the supreme court, which consists of several justices.

Dean Charles W. Joiner, of the Wayne State University Law School, described the function of the appellate courts in a presentation at Williamsburg:

> 1) In the individual case, an appellate court corrects the mistakes made at the lower level so as to prevent miscarriages of justice between the litigants. This action also tends to provide an effective way of encouraging modesty among the trial judges which is important to creating confidence in the system.
>
> 2) In the larger sense, the appellate court, by its opinions, tends to teach other judges, lawyers, and all citizens something about the law, what premises are acceptable, what interpretations are proper. In a sense, the litigation of some individuals has a larger public purpose, particularly at the appellate level. Private litigation provides the vehicle for development and direction of growth in the law, for unifying different interpretations, etc.[2]

The appellate court in some states is a part of the supreme court, which is the court of last resort. In other states, there is a separation of responsibility with the intermediate courts and the supreme court having authority to review different cases. Depending on the volume of the cases that go up from the trial courts, the state may create whatever system that best suits its needs, which might include assigning commissioners or trial judges on a temporary basis to assist with the work load.[3]

[2] Charles W. Joiner, *The Function of the Appellate System*, from Addresses and Papers of the National Conference on the Judiciary, March 11–14 at Williamsburg, Virginia, 1971 (Washington, D.C.: Government Printing Office), pp. 97–102.

[3] Joiner, *The Function of the Appellate System*, pp. 99–104.

Jurisdiction of the appellate court extends to case review that may be a court-determined, or legally prescribed right to review, and to other cases that the appellate court reviews at its discretion upon petition for such review. The effect of the appeal may be a reversal, which puts the litigants back at their original starting point, or the case may be returned to the trial court to correct earlier errors that had been made during the trial, or a new trial may be ordered.

State Supreme Court. The court of last resort in the state, the supreme court, is the highest appeals court to which most cases may be taken from the trial courts or the intermediate appeals court. Exceptions, of course, involve issues of the U.S. Constitution and other matters that are clearly within the purview of the U.S. Supreme Court. With great respect for the sovereignty of the states, the rights of the state supreme courts are recognized and enforced. The chief justice and the justices of the supreme court hear cases on appeal or by their direction in matters described briefly in Chapter One of this text: equity, probate, capital convictions, writs, applicants to the state bar, and numerous other issues involving interpretations of laws and the constitution of the state.

The cases appealed to the supreme court are decided upon and disposed of in the same manner as are those that are handled by the appellate courts. In states where there is no intermediate court of appeal, the supreme court handles all appeals from the lower trial courts.

In a state having a unified court system, that is, one that has been reorganized throughout the state into a true state system of courts under coordinated leadership, the chief justice must have the proper administrative structure and tools, according to Chief Justice Edward E. Pringle of Colorado.[4] These tools include:

1) Reorganized and unified court structure, with elimination of overlapping jurisdiction and integration of minor courts;
2) Constitutional authority and responsibility vested in him for administration of the judicial system (including assignment of judges) and administration of rules (both procedural and administrative), and, incidentally, that authority must include the power to designate chief or presiding judges in the various judicial districts or circuits and the power to delegate to these judges degrees of authority to administer those districts or circuits;
3) Some form of judicial selection and tenure other than partisan elections and based on merit, and including a removal commission;
4) Constitutional provision for a state judicial administrator or administrative director responsible to and appointed by the chief justice or su-

[4] Edward E. Pringle, "The Role of the State Chief Justice," from *Addresses and Papers of the National Conference on the Judiciary, March 11–14, 1971 at Williamsburg, Virginia* (Washington, D.C.: Government Printing Office), pp. 82–83.

preme court, with the administrator having a staff of professional assistants in several disciplines, in addition to adequate clerical support;

5) State funding administered by the judicial branch, under the authority of the chief justice, including budget preparation and submission thereof directly to the legislature; and

6) Separate judicial personnel system administered by the judicial branch covering all court personnel—including probation, if possible, and providing for salaries, appointment, removal, etc.

The Grand Jury

The grand jury is a body of citizens chosen for a specified period of time (usually one year) to serve as auditors of the various offices of government and to conduct investigations of public offenses committed or subject to trial in its county of jurisdiction. The grand jury's origin is in England, when it was instituted in 1215 with Magna Carta. The original principal purpose of the grand jury was to protect the people against

Simulation of the Grand Jury examining a witness.
Courtesy, Grand Jury, County of Sacramento.

the tyranny of their own government. This has been extended considerably to include the examination of evidence and witnesses to determine whether a person should be held to answer for a felony, which is an alternative to the municipal court preliminary hearing in some states, but which is routine in all felony cases in other states. Other functions of the grand jury include visiting and inspecting all branches of government, such as county hospitals and jails, coroner's offices, the courts, and various other government operations to perform in an audit capacity. The jury recommends corrective action in such cases that require structural or procedural changes in government operations: In criminal matters, the jury issues a true bill, which is an order to the prosecutor to file an indictment in the superior court charging the accused with a specific crime. A federal grand jury operates similarly with the federal courts.

Although utilization of the grand jury for all felony prosecutions would be an unwieldy and virtually impossible process in some jurisdictions, there are advantages to the grand jury *indictment* over the *information,* which the prosecutor files at the direction of the lower court after the preliminary hearing. Two advantages of the grand jury proceeding are confidentiality and objectivity. The objectivity of the prosecuting attorney is essential to all cases, and there is little problem in most cases. But, consider the situation when a public official, a police officer, or some other person who may be in a close working relationship with the district attorney is suspected of or has been accused of a crime. Regardless of the action taken by the prosecutor, there will be many people who will believe that he acted in deference to that relationship. By taking the matter to the grand jury, the prosecutor is passing on the responsibility to that body, and any decisions will be those of the grand jury.

The secrecy of a grand jury indictment is in sharp contrast to the open court procedure of a preliminary hearing in municipal court. In the first place, members of the grand jury are sworn to secrecy, which means that all matters that come before that body for inquiry or investigation are kept confidential. Attendance at the meetings is by invitation only and attorneys are not allowed to accompany their clients who are subpoenaed before the grand jury. A witness may give information and present evidence to the jurors, who continue with the inquiry until they have satisfied their need for a complete investigation, which may include many people participating in various activities over a long period of time. While the investigation is going on, the grand jury may be making determinations that certain individuals should be held to answer for specific crimes, then at the conclusion of the investigation a series of secret indictments are issued by the jury.

An example of how a grand jury may be utilized for the greatest advantage might be found in a typical "buy program," or an extended narcotics investigation. The typical arrest for possession of narcotics or dangerous drugs leads to a preliminary hearing, at which time the evidence is produced, the witnesses examined, the legality of the evidence challenged by the defense and established by the prosecution. Then the magistrate directs the district attorney to present an information to the superior court for the trial. Using this procedure, there is little likelihood of doing much about the problem of narcotics traffic in the area. The "grand jury method" would be for the officer to make contact with the user of narcotics in some undercover role as another person who "makes the scene." Through a period of contacts and various associations with several users, the undercover agent is able to gain an introduction to a peddler. Still in his undercover role, he makes a purchase. Armed with the evidence, the officer goes to the prosecutor and they present the case before the grand jury, which may also include several separate indictments against persons for possession of drugs with whom the officer has associated during the investigation. The grand jury votes for indictments, but they do so in secrecy. The case continues, however, because the dealers and users are not aware of the investigation.

The undercover officer goes back to the scene of his earlier investigative activity and continues to make purchases and continues to go before the grand jury and present the evidence that leads to more secret indictments. As the officer gets better known in his assumed undercover role, the dealers who are unable to supply his growing demands for narcotics introduce the officer (who is not known to them as anything but a user or dealer who has a great demand and who is—to them—a good customer) to suppliers higher in the system of narcotics dealers. The officer continues to build cases, and the grand jury continues to vote for indictments. Finally, when the officer can no longer continue the investigation with safety or further yield to the investigation, the prosecutor secures warrants for several people who are to be charged with the various narcotics violations, and then arrests are made simultaneously throughout the area. By using this method of investigation, and with the aid of the secret grand jury proceedings, the police are able to more effectively address the narcotics problem because they have been able to identify the higher-level suppliers instead of just arresting the users. This type of investigative strategy, with the cooperation and assistance of the prosecutor, the grand jury, and many assisting agencies, is also effective in organized crime activities and other crimes such as prostitution, gambling, and dealing in stolen property.

Disadvantages of the grand jury have been pointed out by various

study groups and commissions. Following is an excerpt from one such
report that points up some of the reasons why use of the grand jury
for indictments be abandoned:

> Those states still requiring indictments to be returned only by grand
> juries should eliminate that rule. Grand juries should focus attention upon
> special situations, such as those involving official corruption.
>
> Many of the 50 states have eliminated the rigid requirements that grand
> juries must hand down all indictments for serious offenses. There is a
> growing consensus that this is archaic. Grand juries place heavy burdens
> on the prosecution and create long delays in resolution of criminal charges.
> The composition of grand jury panels is also subject to challenge. States
> now using other arrangements show no signs of return to the former
> practice, nor of any resulting denial of substantive justice. Professional,
> tenured, and properly supervised prosecution would make the rigid grand
> jury requirement obsolete. Prosecutors could then be trusted to bring
> cases before the courts without delay, upon presentation of information.[5]

Prosecution and the Defense

Presentation of cases in a court involves the adversary system. In a non-
criminal—or civil—case, the *plaintiff* and the *respondent,* or *defendant,*
both enter the trial at an even point, with an equal advantage. The *litigants* each present their case by introducing evidence and testimony. The
case is weighed by the judge or jury on its merits, which consists principally of the evidence presented. Whichever side in the case has the
preponderance of weight in favor of his side of the case will win the law-
suit. The process involves a balancing of the scales with each side having an equal weight at the outset of the case. In a criminal trial, the
issue is much different. The accused is presumed to be innocent, or the
preponderance of the case is immediately in his favor. In accordance
with the American system of criminal law, the accused stands innocent
until *proven* guilty. The burden of proving the accused guilty of the
crime rests on the prosecutor. The defense at no time has to prove innocence. As a matter of fact, and procedure, the defendant shall be
considered innocent at all times until he is proven guilty *beyond all
reasonable doubt* in the judgment of the judge or—in a jury trial—the
jury. "Beyond all reasonable doubt" does not mean absolute certainty,

---

[5] Committee for Economic Development, *Reducing Crime and Assuring Justice:
A Statement on National Policy,* prepared by the Research and Policy Committee
(New York: Committee for Economic Development, 1972), p. 27.

but the courts have held that there must be a moral certainty that the accused did commit the crime.

Prosecuting Attorney. For the federal government the prosecutor is known as the U.S. Attorney, for the state he is the attorney general, for the trial courts the prosecutor is the district attorney. The district attorney usually prosecutes misdemeanors and felonies in the courts. The lower trial courts may use corporation counsels or city attorneys to prosecute misdemeanors. In civil cases the attorney general, county attorney, city attorney, or corporation counsel will represent the government. There are variations throughout the country, but one will usually find the DA as the prosecutor of most criminal trials.

An elected official and officer of the court, the district attorney represents the people of the state as the victim of the crime committed in the state (a crime being a *public* offense). The prosecuting attorney is generally responsible for determining—upon examination of reports and other inquiries he deems appropriate—whether or not to seek a complaint charging an individual with a crime and what charge will be filed against that person. In addition to the assessment of the crime by the prosecuting attorney and his decision to prosecute or not, the grand jury is used extensively as a body to hear testimony and examine evidence presented by the district attorney to determine whether or not a prosecution will be pursued by way of an indictment.

The district attorney is the legal advisor to the county grand jury. Other responsibilities include the initiation of proceedings against inebriates, the mentally ill, narcotics addicts, and nonsupport of minor children cases. Many district attorneys employ their own staffs of investigators.

One may ask why there is an entirely different staff of investigators for the prosecuting attorney when the police agency with primary jurisdiction conducts the investigation that leads ot the arrest. Although there may be a problem caused by an incomplete investigation by the police detective, this is actually a secondary purpose for the district attorney investigator. The emphasis is different once the case is on its way through the courts, and the DA's investigator works as the attorney's field man, who assists the DA in lining up witnesses and evidence, handling last minute details, and conducting background data for the trial that may not have a direct bearing on the evidential value of a bit of evidence but is critical to the case in a variety of other ways. The investigator serves as an assistant to the prosecutor during the trial while the police detective is busy attending to dozens of other cases. In some jurisdictions it is not unusual for a prosecuting attorney to operate his own intelligence unit in cooperation with other local agencies to combat organized crime, which is directly related to so many of his other prosecutions.

In a criminal case, the procedure usually begins with the field police officer, who is the first on the scene of the crime. Either he makes an arrest at the scene or following a pursuit, or he carries the investigation through as far as he can, gathering and preserving the evidence, taking statements from the victims and witnesses, and preparing his reports. He may or may not identify the culprit at that phase of his investigation. In most cases he does not identify his suspect at that time. The follow-up investigator, usually an officer assigned to a "plainclothes" or detective detail, is responsible for continuing with the investigation. At some point in the investigation the case reaches the stage when the investigator must seek a complaint and a warrant that will lead to the arrest of the person responsible for the crime. As soon as the investigator has compiled sufficient evidence to prove that a crime has been committed, and he has built up sufficient proof that a specific individual should be held to answer to the charges, the investigating officer presents the case to the district attorney or one of his deputies, who are also attorneys and serve in the same capacity as he.

The prosecutor is responsible, as an officer of the court, to inquire into the officer's investigation sufficiently to convince him that the facts are as the officer has presented them in his reports and discussions. This should in no way be misunderstood to infer that the prosecutor is determining guilt, as that is strictly the prerogative of the court, but he must be reasonably convinced that the individual to be charged is guilty in his mind so that he will proceed with his part of the series of events. The district attorney makes a determination at this point whether to proceed with the prosecution. If he makes the decision to prosecute, he next approaches the judge, who is functioning as a magistrate. The prosecutor files a complaint with the magistrate. The magistrate reviews the information presented on the complaint. The information is very minimal, just enough to convince the magistrate that a crime has been committed and that the district attorney has sufficient cause to charge the individual he has named as the accused. It is important to continue with the notion that at this time the accused is still innocent, because he has yet to appear in court to be proven guilty. The magistrate is not passing judgment on the accused, only on the merits of the case. If he agrees with the prosecutor, whose responsibility to the court as one of its officers is recognized by the magistrate, he then issues a warrant for the arrest of the suspect, who must be brought to the court to answer the charges.

After the arrest, the accused selects an attorney to represent him, or the court assigns an attorney to him. Throughout the process at every step along the way, the district attorney represents the people and the defendant has his attorney to protect his interests. The district attorney may meet and confer with the accused and his attorney and recommend that the accused plead guilty of the charges to avoid prolongation of the process. The accused must be proven guilty if he chooses—on advice of his counsel—to proceed with the trial, but he may waive that right to the trial by entering a plea. He may agree to plead guilty to a lesser charge, which may be negotiated with the combined consent of the prosecutor, the defense, and the judge. This process is known as *plea bargaining,* which is utilized by the prosecutor with the approval of the courts to speed up the processing of so many cases in a busy court.

In court, the prosecutor presents evidence and witnesses who give testimony to substantiate the charges earlier developed during the investigation and as briefly recounted in the complaint. The defense cross-examines, which is usually a device to raise questions of doubt as to the validity or veracity of the evidence or testimony and to make points supporting inocence of the accused. In a misdemeanor case, the trial is held in the lower trial court and the prosecutor presents the case in that court. If the charge is a felony, this first court appearance is not a trial at all, but what is known as the *preliminary hearing.* In a preliminary, the judge sits as a magistrate and determines only if proof has been presented by the prosecutor that a crime has been committed and if there is sufficient information to instruct the prosecutor to file an information in superior court charging the accused with the offense charged in the complaint.

During the trial, a judge presides over the proceedings. If a jury has been chosen and is sitting as a part of the trial, the jury is responsible for making a value judgment on guilt beyond a reasonable doubt based upon their unanimous assessment of the evidence and information presented by the prosecutor. The judge determines whether each item of evidence shall be introduced, and he serves as the legal arbiter; in other words, the judge determines legality, while the jury determines fact. In the absence of the jury, the judge decides both legality and fact and it is he who declares guilt. In the absence of a guilty finding, the accused goes free, still an innocent person.

Defense Attorney. Every person accused of a crime shall have legal representation. This is a provision of the Sixth Amendment to the U.S. Constitution. The accused shall have a fair trial, and he has the right to "due process," which essentially means that his trial shall be in accordance with established procedures. This is a provision of the Fifth Amendment to the U.S. Constitution. Without competent legal representation an accused individual who is innocent may be denied the rights assured him by the Constitution. The courts recognize this as a possibility, therefore they assign counsel to the accused when he has not chosen one himself, and such assignment may be made even over his objections. In the event that the accused wishes to represent himself without counsel, the court very carefully examines the matter and renders its legal decision on whether the accused is competent to represent himself. Only then does it allow for the matter to proceed.

Throughout the process, beginning when the accused and his attorney first meet, the attorney as an officer of the court and also as the legal representative of the accused is obliged to advise his client on the points of law and proceedings throughout the entire process. His role is to assure his client of a fair and impartial handling of his case from beginning to end. You may ask the question "What if the defense attorney knows that his client is guilty, should he still serve as his attorney?" The answer is a qualified yes. Qualified for this reason: Although the attorney is convinced of his client's guilt perhaps by that person's own admission, he has yet to be proven guilty. Certainly, the accused must be represented by competent attorneys, whether they committed the alleged crimes or not. With his knowledge of the facts as presented to him by his client, his responsibility to the court as an officer of that court as a skilled attorney, is to advise his client in the best interest of justice and of his client. Such advice may well be that the accused should agree to a negotiated plea for a lesser charge offered by the district attorney, or a recommendation that he plead guilty to the charges. The attorney must maintain the confidence of his client and cannot disclose information given to him in confidence in this attorney-client relationship. For example: An individual commits an aggravated assault and contacts his attorney. There is an understanding that the attorney-client relationship exists because the culprit asks for advice and the attorney agrees to hear him out and advise him. After hearing the details, the attorney tells his client to give himself up to the police and plead guilty. Not accepting this advice, the client dismisses the attorney and goes to another one who advises him to do nothing and to keep his mouth shut. Although the relationship is severed, and there is even some doubt as to whether a true client relationship was established—there was certainly none of the usual rapport—there is no doubt that the attorney cannot disclose the information without violating his code of ethics as an attorney. The defense attorney must staunchly defend his client, even the "guilty ones." A mistrial may be declared if at any time during the proceedings it becomes evident that either the prosecution or the defense is not adequately representing his client.

There are many defendants who cannot afford what might be considered a "good attorney." Upon certification that the defendant is indigent and cannot afford to pay an attorney, the court will provide one for him at the state's expense. As an officer of the court, an attorney may be assigned to handle the defense except when it would interfere with the other demands of his responsibilities to his clients and the court. In a great many jurisdictions the county position of public defender has been created. This officer is responsible to the indigent accused, to defend him and to assure him of his constitutional guarantee to a competent defense. Although not a new office, the tax-supported defense attorney has taken on new meaning and emphasis to assure the accused of every possible means of well-qualified legal representation.

The Jury Trial

The accused has a Constitutional right to a jury trial. As a matter of routine, and also as a simple matter of logistics, it is virtually impossible for every criminal trial to be attended by a jury. In the majority of cases, therefore, we see the encouragement of—and the practice of—trials without a jury. Such a trial is called a *court* trial, and the judge functions in the dual role of judge and jury. Jurors are selected usually by a lottery system from the county's rolls of registered voters, assumed to be the peers of the accused, who is likely to be a resident of the same county occupied by the jurors. Various methods are used to summon the jury and to provide for their service, but once empaneled to sit as a jury in a criminal trial they function as the judges of fact in the case. While the judge determines which evidence and witnesses will be authorized for presentation during the trial in accordance with the rules of procedure and evidence and serves as the arbiter on the law, the jury determines the truth and weight of the evidence and then passes judgment on the guilt of the accused.

Juries usually consist of twelve members, except when waived in accordance with accepted practice, or in some jurisdictions where a jury of a lesser amount of jurors has been established by law. They hear testimony and examine evidence, receive instructions from the judge as to the legal considerations as to their role during the trial, and form opinions about the guilt or innocence of the accused. At the conclusion of the trial, the judge instructs them as to their role in the matter, and provides them guidelines to follow when arriving at their conclusions. The jurors then retire to their chambers where they meet as a committee to discuss and to vote on the issues. In a criminal trial, the jury must vote unanimously for a guilty verdict. They may decide that there is no justification for a guilty verdict, or they may become hopelessly deadlocked over the issues. In the third instance, the judge may declare a mistrial, which would necessitate a new trial at the initiation of the prosecutor again. In the absence of a finding of guilt, the jurors vote for a not-guilty plea. The jury advises the judge that they find the accused guilty or not-guilty, at which time the judge assumes his role in the case to proceed with sentencing or to order the release of the accused.

Coroner's Inquest

Although not a court, the coroner's inquest has a quasi-judicial appearance in procedure and outcome. The coroner is charged with the responsibility for determining the cause of death under a list of many different conditions, including deaths occurring during surgery, death occurring under suspicious circumstances, death of a person who had not had the attention of a physician for a specified period of time, and many other occasions. There are certain situations when the cause of death may be obvious, but the circumstances surrounding the death may be open to question. An example of a death might be a self-defense situation between an occupant of a house or operator of a business who kills a burglar during the commission of what appears to be a crime, but there is some question as to whether the death was necessary under the circumstances as they appeared to the officer at the time he arrived on the scene some few minutes after the occurrence.

The investigating officer would take the statements of the witnesses and gather the evidence that may or may not substantiate the statements of the person who claimed the need to kill his assailant in self-defense. The coroner's responsibility is to determine cause of death, and the police responsibility is to investigate the case from a criminal prosecution standpoint. In addition to performing an autopsy and establishing the time of death, the type of wound and weapon used, the coroner may determine that further inquiry is necessary. Sitting in his role as hearing officer, the coroner may impanel a jury from available adults he is able to summon to the place of the hearing, which may be a room in the funeral home or an available courtroom or other public place. The coroner subpoenas witnesses and they are sworn in to testify to their observations and the role they played in the investigation. Witnesses may include the individual whose actions caused the death, the officers on the scene, and any other witnesses the coroner may choose to testify including the doctor who performed the autopsy. At the conclusion of the hearing, the jury makes a determination as to cause of death. The decision may be "accidental" or "caused by the criminal act of another," or "by negligence," or other decisions.

In the event the coroner's inquest yields a conclusion that the death was a criminal act of someone, the coroner recommends to the prosecutor that some criminal action and/or further investigation should follow. The prosecution, of course, is the prerogative of the district attorney and the recommendation of the coroner is just that: a recommendation. Inquests are not held on a regular basis, nor are they automatic in all suspicious deaths. Neither are autopsies held in all cases. The coroner has the authority to make his decisions about how to pursue his inquiry, although he may act at the request or recommendation of the prosecutor, or perhaps at the insistence of the survivors when they may raise questions that the coroner believes should be asked during a formal inquiry.

Administrative Hearings

Various governmental bodies have the authority to subpoena witnesses and to conduct such inquiries that are necessary to their operations. City councils, county boards of supervisors, personnel commissions, licensing boards, school boards, human relations commissions, and numerous other agencies hold hearings and make administrative decisions that have binding effect on the individuals who are the subjects of their inquiries. For example, a school teacher may be charged with some type of administrative violation that may or may not concurrently be a criminal matter. The administrative hearing is held independent of any other issue and has no direct relationship to any other action. The board may sit as a body and swear in witnesses, hear testimony, and conduct its inquiry with the chairman or president of the board presiding in his quasi-judicial role, or the board may appoint an attorney to sit as the hearing officer to preside at the hearing and to present to them a summary of the hearing and his recommendations. In either case, the board makes the final determination as to the fate of the accused teacher and it may vote to suspend or to withdraw his credentials or license. The result is that this professional individual has been denied, by board action, the right to practice his profession anywhere in the state.

Arbitration boards have been established to relieve the burden on the courts in personal injury cases involving competing insurance claims resulting from traffic collisions or industrial accidents. Labor-management relations have been handled by arbitration boards as well. The result in these various types of quasi-judicial hearings has been a reduction of the burden on the courts and a considerable speeding-up of the litigation, which previously would have taken several years in some cases had it gone to the courts for disposition.

Presentence Investigation

Following the guilty verdict and preceding the judges imposition of the sentence, the judge may order a presentence investigation to be conducted by the probation officer. The defendant may demand immediate sentencing, and he will if he believes that it will be to his advantage that he do so, but most defendants welcome the investigation. The purpose of the presentence investigation is to inquire into the background and the personal life of the defendant, his work and personal history, his integration in the community, and the various factors that will provide the judge with the insight to use his wisdom in imposing the sentence that the judge deems most appropriate for the offense, the temper of the community, whatever other pressures play on his conscience, and that he believes will be most appropriate to lead to the eventual rehabilitation and reintegration of the defendant.

The Sentence

Although there are a few mandatory sentences in certain types of offenses, the judge has a wide range of discretion within which he may operate when imposing sentence. There are maximum fines and terms of imprisonment in the county or city jail in misdemeanor cases, and prison sentences for felony convictions may be somewhat static. The judge may suspend sentence altogether, or he may sentence the defendant who has been found guilty of a felony to a long period of probation with a short term in jail as a condition of that probation. The judge may sentence the defendant to a definite period of time in the penitentiary, or prison, or he may preside in a state that provides for indeterminate sentences. In that case, the judge merely remands the convicted defendant to prison "for the term prescribed by law," which may consist of a minimum and a maximum term with the exact amount of time to be established by a state board of corrections. Whatever the sentence is to be, the judge relies with some confidence upon the findings of the probation officer during his presentence investigation and his recommendations regarding the sentence.

Summary

In a few brief pages we have attempted to cover the highlights of the court system and various processes related to the court function as a part of the criminal justice system. The court is the "process" component of the system, which acts upon matters brought before the court by the law enforcement component through the prosecuting attorney, and then passes the matter on to some other component of the system, such as corrections or some anciliary agency or function to assure the best possible disposition of the case.

The court system consists of a separate federal system for matters involving the federal government in civil or criminal matters, and a network of state court systems functioning with considerable autonomy in their respective states. The state system consists of a series of trial courts at the local level, and appellate courts, which serve several trial court jurisdictions from a fixed location, or on a circuit court rotational system. The court of last resort for appeals within each state is usually that state's supreme court. Appeals beyond state level to the U.S. Supreme Court may be initiated when the cases involve matters of the U.S. Constitution, issues between states, or certain other specified cases.

In this chapter we have covered some of the factors that are involved in the court process and some of the offices and individuals who perform within the court component of the system. We made no attempt to cover in detail all of the mechanisms of the system. That, of course, is the subject of another text and another course of study. The attempt here was to briefly review the court component of the system as a part of the total system in the administration of justice.

Exercises and Study Questions

1. Based on what you have studied in this chapter, draw a flow diagram on the progress of a misdemeanor case from arrest to final court disposition.

2. Draw a flow diagram on the progress of a felony case from arrest to final court disposition, being sure to include both the lower preliminary process as well as the trial.

3. Explain the relationships of the prosecutor and the defense attorney in a criminal trial.

4. Draw a chart of the court system in your state and in your county, and compare the chart with what you have read in this chapter. What are the differences? Similarities?

5. Which official is responsible for custody of the deceased in a homicide case?

6. Explain the phenomenon the author calls "judicial supremacy."

7. In the jurisdiction where you live is there a justice court?

8. What is the function of a small claims court?

9. Describe the difference between a judge and a magistrate as described in this chapter.

10. When a grand jury determines that a person should be held to answer to a criminal charge, what does the district attorney file in the superior court?

11. Contrast and compare the coroner's inquest with the municipal court trial.

12. How does an administrative hearing compare with the criminal trial?

13. What is the substance and effect of the presentence investigation?

14. Recommended semester project: Visit your local municipal court and follow a criminal case through the preliminary hearing to the felony trial in the superior court. Prepare a written chronicle of events outlining the program of the case, the final results, and your impression.

Suggested for Additional Study

For this chapter, refer to the Government Code, the Criminal or Penal Code, and other government publications for your own jurisdiction to contrast and compare the court system.

ADAMS, THOMAS F., *Criminal Justice Readings*. Pacific Palisades, Calif.: Goodyear Publishing Co., Inc., 1972.

BRISTOW, ALLEN P. and JOHN B. WILLIAMS, *A Handbook in Criminal Procedure and the Administration of Justice*. Beverly Hills: Glencoe Press, 1966.

WESTEN, PAUL B. and KENNETH M. WELLS, *The Administration of Justice*, (2nd Ed.). Englewood Cliffs: Prentice-Hall, Inc., 1972.

WRIGHT, R. GENE and JOHN A. MARLO, *The Police Officer and Criminal Justice*. New York: McGraw-Hill Book Co., Inc., 1970.

7

Corrections

Introduction

Once the defendant has been found guilty, sentence is imposed and the subject is introduced to the next component of the three part criminal justice system: corrections. Actually, however, the system and its parts are not that clearly separated from one another. When the defendant is arrested for the suspected offense he is introduced to one segment of the corrections component when he is booked into the city or county jail. He is innocent until proven guilty, but nevertheless he is in custody and must remain in that state until he is released on bail or on his own recognizance (his word is his bail) or until he goes to trial. He may remain in custody throughout the entire time of his hearings and trial as an unsentenced prisoner. During the trial and under special conditions, another segment of the corrections component might get involved in his case sometime prior to a finding of guilt or innocence: probation.

In some jurisdictions, and under conditions that are agreeable to the defense, the court, and the prosecution, probation gets into the act somewhat prematurely when the judge orders a presentence investigation so that in the plea-bargaining sessions the accused has an opportunity to anticipate what the probation officer would recommend in the way of punishment—and the judge would probably impose—if he were to plead guilty to the charges as they stand, or to some reduced charge. This is an extension of the "bartered plea" concept when there is some negotiating to determine if the defendant will enter a guilty plea to avoid the delay and time of a trial. This is not a routine situation, it should be pointed out, and the most common type of presentence investigation is carried out after the defendant has been found guilty—or has entered his plea of guilty—and the judge wishes to have some substantive information about the defendant and his crime in order that he might impose sentence with more knowledge and considered judgment.

The judge pronounces the sentence. Except for a suspended sentence with no conditions attached, the defendant begins his experiential journey under the watchful supervision of one or more of the several segments of corrections: probation, institutions, and, in many cases, parole. In this chapter, we shall explore each of these segments in approximately the same order as the defendant who might encounter the full cycle, beginning with probation.

Probation

The probation officer is either a federal or a county officer, depending on the jurisdiction of the case in which the defendant is involved. Although we shall briefly discuss federal probation later, this section generally refers to the local county probation officer and his department, an arm of the courts, with principal responsibilities as a correctional agency. The probation officer and his deputies serve at the pleasure of the superior court and function within the general policies and guidelines prescribed by that tribunal.

Probation Defined.   Probation is a conditional imposition of supervised liberty in lieu of imprisonment in jail or some other institution, which continues for a specified period of time of good conduct. Probation may include a short term in confinement in a local jail followed by an extended period of this supervised freedom as a condition of suspension of a sentence to state prison. The objective of probation is to accomplish rehabilitation of the guilty offender through a series of supervised experiences and types of treatment without removing him from the social milieu. The process may be described as a means of protecting the community by contributing to the rehabilitation of an offender through constructive control. From the variety of definitions one may find, three factors seem to be constant: supervised liberty, threat of imprisonment as an alternative, and rehabilitation as an objective.

Probation is imposed by the judge in the same manner as he would impose a sentence of imprisonment in jail or state prison. It is one of the alternatives open to the judge when passing sentence, which he feels is the most appropriate course of action to lead to the eventual rehabilitation of the offender and to (hopefully) prevent him from repeating his criminal behavior. It is at the time the judge is contemplating the sentence that the probation officer or one of his deputies is assigned to the case. The judge orders a presentence investigation.

Presentence Investigation

There are at least four functions of the presentence investigation: (1) Compile all available data about the crime and the circumstances surrounding it, including any contributing or mitigating circumstances that might provide insight into the reasons for the crime; (2) find out as much as possible about the offender, his personal behavior characteristics, his family and work environment, and such other personal insights about the individual that will serve the judge in making his determination as to the most effective sentence to impose for the protection of the community and rehabilitation of the offender; (3) articulate the alternatives available to the court in the imposition of sentence; and (4) recommend to the court the alternative that the probation officer believes to be the better choice.

Uses of the presentence report, according to a Pennsylvania training manual, include:

1. a base of information to assist the court in determining the most appropriate disposition of the case
2. basis for case planning by the probation officer
3. source of information to institution when classifying offenders
4. resource for parole planning and supervision
5. a base of information for referrals to noncorrectional human service agencies
6. source of information for correctional research [1]

The probation officer provides a very critical service in the sentencing as well as the rehabilitative process when he conducts his investigation and presents his report to the court. The information he gathers, his interpretation, and his reporting of that information strongly influence the court in making the sentence determination.

The Sentence

Alternatives available to the court are numerous. Criminal definitions and legally prescribed maximums and minimums have some influence, but the judge has almost limitless discretion except in those few cases

[1] Center for Law Enforcement and Corrections, *Probation, Parole, and Pardons: A Basic Course,* Training Module 6913 (University Park, Pa.: Pennsylvania State University, 1969), p. 14.

in which mandatory sentences accompany a finding of guilty. Misdemeanors are punishable by imprisonment in a county or city jail and/or a fine, or any imposition of sentence of lesser severity. A felony conviction by a superior court carries with it a maximum sentence of imprisonment in state prison or a fine, or both. Federal sentences have comparable limitations with federal probation and prison involvement, with some variations in procedure. Definitions of felonies and misdemeanors are used as guidelines. A felony is a crime punishable by death or imprisonment in a state prison, while a misdemeanor lies in the "any other punishment" category.

Although a crime is punishable within certain minimums or maximums, and the designation of felony or misdemeanor is determined by how it is *punishable,* the judge may—in some jurisdictions—change that designation by imposition of punishment in a specfic case. For example, the criminal code may state that a crime is punishable by imprisonment for a maximum of five years in state prison. The judge exercises his discretion in the sentencing by prescribing three years' probation in lieu of prison and thirty days in the county jail. Because the threat of prison prevails throughout the period of probation, the conviction in this case stands as a felony conviction. In another case with the same *punishable* provision, the judge imposes a straight six months sentence in the county jail with no other provisions. By virtue of his action, the judge has not affected the classification of the felony crime that was committed, but he has convicted the offender as a misdemeanant, and his record will show a misdemeanor conviction. A misdemeanor cannot be upgraded into a felony, but it is the court's prerogative in the example just given for the judge to downgrade a felony arrest into a misdemeanor conviction.

Although the stated purpose for imposition of sentence may be for the protection of the community and rehabilitation of the guilty offender, traditional demands on the courts have been that the sentence must also serve to isolate the criminal from the society he offended, and that there must be some revenge on the part of society for certain types of crimes. The offender must be required to "pay his debt" to society. The judge is responsive to the needs and demands of the community he serves, as well as to the justice system. In the final analysis, the decision the judge makes involves an intricate series of decisions that take into account the nature of the offense, the temper of the community, his own moral feelings about the offense, the legal constraints within which he must operate, internal and external pressures that are working on him at the time, the capacity to which the local jail and nearby prison may be extended, his own attitudes about the effectiveness of the alternatives to imprisonment, and the probation officer's presentence investigation report.

Probation

The judge has weighed all of the factors presented to him following the findings of guilt, and he sentences the offender to probation. Although someone may argue about the semantics and state that probation is not a sentence, the threat of incarceration for all or part of a specified period of time stands throughout the duration of the probation. The similarity to a sentence ends at that point, and the probationary period has no resemblance to a similar period of time spent in custody in an institution. The conditions of probation are imposed by the judge, and the probation officer is required to enforce those conditions and to report infractions to the court. Terms of probation generally include the following restrictions and requirements:

1. Strict observance of all laws.
2. Developing and keeping good habits.
3. Maintaining a good work or school record.
4. Associating only with persons approved by the court and the probation officer.
5. Marriage or divorce, or other change in living arrangements with the approval of the probation officer.
6. Attending prescribed counseling or treatment sessions.
7. Abiding by all of the restrictions imposed by the judge who granted probation.
8. Reporting periodically as agreed with the court and the probation officer.

The terms may vary with the individual, and the variations should— ideally—correspond with the recommendations contained in the pre-sentence report. Limitations do exist—realistically—because of the number of individuals who must be supervised by each probation officer. Part of the rehabilitative process involves the building of self-reliance and social responsibility, which includes living by established rules. Upon the successful completion of probation, the probation is automatically ended. A violation of probation must be brought to the attention of the court, and the discretion is again in the hands of the judge. He may order continuation of the probation; he may add restrictions; or he may revoke the probation and order the violator to go to jail or prison for the crime leading to his original conviction on the basis of his inability to perform his probation as required.

Except for recent breaks in the trend at the time of preparation of this manuscript, and at other times in history, this nation has seen continuous increases in the numbers of reported crimes in the Index offenses, as pointed out earlier in this text, and there has been a corresponding upward trend in arrest statistics. At the same time, however, another trend appears to be moving along. Populations, and average daily attendance at the many correctional institutions is showing a decrease. This is the result of many recommendations, and subsequent action on those recommendations for exploration in the use of alternatives to imprisonment for rehabilitative efforts. A 1972 California report to the attorney general stated:

> The trend is, simply stated, one of reducing the number of criminal offenders who are taken into close confinement and reducing the length of time served by those who are held in custody. The orientation of the decision makers toward this trend, and the various available programs, work together to produce a single result, to wit, a steady reduction in institutionalization and a comparable increase in community-based handling of offenders. The trend is nationwide and is clearly manifested throughout the California Department of Corrections, the California Adult Authority, the probation departments of the various California counties, and the court system.[2]

The President's Crime Commission made the following statement about community-based corrections, which includes probation as the principal process of this concept:

> With two-thirds of the total corrections caseload under probation or parole supervision today, the central question is no longer whether to handle offenders in the community but how to do so safely and successfully. Clearly, there is a need to incarcerate those criminals who are dangerous until they no longer are a threat to the community. However, for the large bulk of offenders, particularly the youthful, the first or the minor offender, institutional commitments can cause more problems than they solve.

> Institutions tend to isolate offenders from society, both physically and psychologically, cutting them off from schools, jobs, families, and other supportive influences and increasing the probability that the label of criminal will be indelibly impressed upon them. The goal of reintegration is likely to be furthered much more readily by working with offenders in the community than by incarceration.

> Additionally, other goals are met. One is economy. In 1965 it cost, on the average, about $3,600 a year to keep a youngster in a training school, while it cost less than one-tenth that amount to keep him on probation. Even allowing for the substantial improvements in salaries and personnel

[2] Task Force on Probation and Parole, *Report to Attorney General Evelle J. Younger* (Sacramento, Calif.: State Printing Office, 1972), pp. 4–5.

needed to make community programs more effective, they are costly. This is especially true when construction costs, which now run up to $20,000 for each bed in a children's institution, are included. The differential becomes even greater if the costs of welfare for the families of the incarcerated, as well as the loss of taxable income, are included.

Various studies have sought to measure the success of community treatment. One summary analysis of 15 different studies of probation outcomes indicate that from 60 to 90 percent of the probationers studied completed terms without revocation. In another study, undertaken in California, 11,638 adult probationers who were granted probation during 1956 to 1958 were followed up after 7 years. Of this group almost 72 percent completed their probation terms without revocation.

These findings were not obtained under controlled conditions, nor were they supported by data that distinguished among the types of offenders who succeeded or among the types of services that were rendered. But they are the product of a variety of probation services administered at different times and places and provide some evidence that well planned and administered community programs can be successful in reducing recidivism. These findings, combined with the data from the national survey of corrections showing that probation and parole services are characteristically poorly staffed and often poorly administered, suggest that improvement in the quality of community treatment should be a major goal.[3]

Standard 1.2 of the American Bar Association Probation Standards stresses the desirability of a sentence of probation in these words:

Probation is a desirable disposition in appropriate cases because:
(i) it maximizes the liberty of the individual while at the same time vindicating the authority of the law and effectively protecting the public from further violation of law;
(ii) it affirmatively promotes the rehabilitation of the offender by continuing normal community contacts;
(iii) it avoids the negative and frequently stultifying effects of confinement which often severely and unnecessarily complicate the reintegration of the offender into the community;
(iv) it greatly reduces the financial costs to the public treasury of an effective correctional system;
(v) it minimizes the impact of the conviction upon innocent dependents of the offender.[4]

[3] President's Commission on Law Enforcement and the Administration of Justice, *Challenge of Crime in a Free Society* (Washington, D.C.: Government Printing Office, 1967), Chapter 6, "Corrections."

[4] Samuel Dash, "Challenge: Sentencing, Correction, Rehabilitation," a paper presented at Williamsburg, Virginia, March 11–14, 1971 and published in *Addresses and Papers of the National Conference on the Judiciary* (Washington, D.C.: Government Printing Office, 1971), p. 214.

The probation department operates in two fundamental ways: investigative and supervisorial. Within the framework of the agency, there are essentially two separate subsystems: criminal justice for adults and juvenile justice for youths who have not yet reached the age at which they are no longer considered juvenile. Investigative services are principally carried out for the court in the form of presentence investigations. Other investigations include placement of children in foster homes, financial ability of parents to pay for custodial services of children in juvenile institutions, and investigations related to casework. Supervisorial work involves field casework and operation of the various juvenile institutions. The structure of an agency usually shows two basic subdivisions of operational units within the probation department, adult and juvenile, along with another division involving the support services related to the actual operation of the probationary system.

Adult probation processes involve the presentence investigation, management of the county's parole program for conditional release from jail, counseling services for probationers, casework management of the many individuals who are on probation, and operation of many community-based rehabilitation programs that provide alternatives to imprisonment. Special educational and training programs are sometimes operated in cooperation with local colleges and occupational training schools to enhance the probationer's chances for greater employability and successful completion of probation. Use of probationers as volunteers in working with other probationers is a form of catharsis that is effective with some individuals. Referral of cases to other agencies and organizations also consumes a comfortable amount of time and effort on the part of the probation department. Such referrals include cases involving alcoholics, drug-abusers, physically and socially handicapped, so-called "unemployable," medical and psychiatric services.

A form of probation that has met with varying degrees of success is the work furlough from jail, which requires the out-of-jail supervision of probation caseworkers when necessary. The probationer serves his time in jail, and at the same time goes out for specified hours during the day when he works on a regular job—which may be the same job he worked at before being sentenced to jail—and at regular wages. Sometimes the job is one found for the probationer by a probation officer, whose responsibility it is to monitor that individual while on the job to assure his presence on the job and his return to jail at the end of each working day. The cost to the county is less because the individual is able to continue supporting his family's needs while he serves out his sentence, which means that his family is not supported by welfare agencies during that time, and he is also employed upon his release from jail. This program may be just the moral boost the probationer needs on release from jail: a job and a source of income that he may not have had prior to his arrest and conviction, and an improved self-image.

Juvenile Probation. Probation services for the juvenile involve a wide range of services. The casework responsibilities for the juvenile probationer are similar to those for the adult, with obvious differences because of the ages of the probationers. Other services in the juvenile category include investigations that involve dependency proceedings, matters that involve juveniles who are in danger of becoming delinquent, and investigations of juveniles who have been brought to the attention of the probation department because they violated a local, state, or federal law. Other services of the juvenile probation section are supervision and institutional services. Supervision of the dependent and the delinquent child involve different approaches because the dependent child has been the victim of criminal or negligent conduct on the part of his parents or some other person, and the delinquent child has been charged with some act that calls for behavior modification. The institutional services involve operation of the camps, training schools, and other institutions that provide custody of the dependent and delinquent children.

Investigations of juveniles are conducted for the assistance of the court in making a determination of the better course of action for the welfare of the child. In dependency matters, the court is concerned with placement of the child in the environment most appropriate for his needs to live a normal healthy childhood. The near-delinquent must have similar placement, perhaps, but his needs may be met adequately by keeping him in his own home and at the same time prescribing a program for him that might deter him from continuing in the direction toward delinquent behavior.

The intake interview usually begins the investigation of the delinquent child. In many cases, the interview reveals enough information to the probation officer so that he may consider the matter in view of the report of the arresting officer, and make some sort of disposition on the case without carrying it further. The youth is counseled and released to his parents. Whether the information comes to the probation officer through the intake process, or from reports forwarded to the department for what the referring agent (usually a police officer, but it may come from a school or parents, or other agencies) believes to be the cause for action by the juvenile court.

The Juvenile Delinquency and Youth Crime Task Force Report describes the intake process:

> (intake is) . . . essentially a screening process to determine whether the court should take action and, if so, what action or whether the matter

should be referred elsewhere. Intake is set apart from the screening process used in adult criminal courts by the pervasive attempt to individualize each case and the nature of the personnel administering the discretionary process. In adult criminal proceedings at the post-arrest stage, decisions to screen out are entrusted to the grand jury, the judge, or usually to the prosecutor. . . . At intake in the juvenile courts, screening is an important objective.[5]

The investigator must collect and document all of the available information concerning the juvenile's misconduct, the attitudes and background information on the child and his family, environmental influences, and the various other factors that have a direct and indirect effect upon the juvenile and his conduct. He must then make a decision as to what further action to recommend. The probation officer who investigates the case determines whether to proceed with formal court action or to take no further action. The officer's report contains recommendations for the judge, based upon the information he has accumulated and his assessment of the juvenile's likelihood for rehabilitation. The court relies heavily on the investigation and recommendations of the probation officer, and quite often takes whatever action the officer recommends. The importance of the intake process in the juvenile justice process is underlined by the Task Force:

> At the intake phase a great deal of juvenile misbehavior can be handled through alternatives other than adjudication. Community agencies and organizations such as social work agencies, Big Brother, employment facilities, school programs, and other viable resources can help the child rectify his problem and alleviate his negative situation. One of the primary considerations at intake should be the effect that labeling and the formal adjudication process will have on the youngster. Even though juvenile records are not public records, it would be naive to assume that there would not be a contaminating effect as a result of formal adjudication. Hence, the reason for attempting to make a referral other than formal adjudication in court.[6]

Supervision involves the process described earlier: supervised liberty for a specified period of time and with a list of conditions under which the probationer must perform. The caseworker meets and confers with the probationer in the office, in his home, and at various other places as often as practicable. He counsels the juvenile on family and personal problems, often extending his counseling to the family on matters relating

---

[5] President's Commission on Law Enforcement and the Administration of Justice, *Task Force Report: Juvenile Delinquency and Youth Crime* (Washington, D.C.: Government Printing Office, 1967), p. 5.

[6] President's Commission, *Task Force Report: Juvenile Delinquency and Youth Crime,* p. 5.

to the juvenile and his problems. The officer attempts to identify referral needs and makes every effort to make those referrals to psychologists, employers, schools, youth organizations, and many other resources available to work toward the greatest degree of success with the child's rehabilitation. He also takes appropriate action on infractions of the conditions of probation, and he remands the violator back to the court for a new determination to be made as to how best to treat the child.

Institutional facilities operated by the probation department are basically of two types: (1) housing for dependent children, and (2) detention of juveniles for the treatment of delinquency. The children who are dependent upon the county because of abandonment or abuse, or for some other reason determined by the court, are returned to the custody of their parents or other responsible family adults as soon as possible, or they are placed in foster homes. Custodial, or detention, facilities include institutions most commonly known as juvenile halls, which are for the temporary detention of juveniles awaiting court appearance or placement in another institution, or placement in a foster home or the longer-term institutions, such as camps, ranches, and schools.

The temporary detention facilities provide housing on a more temporary and short-term basis. Consequently, the education and training they provide for the children are on a much more transient basis. In the other treatment institutions there is provision for educational progress, occupational training, various types of recreation and leisure-time activities, and after-care supervision to follow-up whatever programs have been started while the juvenile is in the institution.

Federal Probation. The Federal Probation Service, through the Administrative Office of the U.S. Courts, provides probation and parole services for the ninety district courts in the fifty states, the District of Columbia, and Puerto Rico. The federal probation officer serves at the pleasure of the district court in essentially the same capacity as his counterpart who works as a deputy probation officer for the county. He engages in investigations and casework with individuals who have been adjudged guilty of federal offenses and who are placed on probation or parole.[7]

Correctional Institutions

Throughout the United States there is a vast network of jails, prisons, camps, farms, halfway houses, and private institutions. More than 1.3

---

[7] Richard G. Kleindienst, *Attorney General's First Annual Report, Federal Law Enforcement and Criminal Justice Assistance Activities* (Washington, D.C.: Government Printing Office, 1972), pp. 443–44.

Group counseling, California Rehabilitation Center at Corona.
Courtesy, California State Department of Corrections.

million individuals are housed in thousands of institutions every day of
the year, according to the Federal Bureau of Prisons.[8] Those prisoners
are housed in federal, state, and local institutions, most of them in city
and county jails. How many individuals are housed in each institution
and the list of those places may be found in a several hundred page
volume published by the U.S. Department of Justice.[9]

Local Jails. The local jails are maintained by the city police and
county sheriffs across the nation, usually housing a handful to a few
dozen inmates, many of them awaiting hearings and trials. Until found
guilty in court, or by virtues of a plea of guilty, those people are innocent and have to be proven guilty. Their presumption of guilt by the
arresting officers and the prosecutors causes them to be housed in the

[8] President's Commission, *Challenge of Crime in a Free Society,* p. 159.
[9] National Criminal Justice Information and Statistics Service, *Local Jails: A
Report Presenting Data for Individual County and City Jails from the 1970 National
Jail Census* (Washington, D.C.: Government Printing Office, 1973).

jail, but how to maintain their custody under maximum security conditions is a dilemma. Custody and transportation, and related matters concerning the feeding and control of these persons is the chief concern, while rehabilitative efforts are directed toward those who have been determined by the courts as guilty of some criminal conduct.

Short-term imprisonment with little or no attempt to rehabilitate the inmates describes the average jail. The prisoner who is serving a sentence of a few days may be assigned simple tasks that might attempt at keeping the individual busy to make the situation more tolerable for everyone concerned. For those whose sentences are somewhat longer, perhaps up to one year, there are work assignments both inside and outside the institution that they may take part in. In addition to keeping busy, the inmates may earn "good time" off their sentences for their conformance to the rules and participation in jail programs.

Efforts at rehabilitation in the county and city jail are necessarily short-term programs because of the nature of jail sentences, which are usually for terms of a few days to a few weeks. Any treatment programs must be brief and intensive in nature, and they must show some results in that short time, however slight those successes may be. The National Sheriff's Association *Manual on Jail Administration* discusses the short-term treatment program:

> Most jail personnel recognize the fact that the great majority of persons committed to their custody have some problems of a personal, social, and/or medical nature, that such problems vary according to the individual, and that the community and jail personnel should be doing far more to help resolve the problems of prisoners, if the real and sensible objective of the jail is to be accomplished. That objective is properly to confine, supervise, and help solve the problems that prisoners have so that they are less likely to come into further conflict with the law after release. If these functions of custody and treatment are effectively performed, future crimes by current prisoners will be reduced. Thus, the community will be a better and safer place in which to live for the prisoner and the citizens in the community.[10]

The treatment programs must help the jail inmates solve personal and social problems, and must address the problem of both the sentenced prisoners as well as those who are in custody while going through the various phases of the judicial process, still innocent in the eyes of the law but confronted by serious legal problems. The treatment activities are as varied as they are intense, and they must meet the needs of "the

[10] National Sheriff's Association, *Manual on Jail Administration* (Washington, D.C.: National Sheriff's Association, Inc., 1970), p. 190.

different types of inmates such as the pretrial, the first offender, the juvenile or youthful offender, the alcoholic or drug addict, the mentally or physically ill, and others." [11] Treatment programs include the obvious ones of medical and psychological, dental, and physical conditioning. Other treatment programs in the jail include counseling and guidance on a one-to-one relationship, therapy in groups or individual sessions for problem solving or behavior modification, educational programs to enable the inmate to experience genuine success in some significant way, religious participation, and an organized system of recreational activities. Occupational programs may be added to the list for the longer-term prisoners, although facilities and equipment are limited so that only a few basic occupational skills may be covered by an institution.

Housing and movement of the prisoners in jail are most challenging because of the transient nature of the institution. Booking and temporary housing until bail is raised for an early release, or placing in cells for overnight or a day or two while awaiting arraignment or trial involves classification and housing according to alleged charges, physical condition, criminal history, and age, not to mention special problems such as persons arrested for child molestation, drugs and intoxication, disorderly conduct, and the entire spectrum of criminal conduct that may involve special security problems. Once the individuals are placed, a continuous process throughout the day and almost without interruption, they must be processed through very thorough inspections and other procedures for security and health requirements. They are outfitted with jail clothes but must make frequent changes into street clothes for court appearances. Just the process of scheduling and moving the prisoners out of the jail into the maze of courtrooms according to some semblance of an organized pattern would challenge the mettle of a choreographer.

Visiting rights of attorneys and members of the family, inspection of visitors, arranging for privacy *and* security during visits, controlling the movement of people and prevention of smuggling contraband, providing supplies and equipment, such as paper, reference books, and a typewriter, for the inmate who chooses to handle his own defense, and special problems with the newsworthy prisoner are all individual problems that must be handled on a continuous basis in such a manner that it all occurs without incident and at a low visibility level. For the prisoner who is eventually sentenced to prison, the jailors transport them to the state prison or reformatory.

Juvenile Institutions. The two basic juvenile institutions are the home or house for dependent children, and the juvenile hall. Although their orientation is different, because the former involves children who

[11] National Sheriff's Association, *Manual on Jail Administration,* p. 190.

are the victims of their circumstances, and the "hall" is for those who caused the circumstances leading to their detention, housing, control, movement, feeding, recreation, and most of the daily housekeeping activities are similar. These two facilities are for stays of short duration, where the children stay while waiting for placement in foster homes or return to their own homes, or—in the case of delinquent children—while their cases are studied and the court determines the most appropriate disposition for them. The delinquent children also may be placed in foster homes or returned to their parents or guardians although adjudged wards of the court, which means that they are remanded to the supervision of the probation department for behavior modification or other forms of treatment and rehabilitation.

For longer periods of custody, juveniles who have been remanded to the probation department or the state's Youth Authority (or similar agency), are placed in training schools, ranches, camps, or similar institutions. Although each type of institution is unique, their similarities are that they serve as the housing establishments for children under various degrees of supervision while efforts are made to develop in them a life-style that will be carried on following their return to their own homes. Their schedules include educational programs, organized and individual recreation, work activities that may include organized occupational training programs, moral and spiritual counseling and guidance, and different types of treatment geared to their individual needs. Significantly important in the behavior modification process of delinquent children are the correctional personnel assigned to those institutions who serve as models for the children. Through their guidance and direction, the children are able to develop in a positive manner and live delinquency-free lives following their release from the institutions.

Community-based Treatment

Adults and juveniles who have been inducted into the criminal justice system may be directly introduced to processes in the system generally referred to as "community-based," such as private counseling services or supervision by a probation officer, Alcoholics Anonymous, a youth organization, Big Brothers, day camps, or community centers for recreation and counseling services, training schools, educational programs, or places of residence where peer pressures serve to reinforce the legally and socially acceptable types of conduct. Others may be introduced to the community-based phase following a period of incarceration in an adult or youth institution. Such community treatment programs may include intensive sessions in transactional analysis or gestalt theory, behavior modification, or other forms of individual or group therapy. Methadone maintenance programs for drug users may be operating for the purpose of providing a legal source of drugs that substitute for heroin and other hard narcotics with an objective of gradually reducing the use of drugs and eventually total abstinence.

Some inmates of jails or penal institutions are allowed to pursue occupations in the community while they are serving their sentences. The work furlough program is a means by which the convicted prisoner may leave the jail or other institution for the time they work at their regular occupations, or at some other job found for them by the probation officer. Any violations may lead to cancellations of their participation in the program.

Variations of the work furlough program may include short-term "leaves," or approved absences from the institutions. Generally granted to the inmate of the institution whose term of custody is nearing an end, this type of a furlough program is designed to provide for the individual an opportunity to get out and look around, to find himself in relationship to other people in a posture of freedom, and to adjust to society gradually rather than to be suddenly evicted at the end of his term and to be totally disoriented to the world around him upon his release. Some persons become institutionalized and their release has such a traumatic effect on them that they willingly commit a new offense so that they might return to the security of prison or jail.

Neighborhood probation offices may serve as community centers for the probationers who live nearby, and such a base may provide for them a greater opportunity for success than having to visit a distant centrally located "concrete palace" in a civic center. For some individuals, a closer and more constant relationship with their probation or parole officers may provide for them the supervision most appropriate to their needs.

Halfway houses, either public or privately owned and operated, provide for the previously incarcerated individual the "institutional" feeling of security or control that has been his way of life for some time and at the same time provide for him opportunities to become socialized and reintegrated back into the community. Ongoing treatment programs continually operate, and the resident participates concurrently with his residency. The idealistic goal is that the individual will become both socialized and rehabilitated at about the same time as he is ready to leave the halfway house and return to his own community in what is hoped to be an improved condition so that he is less likely to repeat his criminal or delinquent behavior that got him into the system in the first place.

Many private organizations, particularly churches, may actively provide services aimed at the delinquent or near-delinquent child, and the

The center of Synanon is the Synanon Game—a group interaction where there are no verbal inhibitions or restrictions except for a ban on threats of physical violence. Everything else can be and is said, in a wide range of humor and serious discussion.

Each Synanon Game is a cross-section of the community, bringing in all the various points of view of people with all types of backgrounds and the one common interest to better themselves and their lifestyles.
Courtesy Synanon Foundation, Inc.

feeling of belonging to some type of meaningful relationship with peers, and the comfort in knowing that they are wanted by someone else may provide for some the spiritual and moral strength that they may have lacked previously. Self-help organizations composed of former drug users, or burglars, or check passers, alcoholics, or persons with physical and emotional handicaps operate throughout the country with varying degrees of success in crime prevention. Goodwill Industries, The Salvation Army, rescue missions, and various societies and similar organizations have been quite active for many years.

Prisons and Penitentiaries

The state prison system is operated for the custody, rehabilitation, and other institutional corrections services for felons who serve longer sentences than those who are sentenced to county and city jails. Depending on the nature of the offense for which the person has been sent to the prison, the length of the sentence, the diagnostic evaluations of screening and placement personnel, special physical and/or mental problems, the individual's adaptability to the environment, the history of the offender, and many other factors, placement is made in a maximum, medium, or minimum security type of institution. The offender is introduced to the prison system by the judge when he pronounces sentence. In states that have the length of sentences determined by the court, the determination is made by the judge at the time of sentencing. Other states that have the *indeterminate sentence* provide that the judge sentence the prisoner "for the term prescribed by law."

The prisoner is transported to the diagnostic center, where he is tested for educational and vocational skills and knowledge, and he is studied to determine as much as possible about him so that he may be most effectively placed in the prison system. His offense and his background are studied so that efforts may be directed toward his rehabilitation. Following this evaluation, the inmate is placed in one of several different types of institutions. If the system uses the *indeterminate sentence,* it is at this point that the corrections board fixes the time of the sentence, or at least the time when the inmate may apply for parole. When a person is sentenced for the "term prescribed by law," the code describing the offense and the punishment sets both the minimum and the maximum, such as "not less than two nor more than five years in state prison." The judge has completed his part in the act by putting the process into motion. The corrections board now must study all of the facts and impressions presented to it, interview the inmate, and make a determination as to the most appropriate course of action with each individual.

The board may decide that the inmate must serve two years before he may apply for parole. Once that decision is made, there is little likelihood that he will serve less time, but he may serve more. Toward the end of the two years, the inmate's case is reviewed and the prognosis for his rehabilitation is studied; he is interviewed and questioned about his intentions and plans for parole. The board takes a vote and decides if he will be granted parole, or if he will be required to stay longer before his case will be reviewed again. Professor Caleb Foote of Berkeley discussed the California system:

> In addition to the powers usually exercised by a parole board, the California Adult Authority also determines, within the statutory limits prescribed for their crime, how long convicts committed to state prison will remain under the jurisdiction of the correctional system. In carrying out its duties, the Authority is scrupulous in observing the niceties of legal

technicality. It does not engage in "sentencing"—that word is taboo; rather, the Authority "fixes terms." Thus someone convicted in California for robbery, if denied a probation or county jail disposition, is sentenced by a judge to imprisonment whose maximum duration is legislatively prescribed at life and whose minimum, depending on the degree of crime, is either one or five years. At some time later the Authority will almost certainly release him on parole; of the 852 robbers committed to Corrections under life sentences by the California courts in 1962, 49.2 per cent were paroled after less than four years' imprisonment, 77.1 per cent in less than six years, and 94 per cent in less than nine years; only 3.3 per cent were still in prison on the original commitment at the end of 1971. Those who are paroled do not remain on parole for the duration of their "life" sentences, for at the same time the Authority sets a prisoner's parole date it also fixes his term, the difference between his parole date and his term fix representing the amount of time it wants him to be under parole supervision. Thus it may "split a fix" with a prisoner—a term fix of six years, half spent in prison, half on parole. Unless the Authority later changes its mind for some reason, at the end of the six year "term" the prisoner's debt under the life "sentence" will have been fully discharged. Indeed, discharge may come before six years, for current legislative and Authority policy favors discharge after one or two years of "clean" parole time.[12]

As one can see, there is some adjustment and readjustment in the "fixing" of time that will be spent in custody, and one of the primary considerations is the board's judgment on what is more likely to produce the best results for the individual whose case is being considered.

The institution in the system to which each person is sent depends on the term that he will serve, whether he has been in prison before, and which of the several programs will be most appropriate for his particular case. There are institutions of the more traditional type, designated as maximum, medium, and minimum security. The degrees of security are determined by the type of structure, security devices and systems, physical layouts of the institution and the escape probability, type of internal and peripheral controls, and the manner in which the inmates are housed and controlled. In the maximum security prison, the inmates are housed in separate or double cells that are locked to keep the prisoners from congregating; the buildings are made of impenetrable masonry or stone; the perimeter is enclosed by a high wall with double fences; and the entire complex is under the constant surveillance of armed guards. Medium security prisons are somewhere between the

[12] From a paper delivered by Caleb Foote at the Annual Chief Justice Earl Warren Conference on Advocacy in the United States, June 9–10, 1972 sponsored by the Roscoe Pound—American Trial Lawyers Foundation. Published in their final report, *A Program for Prison Reform*, pp. 19–20.

structure and character of that type of institution and those that are classified as minimum security institutions. The latter house their prisoners in dormitories in condominium type settings, and they may be separated from the rest of the world by low fences, with gates that may not even be kept locked, except to keep out the curious.

Camps, ranches, and honor farms of various types, as well as the halfway houses mentioned earlier in this chapter may serve as minimum security facilities. Educational and occupational training programs are carried on in all of the institutions, as are a variety of treatment programs. The location of the institution, such as a forest area or prairie land, may have been selected so as to provide work assignments for the inmates that are directly related to the area, such as forestry and conservation programs of seeding and planting, or cattle ranching, or farming to produce much of the food consumed in the other institutions.

The President's Crime Commission, in its major report, *Challenge of Crime in a Free Society* described its concept of a model for correctional institutions:

> The Commission believes that there is, therefore, value in setting forth, in the form of a "model," the changes it sees as necessary for most correctional institutions. There will, of course, continue to be special offender problems that must be dealt with in other kinds of institutions. But in general new institutions should be of the sort represented by the model, and old institutions should as far as possible be modified to incorporate its concepts.
>
> The model institution would be relatively small, and would be located as close as possible to the areas from which it draws its inmates, probably in or near a city rather than a remote location. While it might have a few high-security units for short-term detention under unusual circumstances, difficult and dangerous inmates would be sent to other institutions for longer confinement.
>
> Architecturally, the model institution would resemble as much as possible a normal residential setting. Rooms, for example, would have doors rather than bars. Inmates would eat at small tables in an informal atmosphere. There would be classrooms, recreation facilities, dayrooms, and perhaps a shop and library.
>
> In the main, however, education, vocational training, and other such activities would be carried on in the community-based resources. In this sense, the model would operate much like such programs as the Highfields and Essexfields projects. Its staff, like probation and parole officers, would be active in arranging for participation by offenders in community activities and in guiding and counseling them.
>
> Some offenders might be released after an initial period of detention for diagnosis and intensive treatment. The model institution would permit

correctional officials to invoke the short-term detention—overnight or for a few days—as a sanction or discipline, or to head off an offender from prospective trouble. Even if initial screening for classification indicates that long-term incarceration was called for, and an offender was, therefore, confined in another facility, the community-based institution could serve as a halfway house or prerelease center to ease his transition to community life. It could indeed serve as the base for a network of separate group homes and residential centers to be used for some offenders as a final step before complete release.

The prototype proposed here, if followed widely, would help shift the focus of correctional efforts from temporary banishment of offenders to a carefully devised combination of control and treatment. If supported by sufficiently flexible laws and policies, it would permit institutional restraint to be used only for as long as necessary, and in carefully graduated degree rather than as a relatively blind and inflexible process.

A final advantage of the concept suggested here is that institutions that are small, close to metropolitan areas, and highly diversified in their programs provide excellent settings for research and experimentation and can serve as proving grounds for needed innovations. Not only are they accessible to university and other research centers, but their size and freedom from restrictions foster a climate friendly to inquiry and to the implementation of changes suggested by it.

The Commission recommends:

Federal and State Governments should finance the establishment of model, small-unit correctional institutions for flexible, community-oriented treatment.[13]

The Federal Prison System. The federal system represents a comparatively small part of the total institution network, housing 5 percent of all prisoners in the United States.[14] The Federal Bureau of Prisons, under the direction of the Attorney General's office, operates the federal prison system, which houses persons convicted for violations of federal laws. The system consists of all types of institutions from maximum security to halfway houses situated in the heart of metropolitan areas. As a part of the federal corrections system, members of the Federal Bureau of Prisons serve as a part of the Interagency Council on Corrections. The council is jointly chaired by officials of the Bureau of Prisons and the Law Enforcement Assistance Administration, and it coordinates all federal corrections programs, and makes policy recommendations in an effort to bring about improvements in the system. Participants in the council include members of the Civil Service Commission, the Office of

---

[13] President's Commission, *Challenge of Crime in a Free Society,* Chapter 6, "Corrections."

[14] Kleindienst, *Attorney General's First Annual Report,* pp. 15–16.

Economic Opportunity, the Board of Parole, the Administrative Office of
the U.S. Courts, Department of Labor, Housing and Urban Development
Department, and the Department of Health, Education, and Welfare.[15]

After a reflective and analytical study of the prison system in the
United States in 1972, the Annual Chief Justice Earl Warren Conference
on Advocacy in the United States presented their final report: *A Program
for Prison Reform.*[16] In that report, the Conference presented twenty
recommendations for prison reform:

I

Criminal sanctions can never be a cure for the ills of society. While at
present they are considered necessary, and are regretfully imposed for
lack of a constructive alternative, criminal sanctions are essentially negative responses to the failings of human beings, to the failure to correct
basic malfunctions and inequalities in society, and to public demands for
retribution.

II

Prisons must be judged by their actual functioning rather than by their
stated objectives. Experience has shown that prisons do not rehabilitate
offenders. For all practical purposes, prisons are wholly punitive. Given
this reality, they accomplish only three limited functions: Protection of
society from a relatively small number of dangerous convicted persons for
a limited period of time; possibly some deterrence of a limited segment
of society at large; retribution for blameworthy acts. Furthermore, recidivism rates indicate that prison "caging" maladjusts prisoners, and thus
actually exacerbates the crime problem.

III

These limitations must be candidly recognized and the employment of
imprisonment and other criminal sanctions must accordingly be sharply
curtailed. Indeed, the release of the majority of the prison population,
coupled with the provision of community programs and services, would
not increase the danger to the public, and ultimately would enhance
public safety.

IV

Imprisonment should be a last resort. The presumption should be against
its use. Before any offender is incarcerated, the prosecution should bear
the burden of proving in an evidentiary hearing that no acceptable
alternative exists. An equal burden should be required for the denial or

[15] Kleindienst, *Attorney General's First Annual Report*, p. 7.

[16] *A Program for Prison Reform*, the final report of the Annual Chief Justice
Earl Warren Conference on Advocacy in the United States, June 9–10, 1972, sponsored by the Roscoe Pound–American Trial Lawyers Foundation, Cambridge, Massachusetts, pp. 9–16.

revocation of "good-time," probation, and parole, which really are only other ways of imposing imprisonment.[17]

V

Nearly half [18] the present potential prison and jail population can and should be placed outside the criminal justice system by decriminalizing behavior which does not involve (a) the threat or use of force against another person or persons, (b) fraud, (c) wanton destruction of property, or (d) violent attacks against the government.

VI

Among the offenses which should be thus reviewed for immediate removal from the criminal law are alcoholism, drug addiction, adult-consenting sexual acts, such as homosexuality and prostitution, and gambling, all of which are usually "complainant-less." [19] It should also be recognized that further social, psychiatric and medical research may place certain forms of behavior now termed "criminal" into discernible, and possibly treatable, disease entities.

VII

The de-criminalizing of offenses does not imply approval of such behavior or that society should ignore it. It recognizes that the criminal law and its agencies are inappropriate, often even exacerbating, to such behavior, and that what is required instead is a concurrent enlargement of available community resources in medicine, public health, vocational training, education, welfare and family counselling. It is important, however, that such "therapeutic" programs not be employed either as a guise under which another form of incarceration is imposed, or as a condition for the avoidance of imprisonment, both of which are often now the case.

VIII

We should further reduce our excessive reliance on prisons by making extensive use of alternatives to imprisonment, such as fines, restitution, and other probationary methods, which could at least as effectively meet

[17] Mr. Peter Preiser was of the opinion that the burden upon the Prosecution would be impossible to fulfill. Instead he suggested, "Accordingly, standards and criteria for the use of incarceration should be enacted by Legislatures, and before anyone is incarcerated, there should be an opportunity for a hearing. The same principles should be required for denial or revocation of parole."

[18] As pointed out by Mr. Hans W. Mattick, this estimate is based on an analysis of the FBI's Uniform Crime Reports. Professor Caleb Foote, on the other hand, believes a reduction of such size would require the adoption of all the prison-reducing recommendations in this report.

[19] District Attorney William Cahn was opposed to the removal of gambling and, to a lesser extent, prostitution from the criminal law. He regarded gambling, particularly, as a "corruptive influence on society" and a source of people's entering "the stream of criminal activity." He also was opposed to "legalization and decriminalization" in the area of narcotics addiction and drug abuse, both as to possession and the sale of drugs.

society's need for legal sanctions.[20] However, such alternatives must be made available to all people who have committed similar offenses, so as not to become a means for the more affluent to buy their way out of prison. And, where some kind of confinement seems necessary, half-way houses, community centers, group homes, intermittent sentences, and other methods of keeping offenders within the community should be preferred to prison.

IX

Even where imprisonment is warranted, we should not normally resort to long sentences. Experience has proved that, beyond a certain length, they are self-defeating.[21] Therefore, those present statutory maximum sentences which are grossly disproportionate to any legitimate social purpose should be drastically reduced. Correspondingly, the average length of actual time served, which now exceeds that of other western nations, should likewise be greatly shortened.

X

The indeterminate sentence has not had the salutary effects predicted. Instead it has resulted in the exercise of a wide discretion, without the guidance of standards, and in longer periods of time served in prison. Those who are least able to mobilize social, economic and legal resources into the sentencing processes thus become the victims of the harshest and most discriminatory sentences. On occasion, even the non-poor may be victimized by an idiosyncratic judge with tendentious prejudices about race or life style. There should, therefore, be strict limitations on the judicial and quasi-judicial exercise of discretion [22] in the fixing of terms of imprisonment, with firm guidelines based on reasonably definite factors such as past criminal record, maturity, and the mitigated or aggravated nature of the particular criminal act being weighed. By way of contrast, the definite sentence would automatically eliminate administrative parole board procedures which now consist largely of an untrammeled discretion which reduce prisoners to little more than suppli-

[20] Several Conferees were of the opinion that fines and restitution without the threat of imprisonment would not be efficacious.

[21] This conclusion was based on the personal judgment of nearly every Conferee. However, Dr. E. Preston Sharp points out that "there is no clear evidence supporting either the negative or positive impacts of the length of a prisoner's incarceration. The major thrust should be to provide funds to support the long delayed and badly needed research capability."

[22] District Attorney Cahn was of the view that a strict limitation of discretion was insufficient and that "certain violations of the law should carry prison sentences as punishments without alternatives and without discretion." It was his position that such totally-fixed sentences would eliminate more clearly the necessity and the expense of the parole system. He also added that the prosecution should have nothing to do with sentencing.

cants. The ultimate goal should be no indeterminacy whatsoever in sentences.[23]

XI

The presumption of innocence should pervade our system of criminal justice at all pre-conviction stages. But our present bail and release-on-recognizance systems do violence to that principle and are discriminatory and arbitrary.

Studies have demonstrated that most often bail is unnecessary and merely an unjustifiable impairment of the right of an accused to be free pending trial. Yet under our present practices half or more of accused persons are detained in jail pending trial.

Some members of the Conference recognized that short and specified pretrial custody may be required for society's protection in a few extreme cases, such as where a person is irrational and dangerous due to severe mental illness or when the state can establish the highly probable imminent occurrence of a specific dangerous crime of personal violence.[24]

But all agree that bail as a prevailing system should go. An end to it would, of course, also serve to further reduce prison and jail populations.

XII

The drastic reduction of our prison population would enable us to employ better our resources in the penal institutions which would remain.

Prison personnel must be adequately trained and compensated, and the racial and ethnic composition of the prison population should be taken into account in the formulation of staff recruitment policies.

XIII

We must take immediate steps to ensure respect for the rights which a democratic society must grant even to prisoners. Though he is suffering a punishment, a prisoner is still a citizen and a human being. Therefore, except to the extent absolutely necessary for custodial purposes, he should not be deprived of any of the individual rights recognized in a free society.[25] These include, but are not limited to, such basic dignities as freedom from racial discrimination, freedom from physical and mental

---

[23] Mr. Henry J. Mascarello, while agreeing that imprisonment should be a last resort only, thought that it would be better achieved if sentences were indeterminate "leaving it up to a professionally-constituted parole board to decide (later and on the basis of more information) when the 'no other course' ceases to exist."

[24] District Attorney Cahn would also provide for custody (not bail) where the prosecution can "prove" substantial reason to believe defendant will not appear for trial.

[25] In the words of Mr. Robert L. Smith, "emphasis should be made on a justice or economic model which would force the correctional system to come closer to approximating the outside world."

brutality,[26] the right to adequate diet, clothing, and health care, the right to furlough or institutional accommodations to maintain social and familial ties, including being located as close to home as practicable, freedom from censorship of mail and other literature including law books, the right to participate in local and national elections, and the right to procedural and substantive due process to guarantee such rights.[27] Judicial, administrative, and legislative action to promote and develop these rights is imperative. The presumption should always be strongly in favor of full entitlement to such rights and not against them as is all too prevalent today.

XIV

As a further concomitant for the securing of such rights, prisoners should be permitted to organize, without fear of reprisal, for the purpose of effective expression and negotiation of grievances. Even in the absence of grievances, and as a method of avoiding abuses leading to grievances, there should be regular meetings between duly elected prisoners' representatives and prison authorities.[28]

XV

Under current practices, the initial sentencing, as well as the later parole hearing that determines the ultimate sentence, is usually conducted absent the right of a prisoner to present open proof, to cross-examine witnesses and probation officers, and to exercise the other elements of due process. The right to full due process should accompany the sentencing procedure through all its stages, including the denial of probation, or to any other decisional stage that substantially affects the term of imprisonment. Until such time as the present parole system is eliminated by short definite

[26] Dr. Irwin M. Greenberg comments, "In particular, solitary confinement should be abolished as a punitive measure. Enforced seclusion should only be utilized for the prevention of physical violence in cases where no medication can reduce the threat of such violence. It should be noted that recent research has indicated that therapeutic agents such as lithium carbonate may be highly useful in aggressive prisoners. In addition, it should be recognized that special sections for such prisoners, even in the absence of solitary confinement, only serve to promote aggressive behavior, and that too, should be abolished."

[27] Interestingly, Mr. D. Lloyd Macdonald would specifically add to a "right to personality," commenting that: "The rapidly expanding medical and technological field of behavior modification through hormonal regulation, brain surgery, electric stimulation of the brain, and aversion therapy will soon allow corrections people to fundamentally change the behavior patterns and personality of persons in their custody. There is some promise in this, but the dangers are of profound dimensions for our social system. Any application of behavior modification techniques should be postponed pending full medical, jurisprudential and philosophical exploration of the implications. In any event, there ought to be an absolute bar against any use of such techniques without the inmate's consent and the concept of consent itself needs new attention and reformulation."

[28] District Attorney Cahn expressed a preference for an ombudsman concept as a means of dealing with grievances, rather than encouraging the organization of prisoners.

prison terms, due process should apply to both the initial granting and revocation of parole or good conduct time. These events are now at least as critical in the sentencing process as is the original judicial decision.

XVI

Since most prisoners are without means to engage counsel for the protection of their rights, it is essential to the implementation of such rights that the availability of properly trained and experienced Publc Defenders or private counsel, with adequate staff support, be assured to all. Such legal services should be available to challenge the conviction, to aid the prisoner with any civil problems, and to represent the prisoner in grievances against the institution.

XVII

Like most other public institutions, prisons must be open to public scrutiny and not be hidden away beyond easy observation. To assure such high visibility, the press and other media, upon request, should have ready access to our prisons, provided that each prisoner's right to refuse interviews or exposure shall be respected.[29]

XVIII

The fact that rehabilitation is not a legitimate purpose of imprisonment does not imply that "helping" programs should be removed from prisons. The state has a duty to provide economic, social, educational and medical services in prisons, as well as in the communities, but since such services bear no relationship to the legitimate purposes of imprisonment, their acceptance by prisoners should be voluntary. Especially since there is no convincing evidence of the effectiveness of rehabilitative programs in prison, they should have no bearing whatsoever on the length of a prisoner's incarceration.[30]

XIX

Upon completion of their sentences, prisoners should return to full, lawful membership in society. No discrimination should be permitted against former offenders regarding work,[31] education, voting or other civil and human rights. Legislative reform in this regard should be undertaken, and existing agencies engaged in such functions as job placement and training should coordinate their efforts with those of the prison system. Changes should not have to await judicial intervention.

[29] District Attorney Cahn would set out guidelines to avoid press "fishing expeditions" not directed toward specific complaints.

[30] A small minority—two—of the Conferees were not ready to write off the value of prison rehabilitation programs. One of them believed the acceptance of such programs by prisoners should be mandatory. The other felt that the fault was with the imperfections in "previous rehabilitation programs."

[31] Except on the basis of explicit and narrowly-defined standards directly related to the circumstances of convictions for past offenses. (This qualification stressed by Messrs. Macdonald and Cahn.)

XX

To focus, as we have done in this Conference, on that portion of the criminal justice system which begins with judicial sentencing and terminates with restoration of civil and political rights is not to imply that other areas of our criminal justice system are not also in need of reform. Our entire criminal law should be reviewed periodically and systematically so as to keep it abreast of the contemporary needs of a free society.

Parole

The third part of the corrections component of the justice system is that phase in the process that follows imprisonment in the state and federal prison systems. There are county jail paroles, which are granted along similar lines with the same objectives, but parole generally involves the men and women who have already spent some time in prison and who are provisionally released for the last part of their prison sentences. During the time of his supervised freedom, the inmate-turned-parolee is still constructively in custody. Although the parolee has most of his constitutionally guaranteed rights throughout the term of his parole, he must perform according to certain standards and he is expected to subscribe to whatever treatment programs are made available to him.

Who is qualified for parole, and at what point in time he may apply for consideration is generally the responsibility of the parole board, a body of individuals who have been selected from throughout the state and who have been appointed by the governor to serve for a specified period of time. Criteria for their selection are as varied as the people who make the appointments to the board. The members are as representative of the communities as are the grand juries throughout the nation. Among the many other qualifications of the board's members is their willingness to serve and their available time to devote to the task. The board meets at regular intervals and reviews applications for parole. The amount of time demanded of the board's members depends on term-fixing policies, such as the indeterminate sentence when the inmate's term has no exact time when it must come to an end, except for those limitations imposed by the statutory maximum. To what extent the board actually gets involved in the process also dictates the amount of time necessary to carry out their duties. With the background information provided by the professional staff, and recommendations as to the suitability of the applicants for parole, the board makes the actual determinations whether or not to grant parole.

Factors in Determining Whether to Grant Parole

When the parole board reviews the individual cases of the applicants for parole, there are several factors they must take into consideration. Some of the factors are external, which involve the community's attitude and the response of the policeman, prosecutor, judge, and the victims of the crimes. Other factors are social, which involve the individual's ability to cope with the world around him. Still other factors are internal, and they involve the INDIVIDUAL's prognosis for success once he is released. Considering many of the factors in a single listing, they include the following:

a.   The nature of the offense for which the inmate was convicted.

b.   The public sentiment in general, and their particular reaction to the individual being considered for parole.

c.   Recommendations of the prosecuting attorney, the judge who issued the sentence, and the law enforcement officers who made the arrest.

d.   The environmental factors leading to the individual's criminal involvement.

e.   The inmate's personal history, and that of his family.

f.   The individual's potential for continuing his education once released.

g.   The employability of the inmate in some salable skill.

h.   Plans and preparations for living and working arrangements on the outside.

i.   Somewhere for the inmate to go where he will get the reinforcement or treatment he needs, such as a halfway house or other community resources that may be available to him.

j.   The present attitude of the inmate towards himself and his behavior modification in relationship to the time when he was admitted to the institution.

k.   The inmate's present state of mind, conduct, and adjustment ·as reported by the staff.

l.   A counselor's evaluation of the candidate's likelihood to succeed on parole.

m.   The individual's conduct during the interview, and his ability to convince the board that he is ready to go out on parole.

n.   The decisions of the board whether or not to grant parole.

The board may sit as a total unit, or may break up into smaller groups for the purpose of interviewing candidates for parole, and they pass upon the applications. An advantage of parole, if it could be considered as an advantage, is that the inmate's reintegration into society is accomplished under the guidance and supervision of a parole officer, who is a specialist in behavior modification and who can initiate revocation proceedings if the parolee is not conforming to the conditions of his release. The individual who serves out his full sentence, or who is granted a discharge without parole, has no such supervision. Institutions have various effects upon the individuals, and a supervised transition period may be the far better course of action than a sudden implantation into what has become an alien world.

Professor Charles Newman's study group at Pennsylvania State University breaks down the task of the parole officer into three major categories: (1) surveillance, (2) service, and (3) counseling.[32]

Surveillance, as applied in parole, involves actual observation of the parolee under a variety of situations, often without his knowledge. The purpose of surveillance is to determine if the client is performing as he should even out of the presence of his probation officer. Surreptitious surveillance may be conducted to determine that the parolee is no longer in need of close supervision if he demonstrates sufficient internal controls. The process of surveillance may also determine that the parolee is associating with people who are negatively influencing him, and he may be found incapable of adjusting in conformance with the laws and the restrictions of his parole.

Services the parole officer provides include giving assistance in locating a new job or place to live, purchasing an automobile for transportation to work, channeling the parolee into community resource agencies that can help him in his reintegration into the community, and generally showing the parolee the way to solve his own problems. Supervision may be considered as a service, as it is through the parole officer that the parolee is going to demonstrate to the board that he is successfully accomplishing the objectives of his conditional release on parole.

Counseling is accomplished by the agency in a variety of ways, but most often involves the individual and his parole officer in one-to-one counseling situations. Other types of counseling may be attempted for parolee groups in an out-patient environment in which they hold sessions to address a host of problems. The function of the parole officer is to act as a change-agent, one who implements the modification of behavior and causes the parolee to redirect his own goals and values so that he will succeed on parole as an effective and self-respecting member of civilized society.

Since 1934, all of the states in the country have adopted an Interstate Probation and Parole pact, which provides for the movement of both probationers and parolees to another state to relocate families or to

---

[32] Center for Law Enforcement and Corrections, *Probation, Parole, and Pardons: A Basic Course*, p. 46.

accept employment, or for some other legitimate reason. As a condition of this pact, the individual makes the application to make the move and then there is a transfer to a new probation or parole agency in the receiving state. The training module of the Center for Law Enforcement and Corrections, *Probation, Parole, and Pardon: A Basic Course* explains the concept:

1.   Any state may permit a parolee or probationer to go to another state if the person is a resident or has his family residing within the receiving state and can obtain employment there or if the receiving state consents to such person being sent there even though the residence qualification cannot be met.

2.   The receiving state agrees to handle the task of treatment.

3.   The state whose jurisdiction he left may apprehend and return him with no formalities other than establishing the authority and proving the identity of the person to be arrested.[33]

Federal parole is managed by the United States Board of Parole, which considers all applications for parole by prisoners of federal institutions, decides whether parole should be granted, and maintains control over the parolees once they are released. The Federal board of parole issues release certificates for the parolees and may issue warrants for those who do not succeed on parole by living up to the terms of the conditions of their release.[34]

Parole Concepts.   The parole officer, with objectives and goals that are similar to those of the probation officer, consisting principally of behavior modification, performs as a caseworker in the field. He performs the three basic functions of surveillance, providing services, and counseling. As stated in the Training Module of Pennsylvania State University on probation, parole, and pardons,[35] the parole officer guides his client through the reintegration into the community. The officer knows the client and the community, and provides him with a positive relationship and pracitcal support in dealing with his problems. He manipulates the environment (within reason) to aid in the readjusment. In as many ways as possible, the parole officer works with his client and the client's family in adjusting and strengthening his family and social life, and he calls upon various community agencies for problem-solving referrals. The services he seeks out and makes available for his client include educa-

[33] Center for Law Enforcement and Corrections, *Probation, Parole, and Pardons: A Basic Course*, p. 79.

[34] Kleindienst, *Attorney General's First Annual Report*, p. 261.

[35] Center for Law Enforcement and Corrections, *Probation, Parole, and Pardons: A Basic Course*, pp. 51–52.

tional and occupational counseling and assistance, leisure-time resources, family diagnostic services, financial and legal assistance, physical and mental health services, and home-finding. In general, the parole officer serves as a model for the client and shows him the way to experience successes, however slight they may be.

Herman Piven and Abraham Alcabes describe the "social worker" concept of the relationship of the probation-parole officer to his clients:

> The relationship of the social worker to the probationers and parolees on his caseload is a professional one. This means, first of all, that the offender is a "client" and that the focus of the relationship is on his needs, his concerns, and his situation. Secondly, the professional focus is limited to consideration of those factors which bear on the offender's problems and goals and about which the probation/parole officer can exercise his technical skills. Thirdly, the quality of the probation/parole officer's relationship to the offender must be one which accepts the offender as a worthy person and is devoid of the officer's personal judgment.[36]

In other words, say Piven and Alcabes, the "social worker" probation/parole officer's relationship with his client is guided by the following norms: (1) He provides a service; (2) there is a focus on problems that the officer has the skills to attack; and (3) there is an emotional neutrality on the part of the probation/parole officer.[37]

Two other caseworker approaches are discussed by the same authors, Piven and Alcabes, who have done extensive research in corrections. They are the "punitive" and the "protective" officers, whose methods of operation are described as follows:

> The punitive officer's supervision methods reflect his conception of offenders as malingerers and his goal of compelling conformity with ideal standards. The punitive officer's ongoing task is to define for the offender the full range of his social responsibilities.[38]
>
> . . . The punitive officer relies upon negative sanctions to obtain conformity. He uses lectures, reprimands, and threats as devices to make the offender aware that the price of non-conformity is too high. (He uses threat of revocation, increased restrictions, and "shock-treatment" short-term jailing to emphasize his points.)[39]

---

[36] Herman Piven and Abraham Alcabes, A Study of Practice Theory in Probation/Parole (Washington, D.C.: U. S. Department of Health, Education, and Welfare, 1971), p. 39.

[37] Piven and Alcabes, A Study of Practice Theory in Probation/Parole, p. 39.

[38] Piven and Alcabes, A Study of Practice Theory in Probation/Parole, p. 47.

[39] Piven and Alcabes, A Study of Practice Theory in Probation/Parole, p. 49.

. . . The protective agent does not adhere to a systematic theory of human behavior that identifies certain facts as relevant and others as irrelevant in controlling and rehabilitating an offender. Instead, attempting to "get to know" the offenders, he probes and proceeds or withdraws depending upon reactions. Unlike the punitive officer who restricts interviews with offenders to specific issues of conformity with social responsibilities, the protective agent has no analogous focus that prevents agent-offender interaction from developing more or less spontaneously.[40]

. . . In serving offenders, the protective agent sees his job as getting the offender to like him so that the probationer/parolee will accept his advice, and internalize his values. In protecting the community against offenders, his activities are similar to those of the punitive officer. In attempts to "rehabilitate" offenders the agent relies heavily on direct techniques; he finds a job *for* a man, he goes with him to apply for financial assistance, he loans him money out of his own pocket. Direct services are supposed to have two results. First, they value "problems" for the offender which block the offender's attempt to redirect his goals and to strengthen his internal controls. Second, they assist the agent's efforts to make the offender like him.[41]

Concerning the counselor role of the probation/parole officer, the objectives of the officer are to guide and direct the client to eventually develop a strong self-image and self-reliance. If the officer were to continue to make his decisions for him, there would be a reinforcement of the supportive role of the officer. To prolong the role of doing the individual's thinking and performing for him would prolong the term of parole or probation. The goals of probation and parole are to bring about behavior changes that are long-lasting and positive in harmony with social and legal requirements of crime-free behavior. Foremost among the obligations of the change-agent, then, is the task of stimulating the individual to think for himself. To illustrate that task, Piven and Alcabes have this to say:

Within the limits of the law, the right to ultimate choice of action resides with the client. When an offender tells the probation/parole officer that he wishes to marry, buy an automobile, change his place of employment, etc., the officer's obligation is to discuss the plan with the client by examining its probable consequences and alternatives, and with maximum considerations of the offender's views, feelings, capabilities, and goals.

When the offender has already made a choice and taken action, the officer may find it wise to review with him the meaning of the client's decision

[40] Piven and Alcabes, *A Study of Practice Theory in Probation/Parole*, p. 50.
[41] Piven and Alcabes, *A Study of Practice Theory in Probation/Parole*, p. 51.

and help identify options that are still available. Whether a choice is being contemplated or has been made, the officer has an additional obligation: to allow and encourage the client to make the final decision.[42]

Summary

The role of corrections, to paraphrase the word, is to correct certain modes of conduct and behavior in literally millions of individuals over a period of years. This, the third component of the criminal justice system, addresses the problem of criminal and asocial behavior and attempts to show the individuals involved how to modify their own behavior so that the goals of crime-free behavior on their behalf may be reached. In this chapter we have covered the entire spectrum of correctional programs and different parts of the entire corrections component. There is no doubt that we have missed more than we have covered, but for the purpose of this text, it has been our intention to briefly explain each of the many correctional philosophies, agencies, and the roles that the individuals play in this important part of the administration of justice process.

Probation and parole, while perhaps addressing individuals with different degrees of sophistication in the ways of crime, are quite similar in their goals and objectives and in their methods of operation. The officers who fill these roles operate as behavior modification specialists, or change-agents. Through their own strong self-image they are responsible for providing a model for their clients, and for encouraging and assisting those clients to positively cultivate their own self-images and to undergo positive behavior modifications that redirect them back into the mainstream of social conformity. The approach of the caseworker is community-based, as are many of the other community-based treatment programs, including halfway houses, group counseling, and immersion in community-oriented social programs.

The institutions provide a multipurpose need of society. They serve to isolate certain individuals from the society they offended and committed crimes against, to hold them in some place where they may pay their "debt to society" or receive their punishment for their crimes. The penal institutions also protect society from those individuals who are not safe to society. Besides being responsible for providing the isolation and warehouse facilities, the institutions must also bring about some positive behavior changes, educational and occupational preparation, and some preparation for socialization in the society with which the criminal

[42] Piven and Alcabes, *A Study of Practice Theory in Probation/Parole*, p. 56.

could not cope prior to his incarceration. There is a need for attitudinal and behavior changes on the part of individuals so that they may be reintegrated back into the society from which they originated.

Exercises and Study Questions

1. What is the basic difference between probation and parole? Similarities?

2. What is a community-based corrections program (define)? Give an example.

3. Describe how a presentence investigation is carried out, and explain its intended purpose.

4. List the different alternative types of sentences available to the court.

5. If you were the judge, what would be the restrictions you would impose on a probationer who had committed the crime of auto theft. Armed robbery?

6. How many different types of institutions are operated for juvenile delinquents?

7. What is the function of "juvenile intake"?

8. What is the average daily population of correctional institutions in the United States?

9. What efforts at rehabilitation are being made at the jail in your jurisdiction?

10. What is an indeterminate sentence, and how is it administered?

11. List and discuss the changes you would recommend to improve our present prison system.

12. Recommended semester project: Visit your local probation or parole agency and interview at least three different officers with similar responsibilities. Based on the information you have about the different philosophies of probation/parole officers, ask them enough questions to determine which type of officers they represent (social, punitive, protective) and write an opinion paper on the strong points on each of the three approaches.

Suggested for Additional Study

ADAMS, THOMAS F., Ed., *Criminal Justice Readings*. Pacific Palisades, Calif.: Goodyear Publishing Co., Inc., 1972, Section 6.

ALEXANDER, MYRL E., *Jail Administration*. Springfield, Ill.: Charles C Thomas, Inc., 1957.

AMERICAN CORRECTIONAL ASSOCIATION, *Correction Officers Training Guide*. Washington, D.C.: American Correctional Association 1969.

————, *Manual of Correctional Standards*. Washington, D.C.: American Correctional Association, 1966.

CENTER FOR LAW ENFORCEMENT AND CORRECTIONS, *Probation, Parole, and Pardons: A Basic Course*, Training Module 6913. University Park, Pa.: Pennsylvania State University, 1969.

————, *Probation and Parole*, Training Module 6907. University Park, Pa.: Pennsylvania State University, 1969.

DINITZ, SIMON and WALTER C. RECKLESS, Eds., *Critical Issues in the Study of Crime*. New York: Little, Brown, and Co., Inc., 1968.

GIBBONS, DON C., *Changing the Lawbreaker*. Englewood Cliffs, N.J.: Prentice-Hall, Inc., 1965.

KAY, BARBARA A. and CLYDE B. VEDDER, *Probation and Parole*, 2d Ptg. Springfield, Ill.: Charles C Thomas, Inc., 1971.

NEWMAN, CHARLES L. *Personnel Practices in Adult Parole Systems*. Springfield, Ill.: Charles C Thomas, Inc., 1971.

————, *Sourcebook on Probation, Parole, and Pardons*, 3rd Ed. Springfield, Ill.: Charles C Thomas, Inc., 1970.

8

Selection, Education, and Training

Introduction

So far the text has been directed toward establishment of a broad base of information concerning the criminal justice system: what it is, how it operates, and something about the philosophies of the people who function as professionals and paraprofessionals within the system. In this chapter, we shall address three critical aspects of the effective management of the various components of the criminal system: (1) selection of the people who are best qualified for the literally hundreds of different classifications of positions filled by hundreds of thousands of individuals, (2) pre- and in-service education as presented in the college setting, and (3) training in the proficencies necessary to perform correctly. There is such variation throughout the United States in these matters that this chapter will not attempt to address all of the differences. Rather, we shall keep the topics as general as possible, but much of this chapter will reflect my knowledge and experience on the subjects, which has a California orientation. I might hasten to add, however, that I am not attempting to profess that California methods or programs should be used as models to be emulated by anyone. It is my hope that the professor and student alike will use this chapter as a base from which to project local techniques and programs and to make objective comparisons for the purpose of increasing awareness of the differences as well as the similarities. Just the fact that there are so many differences throughout the United States is one factor that underlines the reality that the professions in the system are still developing and emerging.

The Selection Process

The Position Announcement. Because most of the many positions in the justice system are government occupations, they are covered by civil service regulations. The position announcement is usually widely disseminated, and it should reflect the following information: position description, general duties and responsibilities, any special talents or proficiencies that are required (type sixty words a minute, fly fixed wing aircraft, operate a motor vehicle, special language requirements) and special qualifications desired (work with the public under trying circumstances, knowledge of competitive sports rules, able to relate well with people of various ethnic cultures) and any unusual requirements, such as night work.

The civil service announcement will list educational minimums, experience requirements, physical requirements (including height, weight, color perception, no disabilities) when specifically related to the job demands, and any other local considerations that may have been mandated, such as local residence or other similar matters. The anouncement should also list a brief but concise description of the position and expectations of the individual who fills it. It is wise to read that description carefully and to inquire of the employing agency any additional information about the position. The candidate should be confident that he is qualified for the position and that he knows precisely what the position is.

The Application Form. The employing agency may actually use two separate forms: an application, and a personal history statement. The application is usually brief, asking for a sketch of the individual's physical and personal characteristics, work history, and educational background, accompanied by a listing of references and other data that will aid the personnel agency in performing a cursory background pre-employment check. The second form goes into much more detail, and it may include a request for certain data and supporting documents beyond the scope of the application form. For example, if the employer is aggressively seeking candidates in compliance with any equal opportunity and/or affirmative action requirements, it will be necessary for the employing agency to determine the racial or ethnic origin of the candidate. The surname, as you know, does not always accurately reflect one's heritage as it may have been changed by marriage or adoption, or by court action.

The applicant should be careful to read every question and to address the question by responding accurately. It is easy to volunteer information that is not requested or to answer a question in such a manner that the explanation may raise doubts as to an individual's qualifications. For example: the question "Have you ever been convicted for any crime other than a minor traffic violation?" may induce a response of "No, but I was picked up for questioning once in a bunch of burglaries but the police couldn't prove anything." Actually what might have happened is that the individual had no involvement in such a crime but was interviewed because he had been observed in the area at about the time the crimes were committed. The response as written could stimulate all sorts of interpretations. Of course, an investigation will be conducted— or should be, but what would you think if you read that response and were to make a value judgment as to whether you would employ the applicant for a position of public trust?

From my own experience in the business of conducting background investigations as well as performing certain personnel responsibilities for a criminal justice agency, I have found that many applicants somehow have the feeling that a background check does not extend beyond state lines or back very far into an individual's past. Be assured that those feelings are not based on fact. The person conducting the background investigation develops a biography on the candidate, which spans most of the entire lifetime and has no geographical boundaries.

The Written Examinations. Used as a device to screen the number of candidates down to a number that the personnel agency can work with, as well as a determinant of the intellectual capacity and learning capability of the candidate, the written examination usually consists of a battery of tests. Most examinations are objective type, with multiple choice responses for standardization of scoring and rank-ordering the candidates. Usually included is some form of general intelligence test, an adaptability test, and other examinations to test for the specific items listed on the position description. If the job announcement states that a basic knowledge of legal procedure is necessary, the applicant may rest assured that some of the test battery will address itself to a determination of the candidate's knowledge of legal procedure.

Special talents, such as unique memory capabilities, will also most likely be tested. Personality and interest inventories may also be included in the battery because of the agency's desire to seek candidates who are not only qualified to perform the required tasks, but who are likely to stay on the job and to grow within the profession because of strong interests as well as knowledge and adaptability. In short, the test battery should test for those qualities and proficiencies stated on the position announcement.

The Oral Interview. The candidates who pass the written portion of the series of screening devices are next scheduled for oral interviews. Although they are expected to be experts in the profession for which the screening is being conducted, the interviewers may or may not be professional interviewers. In many instances, these individuals have never met each other before this day of the interviews. Their own personal philosophies may differ, and there may be a general concept of what type of person they are looking for to fill the position, but each interviewer may base his decisions upon his own background and experiences. The point of this information is that the oral interview is unpredictable and quite subjective, except in cases when the board members have worked as a team before and they have structured the interviews with a consensus of their value systems operating to make an objective evaluation of each candidate and to rank-order the candidates according to some system.

The oral interview is a type of role-casting, not unlike the procedure used to select actors to play a role in a play. The written examination has been used to determine the candidate's knowledge and adaptability. The oral interview is the time when the members of the board may look for a self-image (particularly if they are confident that their own attributes are the key to successful performance on the job), and to make some value judgement as to whether the candidate would be believeable in the role for which he applied. For example, the police candidate should "look the role," his mannerisms and speech should have certain characteristics that will immediately impress the public that he has the authority and the ability to perform the job of policeman, and his responses to the interviewer's questions must indicate that his personal philosophy is in harmony with the philosophical viewpoints of the members of the interview board.

The oral interview usually lasts from thirty to forty-five minutes, but the first one or two of those minutes may be the most critical. From that point on the members of the board may ask questions and seek responses that confirm their initial impressions about the candidate. According to scientific standards, this may not be a valid method of testing. The point is that—valid or not—the method is relied upon quite heavily and the candidate should be prepared to perform as well as possible, knowing that he is being judged as a whole person from a subjective standpoint. The public does it every day in every single contact the officer makes. Initial impressions are important indeed!

Keeping in mind the subjective nature of the oral interview, the candidate should bear in mind that there are essentially two basic features of the test: (1) the initial impression the interviewee makes upon the interviewer, and (2) the candidate's ability to handle himself well in oral exchange with three or four expert interviewers. There are basically three types of interviews: unstructured, nondirected, and structured. The unstructured interview is usually under the control of the interviewers, but there has been no advance planning and it varies from interview to interview. The nondirected interview is actually dominated and controlled by the candidate, who is allowed to take the conversation wherever he wishes for it to go. The structured interview is directed and controlled by the interviewers as a team. They ask a series of specific questions of all of the candidates and evaluate the responses and the conduct of the candidates according to some sort of agreed-upon criteria. By using this method, it is possible to compare the candidates and to rank-order them according to the criteria established by the interview board in advance.

Although they do not necessarily appear in the following order, questions in an oral interview for almost any position in any profession, including the many agencies of the justice system, will probably include the following:

What do you know about this specific position for which you are applying?

Have you inquired about this agency? and what do you know about it?

Why do you want this particular position? Why this occupation as a choice?

Do you believe that you are qualified for this position? Why?

What are your strongest assets in relation to this position?

What are your weaknesses? or how might you not perform well in one or more areas of the position?

What have you done to prepare for this position? What have you done, or will you do to compensate for those weaknesses?

What characteristics are most essential to this position?

How do you believe you compare with those requirements?

What is your ultimate goal in life—professionally or otherwise?

What would you change about this position if you had the authority to implement change?

How do you perceive yourself in the role for which you are applying in relationship to the roles of the other agencies in the system?

There are various hypothetical situations that may be contrived by the interview board to test for the individual's ability to make value judgement decisions. It would be wise for the candidate to project himself into the position for which he is applying, then to spend some time listing some of the problems or other situations that may arise. Once the list is compiled, the next step would be to contrive as many exigencies as possible and anticipate the alternative plans of action that may solve the problem. The benefit of such an exercise might be that the candidate had rehearsed at least one of the hypothetical problems presented by the interview board. With such preparation, the "extemporaneous" response of the candidate would certainly put him in good stead with the board.

Physical Agility Qualifications. Certain occupations in the justice system require a certain type of physical specimen as well as one who can perform well in psychological and oral interviews. The juvenile hall group supervisor or police officer fall within this category. Brute strength is not as necessary as agility and endurance. The deliberate antagonist or the individual who physically resists arrest or some other form of custody, such as an attempt to escape, is occasionally encountered. They must be handled quickly and effectively, because any prolongation of the altercation will most certainly lead to greater injury to all participants. An individual who is in excellent physical condition and who is then trained by his agency to perform well in weaponless combat situations can usually handle most situations well, provided the odds against him are not too great. The candidate's physical condition may be tested simply by a medical exam, or by both a medical exam and an agility performance test.

The agility test usually starts off with a few basic tests to determine muscular development and coordination, which include a rope climb, sit-ups, and push-ups. It is then followed—or preceded—by an obstacle course with a realistic maximum time limit.

Every part of the course has a realistic counterpart in actual street police duties. Picture the following examples taken from actual experiences: (1) The petty thief captured in the act outside the stadium during a sporting event who ran when an attempt was made to handcuff him. He disappeared among the long row of parked automobiles. (2) The escaping armed robber who alighted from his wrecked car, vaulted a cinder-block wall, jumped on another, ran along the fence, then jumped off into another yard before finally being captured. (3) The car thief who jumped out of the car, dropped down into a drainage ditch, crawled through a culvert underneath the freeway, and escaped across an open field. (4) The frightened juvenile who—for fear his parents would punish him for being out after curfew—sprouted wings and "flew" as though his feet were not touching the ground. In all of these situations, what must the police officer do? Subdue them? Shoot them? Fire warning shots into the air? No. In most cases, the officer is justified only to the extent that he may chase and capture them, using only what force is necessary. The problem is catching them. Success in passing an agility test serves to predict the candidate's agility to take part in chases such as those described.

Medical Examination

Whenever a new employee goes to work, the employer assumes legal responsibility for his physical well-being while actually on the job. He is obligated to provide safety training and safe devices. with which the employee must work. The nature of law enforcement and corrections work, particularly, involves certain hazards that cannot be avoided by safety equipment as in a shop. The gun-crazed madman bent upon killing everyone who gets in his way, the high-speed chase of the traffic violator, the parolee who knows that this violation will lead to his lifetime return to prison, and many other situations that involve emotional trauma take a heavy toll even from the healthy individual.

The man who has high blood pressure (hypertension) or ulcers prior to entering the service is a liability who will certainly worsen as a result of the emotional stresses attendant to even the routine aspects of the work. No matter how badly he may wish to be accepted for employment or how favorable he may look otherwise, an early medical retirement must be expected. Therefore, the decision must be in favor of the agency and he must be passed over.

Because every agency is autonomous in many respects, it has—or may have—different medical requirements. The following is an example of a typical list of medical standards for a policeman:

1. Height 5'8" or 5'9" or no maximum.
2. Height-weight ratios:

Height	Minimum	Maximum
5'8"	140	170
5'9"	145	175
5'10"	150	180
5'11"	155	185
6'0"	160	190
6'1"	165	195
6'2"	170	200
6'3"	175	205
6'4"	180	220
6'5"	185	230

3. Vision and eyes: 20/20 each eye, corrected. Color vision must be normal. Rejection for impaired depth perception, impaired eyelids that interfere with vision or do not protect eye from exposure, and other impairments, such as ulcers, corneal scars, or cataracts.

4. Hearing and ears: ability to hear a whispered voice at fifteen feet with each ear.

5. Nose, sinuses, and mouth: a variable minimum amount of teeth,

with some requirement as to appearance and ability to masticate properly. Rejection for speech impediment, deformity of mouth or lips, pyorrhea, acute or chronic sinustis, enlarged tonsils and adenoids, or nasal obstructions.

6. Skin: must be free from gross disfigurements or blemishes. A candidate may be disqualified for obscene tattoos.

7. Extremities: must be in excellent condition. Disqualification for recurring dislocations; loss of joints from certain fingers, particularly the thumb and index finger; and healed fractures of bones that inhibit or limit the strength or use of any limb. X-rays may be ordered.

8. Cardiovascular: pulse limits 50 to 90. Blood pressure not to exceed 140/90. Candidates rejected for history of heart disease or heart damage, past or present syphillis.

9. Respiratory: chest x-ray and skin test for tuberculosis recommended. Disqualification for any acute or chronic disease of the respiratory system.

10. Gastrointestinal: rejection for any acute or chronic disease of stomach, including existing or history of ulcers. Other disqualifying features: diseases of the intestines, liver, pancreas, spleen, and gallbladder, or hemorrhoids—other than minor—until repaired.

11. Genitourinary system free from acute or chronic disease.

12. Disqualified for disabling disease or demormity of the bone structure. Of particular interest to the medical examiner: the spinal structure, the feet, and any presence of arthritis.

13. Neurological and psychological: rejection for any acute or chronic organic disease or history of epilepsy, vertigo, or paralysis.

14. General: on completion of the medical examination and the accompanying chemical analysis that the doctor may order, he may pass the candidate as qualified for the position, or he may reject the candidate for any cause or defect that he believes would impair the health or inhibit the usefulness of the candidate if accepted.

The personal confrontation and emergency characteristics of the police officer's position have brought about the medical minimums set forth above. Although there are certain characteristics that are subjected to attack, such as the height, teeth, and eyesight requirements other than color perception, most of the qualifications are essential because of the task requirements. For other, nonuniformed and nonemergency, services the qualifications may be simply stated as "must be in excellent physical condition as determined by the county physician." Under those conditions, there is probably little that would disqualify other than general poor health.

Personality Evaluation. This phase of the selection process is usually conducted by a licensed psychiatrist, or a psychologist. Although limited to the selection of police officers and sheriff deputies, the practice could be extended to include many of the other positions in the system. It is imperative that the officer be free from psychological or emotional problems that would adversely affect his ability to function with objectivity and with a maximum effectiveness. There is no place among the police ranks for the homosexual, sadist, masochist, or the coward. Certain fears—or phobias—may be so great as to make it impossible for the police officer to function effectively. Some of those fears may be of high places, pain, being in a closed place, or fear of fear. The psychopath, sociopath, or person suffering from any other mental or neurological disorder should be screened out, and such a screening process cannot be accomplished exclusively by a pencil and paper test. Therefore, only an expert can handle this phase of the selection process.

The psychiatric exam usually consists of a battery of tests including the Minnesota Multiphasic Personality Inventory, the Rorschach Ink Blot Test, and another test of a freehand drawing that is later evaluated by the psychiatrist. The final test in the battery is usually a personal interview.

It is the responsibility of the psychiatrist to recommend the candidate as qualified or not qualified for the position. Even this method of psychological selection is not perfect because many latent tendencies are not identified, but it is considered an invaluable tool in the selection process because the *obvious* misfit is obvious only to the psychiatrist in many cases. An example of the value that the psychiatric test may have is the candidate who is passed as acceptable and later becomes disgruntled with the department's policies. In one Southern California city several "hate" letters were given to the psychiatrist who had originally examined all of the policemen then on the job. From his files, the doctor collected several samples of written material from previous tests and compared them with the writing style of the anonymous letters. He provided the chief of police with a list of possible suspects, which later was narrowed down to the true culprit. Although the latent personality trait involving anonymous letter writing did not reveal itself at the time the officer was admitted into the ranks, it did later and the end result was removal of an unfit policeman. There are many other examples, both positive and negative, but the one cited was clearly unique.

Fingerprints

Any time a person applies for a position with any governmental agency he is fingerprinted and sometimes photographed. Whenever a person is arrested for any offense he *may* be fingerprinted, but when a person is "booked" into jail for any offense, he is *usually* fingerprinted. Whenever a person is committed to any state or federal institution he is fingerprinted. Private corporations involved in sensitive productions involving government contracts fingerprint all applicants. Whenever fingerprints are taken by any of the foregoing agencies, they are classified by the individual agencies for their own files, then one set is mailed to the Federal Bureau of Investigation central clearing house and another set mailed to the respective state clearing houses. At each of the many clearing houses, each set of fingerprints is classified and a record of the prints' owner added to a cumulative file maintained on each individual. Because there are no two sets of fingerprints alike, the prints are a positive means of identification, and a single individual may have a fingerprint record under more than one name.

Whenever an agency submits a set of fingerprints to a clearing house such as the FBI, that agency sends back by return mail the cumulative list showing all the times that individual has been fingerprinted for any reason under any name. For example, a "rap sheet" (a chronology of the times and places a person has been fingerprinted) on a single individual may read as follows: At age fourteen, Jerome Ford was committed to a farm for delinquent boys in Virginia for a series of delinquent acts. At age seventeen, Jerry enlisted in the U.S. Navy at Bethesda, Maryland. At age twenty-three, our subject was arrested for auto theft in Chicago and used the name of Jerry F. Queenbury. At age twenty-seven, Mr. F. changed his name in a lawful court procedure in Seattle to Jerrold Fillmore Quick. Finally, our subject—true name Quick—applied for a job as a policeman in San Francisco under his true name. As far as we know from the information furnished in this account, the subject has been fingerprinted in Virginia, Maryland, Illinois, and California under three different names. Although his name has been changed, his fingerprints have not. When the San Francisco Police Department sends the candidate's fingerprints to the FBI and the California Bureau of Criminal Identification and Investigation, they will receive replies from both of those agencies. The "rap sheets" will show the dates, the reason for the taking of prints, plus the name given at the time, and the disposition—if provided by the contributing agency—of each particular incident, such as "released, no complaint filed."

In addition to what we already know, the information sheet from the FBI may also show Mr. Quick as an applicant for the position of policeman in San Diego and Eureka. He had either forgotten or deliberately failed to mention when making his application in San Francisco that he had applied at the other two agencies. A check with those agencies might possibly reveal that Quick actually did become a member of one of those departments and was dismissed two months later for the use of excessive force.

In the case of some juvenile arrests, individual agencies maintain fingerprint files but—because of the tender age of the children—do not submit them to state or federal agencies. In an actual case worked by the author, one young candidate's background checked perfectly except for a lapse of about three years during which time the candidate's mother was married to one of her several husbands in one of the Southern states. Although the FBI reported no fingerprint record on the candidate, a copy of his fingerprints was mailed to police departments in the two largest cities where the candidate had lived during that specific three-year time span. As a result of those inquiries, one of the two agencies reported that the candidate had been arrested under another name as one of the leaders of an auto theft ring that had operated in that state for several months until they were apprehended transporting one of the cars across the border. Had the check not been made, the candidate would—no doubt—have been appointed to the ranks of the police department.

Polygraph

Polygraph operators theorize that virtually everyone has at least one skeleton in his closet. Verified deceptive patterns are noted in replies to such questions as: Did you ever steal anything in your life? or Did you ever cheat on a test in school? or Did you ever tell a deliberate lie to hurt someone else? Doctor Kinsey's reports on the sexual behavior of the American male and female further bears this theory out with respect to our social mores. If this device—the polygraph—is utilized as a part of the selection process, a great deal of discretion and good judgment must be exercised. Indiscriminate use of polygraph files could be devastating. The examiner must be absolutely above reproach, and there must be no question as to his professional competence. His examination should pertain only to those character traits that directly relate to the applicant's suitability for the police service.

When preparing a set of questions for polygraph examination for preemployment screening, it is first necessary to determine exactly what type of person the chief administrator wishes to employ. Sexual promiscuity or immorality cannot be condoned in the police employee. There is absolutely no place in the organization for a burglar, a robber, or a thief. Many other traits must be identified and evaluated. The examiner must determine whether a single act of theft or certain acts of moral indiscretion at some time in the candidate's lifetime makes him a thief or sexual deviate. Individual departments utilize their polygraph examination phase of the selection process differently. A personal inquiry of

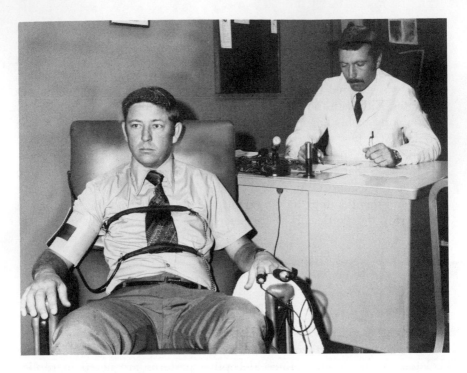

The polygraph is a valuable aid to the investigation.
Posed by Officers J. Birkes (left) and R. Lindley.
Courtesy Police Department, Santa Ana.

each department's personnel division would be necessary in order to ascertain their specific utilization of the polygraph.

The Background Investigation

The initial application submitted by the candidate is usually relatively brief compared with the personal history statement required by the department personnel unit. The form is actually an autobiography in question and answer form, and it is used as the basis for the background investigation. The investigation is primarily conducted for the purpose of screening out the undesirable applicants who have derogatory personal histories. Secondarily, the investigation provides the administrator with a complete biography of each employee. Typical questions asked in the personal history statement form will be listed in the following paragraphs, along with a discussion of the background investigation and how they are related. The order of the investigation may not necessarily coincide with the order of the form, but they will be discussed in that order in this chapter.

1.   List all other names you have used or been known by, including nicknames, maiden name, adopted name, other. State during what period(s) of time each other name was used. School attendance and work records often reflect a variety of names for many reasons. Married women have all used at least two names: maiden and married.

2.   Description of your automobile(s). As a matter of routine, automobile license numbers may be checked against hit-run wants. Another purpose for this question is that an individual's automobile sometimes reflects his personality, or social needs. Some neighbors who are good sources of information about the candidate only know their neighbors by the description of the car they drive.

3.   Education record. This category includes high school, college, vocational, and trade schools. Personal visits to these institutions are made by the investigators, if possible, or mail inquiries are made to determine scholastic records in addition to sociability, participation in sports and other school events, and citizenship records. Scholastic grades are naturally of interest to the background investigator. When compared with the intelligence quotient of an individual, it is often possible to determine something about the drive and perseverance he may or may not possess. An individual with an extremely high IQ who made Cs and Ds may prove less desirable as a potential employee than the average IQ with a scholastic record of As and Bs attained by the student who diligently applied himself and made the best of what he had in the way of natural ability.

4.   Degrees, credentials, certificates you hold. Pilot's license, radio licenses, teaching credentials, special certificates, and degrees reflect both the training and capabilities of the individual.

5.   Disciplinary action while in school, including scholastic probation. This information aids in determining behavior patterns.

6.   Employment record, including all places of employment during the candidate's lifetime, and periods of unemployment. Name and address of employer, type of business, dates of employment, high salary, position and duties, name of immediate supervisor, and reason for leaving. The police agency is another potential employer and naturally wants to know something of the candidate's work history. When possible, the

investigator makes a personal contact with all previous employers (out-of-town employers are questioned by mail) for the purpose of talking with fellow workers and supervisors and looking through the candidate's work reords. Rating while on the job, sickness histories, and all other relevant data are collected and evaluated.

7. Military record, if any, including duty assignments, rates or ranks held, any disciplinary action, and type of discharge as well as the actual dates of service is requested—another employer, of course.

8. List relatives, their names, places of residence, occupations, and additional information that will sufficiently identify them. Crimino-genic personalities in a candidate's family may have sufficient influence over him that he might possibly be placed in an untenable position of having to yield to social pressures to take preferential actions for family harmony, such as "clearing" criminal records by removing or altering records from the files or possibly exerting official influence to gain special favors. Community reputation of the entire police agency also depends upon the individual reputations of all of its employees.

9. References. Some agencies require only four or five references. This is of no value to the investigator because the candidate invariably lists the family physician, a clergyman, an attorney, possibly a so-called influential citizen, and perhaps a casual acquaintance who is a deputy district attorney or chief of police. These people are likely to condemn or negatively criticize the candidate because they know nothing about his personal life; most are no more than slightly acquainted. Some agencies require ten to fifteen references who have knowledge of the candidate's reputation, who know him socially, and who have knowledge of his professional or occupational capabilities. Armed with this list of people who have personal knowledge of the candidate's personal and occupational characteristics, the investigator attempts to find out as much as he can about exactly what the candidate is "made of." He also inquires as to the identity of other people who may know him. Out-of-town reference letters are usually mailed to the references and a few confidential questions asked in an effort to glean from as many sources as possible the maximum amount of information that can be amassed.

10. List all surgery or serious illnesses during the candidate's lifetime. Nature of illnesses and/or purpose for any surgery and the names of hospitals and doctors are required. These items are checked out very carefully because the employer assumes liability for the candidate once appointed. Some permanent disabilities are discovered that otherwise may have been overlooked by the medical examiner or omitted from the original application by the candidate. Along with this question there

will usually be others pertaining to sick leave history and any history of the candidate's having been a recipient of any disability allowance for sickness or injury.

11. List additional sources of income, such as earnings by spouse. At first glance, an individual's expenditures may appear to be in excess of his income, and the investigator may draw the conclusion that the subject is on the verge of having his wages attached or going into bankruptcy. Good credit is mandatory for the police employee, and the candidate must have the self-control to live within his means. The total income presents a true picture of the candidate's fiscal status.

12. List outstanding debts and credit references. Other questions along the same line may call for a statement regarding whether or not the candidate has ever been refused credit and any other data relevant to the candidate's credit record.

13. List all places of residence during the candidate's lifetime. Out-of-town places of residence are checked out by the local police having that particular jurisdiction if the agency's investigator cannot drive the distance and conduct his own investigation. All cities and counties in which the candidate lived are either visited in person by the investigator, or a letter of request for investigative assistance is sent to those that are too far distant. Police, court, and school files are searched for any record of the candidate; the local credit bureaus' records are checked, and personal contacts are made with former employers, teachers, neighbors, friends, and anyone else who may have known the candidate. Personality and character traits of the candidate are the object of this phase of the investigation. Many police agencies have established such a favorable working relationship that a request sent by the Santa Ana, California, Police Department Personnel Division to another police department even as far away as New York City or Houston results in the initiation by that agency of an investigation that yields as comprehensive a report as is required.

14. Marital status, name of spouse and children, if any, and vital statistics on all aspects of the marital and familial situation of the candidate, including former marriages are requested.

15. List all traffic citations and/or traffic arrests (not including parking tickets), *including* those received while under the age of eighteen. The question calls for the date and place, charge or violation, and the disposition (fine, forfeited bail, jail, or the like). The driving record of a potential policeman is most essential because virtually all police agencies require their officers to possess a valid driver's license and their

normal duties include driving department vehicles under both routine and emergency conditions. A poor driving record will disqualify the candidate who has proved to be an insurance liability, accident-prone, or citation-prone. Police officers who violate the traffic laws are subject to the same treatment—citation or arrest—given the nonpolice violators.

16. Other than traffic (covered in 15 above), have you ever in your lifetime been arrested, held by the police for investigation or questioning, or otherwise been under investigation by the police? Complete details are required, including the nature of the incident, time, place, and disposition. The background investigator secures copies of all reports, if available, and he looks into the nature of the charge, including recontacting victims, and interviews the original investigating or arresting officer. In many cases, deliberate omission of information that should be included in response to this question is sometimes a serious matter. An example of deliberate omissions or falsification of the personal history statement is the case of the twenty-five-year-old candidate who listed that he had never been questioned by the police under any circumstances. His background investigation revealed that he had been caught stealing some items from an automobile at the age of fourteen, was severely reprimanded by the police officer, and was released to his parents. Other than the one incident when he was arrested and released as a child, the candidate's background was excellent. When the personnel investigator later questioned the candidate about the incident, the candidate denied anything of that nature ever taking place. He was given an opportunity to refresh his memory and make any changes on the form that he wished to make before being considered for the position. He chose to continue his denial of the act, even when the investigator suggested that it had occurred when he was about fourteen and in a specifically named city when he lived at a certain address in that city. The candidate continued to adamantly maintain that he had never been contacted by the police for any reason, and finally conceded with a great deal of reluctance that such an incident had taken place when he was confronted with a copy of the arrest report. He was disqualified—not for the act of theft at age fourteen, but for *falsifying his personal history statement.*

17. If you have applied for employment with any other police agency, list the date of application, name, and location of the agency, and the status of the application (accepted, not accepted, pending, or the like). The purpose for this question is to aid in the investigation and evaluation of the subject. Another agency may already have conducted a thorough background investigation and some duplication will be avoided, and the opinions of other qualified police practitioners will help in what amounts to a reevaluation of the candidate for a similar position.

The final part of the statement is an agreement by the candidate that he understands the terms of the probationary appointment procedure, that he also understands a thorough background investigation will be conducted, and that he will be disqualified for any deliberate falsification or omissions.

Proof of Good Character

Proof of good character is defined in New York Police Department's notice of examination as follows:

> Proof of good character will be an absolute prerequisite to appointment. The following are among the factors which would ordinarily be cause for disqualification: (a) conviction of a misdemeanor or an offense, the nature of which indicates lack of good moral character or disposition toward violence or disorder; (b) repeated conviction of an offense, where such convictions indicate a disrespect for the law; (c) repeated discharge from employment where such discharge indicates poor performance or inability to adjust to discipline; (d) addiction to narcotics or excessive use of alcoholic beverages; (e) discharge from the Armed Forces other than the standard honorable discharge. In accordance with the provisions of the administrative code, persons convicted of a felony are not eligible for positions in the uniformed forces of the police department. In addition, the rules of the city civil service commission provide that no person convicted of petty larceny, or who has been dishonorably discharged by the Armed Forces shall be examined, certified, or appointed as a patrolman.[1]

Selection Interview

Following the background investigation, the next step in the selection process is to schedule the candidate for a selection interview. The interview is usually conducted by at least one staff officer charged with the responsibility for selecting only the best-qualified candidates. In all but the largest departments it is most desirable for the chief administrator

---

[1] George P. McManus, Project Director, *Police Training and Performance Study,* New York Police Department, Project 70–4 (Washington, D.C.: Government Printing Office, 1970), p. 31.

to take an active part in the selection interviews. In any event, the final decision and responsibility is his. The successful candidates are appointed and launched on their careers.

Probation

Public agencies that provide their employees with the protection and many other benefits of a civil service system have a six-months to one-year probationary period that precedes attainment of permanent status, or tenure. The purpose of the probationary period is to give the employee a breaking-in period during which he determines whether he and the job are suited for each other and to serve the employing agency as the final—and most important—part of the selection process. During the probation, the employee may be terminated by the agency for unsuitability with no right to appeal his dismissal. The decision of the department head in the case of any probationary termination is final.

Education for the Justice System

Development of a universal body of knowledge is one of the prime requisites of a profession. Throughout the justice system there have been many professions, particularly the legal profession, and there have been professional individuals scattered throughout in virtually all of the components of the system. As for universality of knowledge about any part of the system, the development of such knowledge has been somewhat piecemeal and far from universal. During the past few years, particularly since the advent of federal financing of program development and of loans and grants to the students who specialize in law enforcement, corrections, or other components of the justice system through the Law Enforcement Assistance Administration, we have witnessed the phenomenal growth of administration of justice educational programs. From just a dozen or so in the 1950s to what might well be more than one thousand by the time of publication of this book, the college and university programs have literally mushroomed. Not all institutions offer degree programs, and may have only a few representative courses, but the offerings are bona fide academic courses.

Along with the proliferation of programs throughout the nation, we have witnessed the development of courses by the thousands. Many courses were designed to meet local needs only, with little or no thought given to what the other colleges and universities were doing, particularly in other states. Law enforcement, the courts, and corrections are all local programs, with some of the agencies operated by the state government, but actually a small minority. Local agencies and local colleges and universities each developed programs and courses that met objectives, and their programs grew. During recent years, we have attempted to develop some sort of uniformity in courses and in sequences of courses to make it possible for our students to transfer from one college to another, or to matriculate from the two year community colleges to the state college or university. As a result of these attempts, we have succeeded in at least agreement that there is a need for such a uniform curriculum. Although a great deal more has to be done in this direction, strides have been made at various locations throughout the country.

General Education Base. Fundamental to the collegiate preparation of any student is the broad general education base. The individual who is preparing for professional development in the justice system must have a large portion of his educational preparation in subjects that are certainly related to his overall academic needs, but which do not fall in the category of Administration of Justice education. Basic subjects include communications skills, including English Grammar, English Composition, Public Speaking, and possibly Mathematics. Anything beyond the minimum requirements largely depend on the individual proficiencies and interests of the students. Whether or not Physical Education is required may be considered a determinant as to whether the student will take P.E. courses. For the purpose of maintaining an excellent physical condition there should be some involvement in sports and/or recreation activities and instruction. The individual who is planning a career in corrections and who is also planning to start at the entry level of group supervisor in a juvenile institution should take courses in officiating competitive sports, and as many different kinds of sports and recreation classes as possible. He will be involved in directing the activities of youths under his guidance during their leisure time as well as at other times of the day and days of the week.

First Aid is important, and it may be required of all students along with courses on personal grooming and health, and a college orientation class, but if an applicant misses it in college there is no doubt that he will be required to take it as a regular part of his orientation training when he begins working at one of the justice system occupations. Certain other courses may be required by the college or by the state, and those requirements must be met.

Natural Science, either a physical science or a biological science, depending on college requirements should also be studied. For those interested in criminalistics, Chemistry is a must. For other students there

is little direct relationship to the needs of the student for performance
on the job. The science course he takes should be whichever one he
wishes for personal interest.

Social Science courses may be required, such as a U.S. History
course and American Government Institutions. In addition to those
courses, there are many others in the social sciences that would prove
most worthwhile both in the *required* and in the *elective* categories.
Special Ethnic Studies courses should be considered, particularly by the
student who plans to work in areas in which there is a significant representation of some ethnic heritage other than his own. Sociology and
Cultural Anthropology are a must for the individual who is planning
to specialize in probation or parole work. Child Development and Human
Services courses would likewise be directly related to the objectives of
the change-agent, or the caseworker. The Social Sciences include a
diverse range of courses of instruction in Psychology that should also be
worked into the student's program as much as possible. Child Psychology, Social Psychology, and Abnormal Psychology are just three of
the outstanding courses that would enhance the student's knowledge and
awareness of the problems he will be facing in the world of the justice
system.

Humanities includes an array of course selections that will serve
to enrich the student's educational progress. The types of courses that
would directly relate to the student's professional choice may include
Philosophy, Logic, Art, Music, Theater Arts, Foreign Language, or additional courses in Speech or Written Communications. Not only should
the student be concerned with fulfillment of his personal life and leisure
time, but he may also become occupied in a position in which he is
expected to either direct or show others how to make healthy and productive use of their leisure time.

Special courses that should be considered as electives may include
Typing, Shorthand, Journalism, Participative Sports, Band or Chorus or
other artistic participation type class, Supervision, Business Management, Bookkeeping, Accounting, Computer Science, and as many other
electives in the Social Sciences, particularly Sociology and Psychology.
All of these courses, which are not classified as "Administration of Justice" or "Criminalogy," or "Police Science," or "Correctional Science," or
any other justice system-oriented programs, make up approximately two-
thirds to three-quarters of the student's total two-year, and then four-year
college or university education. Administration of Justice courses should
be complete and comprehensive, but they should not dominate the entire
educational program. As a matter of fact, many of those courses listed
above are directly related to justice administration and round out the

essential body of knowledge and proficiencies that the college-prepared professional must master.

Administration of Justice.[2]   The student's major course of study for any one of the justice system's components will include at least one-fourth to one-third of his total program in specialized courses under the umbrella of some title representative of the "total system" encompassing most of the components of the justice system. Although there was originally a stronger emphasis on each of the more specific categories of police science, corrections, court administration, criminology, or law enforcement, it seems that the "umbrella concept" has been the principal thrust during recent years. This could be, in part, the result of insistence by the Law Enforcement Assistance Administration that many sources of funding would be meager unless any educational program would address the educational needs of the "total system."

In California during the fiscal year 1971–72 a task force was created by the Community College Chancellor's Office in cooperation with a state justice educators' association.[3] The purpose of the task force was to reevaluate the curricula for criminal justice educational programs with a view to design a basic core curriculum that would serve as a common base for educational programs leading to two-year degrees in the several different options in the fields of criminal justice.

The idea was to provide for all students preparing for—or at least aspiring to—professional and paraprofessional positions in the system five common courses, which would lead into a choice of options. The options would be Law Enforcement, Corrections, and Judicial Process, with certain courses in each of those options to be developed during the second year of the task force's existence. The courses' outlines were to be disseminated throughout the state with a prayer that community colleges wishing to participate in such a standardization of courses would adopt the core curriculum. The goal was to produce a program of academically sound courses that would be transferable to any other institution in the state, and also that would meet criteria for matricula-

[2] Although this portion of the chapter emphasizes the California Community College approach because of the author's direct involvement in the California experience, it is not intended that the student or instructor consider it from a "superior versus inferior" viewpoint in comparison with any other system. It is simply presented here as an example of an approach to the educational preparation for the justice system.

[3] California Association of Administration of Justice Eudcators, Inc. The Task Force was chaired by Professor Robert Blanchard of Riverside and members included J. Winston Silva of the California Community College Chancellor's Office, Robert Ferguson of Saddleback College in Mission Viejo, Paul Howard of Bakersfield, Al Nottingham of Modesto, and myself, Tom Adams of Santa Ana.

tion into the University of California System, and the State Colleges and Universities System. With the consent of the task force chairman and Mr. Silva of the chancellor's office, the following are excerpts from the report produced by the task force in July 1972: [4]

Statement of Philosophy

The many Administration of Justice agencies throughout the State and the Nation have evolved from a variety of historical origins at different times and have developed into what we now see as a conglomeration of professions, occupations, and paraprofessions with each requiring certain tangible skills and bodies of knowledge characteristic to their respective disciplines. The agencies within the Administration of Justice, in broad terms, consist of law enforcement, the courts, and corrections.

During the past several years, Presidential Crime Commissions and numerous other segments representing a cross-section of interests have continuously concluded that education of criminal justice system careerists should be based on two primary theses:

1. Sub-systems are no longer in a position to function in a vacuum of isolation from one another, lacking concern for the impact the operation of one sub-system has on the other; and

2. It is of paramount importance that all system members have a deep sensitivity and understanding of human beings and the society in which they exist. This understanding should include the origin and styles of deviant behavior and current theories and treatment of these human weaknesses.

Historically, members of the Administration of Justice system have been educated and trained in an atmosphere of almost total segregation from their sub-system colleagues. Law enforcement, judicial and correctional personnel were educated individually with only a cursory coverage of the other member's subject matter. The segregation of the educational process has even included the almost total isolation of training facilities. Except for their sometimes concurrent attendance at an occasional college class, the members of each component were kept separate. They learned little of what the other members of the system were required to know, and the result had been what sometimes appears to be a total lack of knowledge and understanding of each other's respective roles in justice administration. Sub-system members, training for future involvement within the system, rarely had the opportunity to cross-pollinate ideas and theories on critical issues involving each of the segments. Generally, the first meeting of system members took place in the crucible of "real life," instead of in a laboratory setting which offers a safer environment to exchange points of view and resolve difficulties. This isolationist attitude continues throughout the system in varying degrees today.

It appears inane to provide in-depth education for current and future practitioners in atmospheres of isolation and then to expect system mem-

---

[4] *Administration of Justice Education, Part I Five Core Curriculum,* funded under the Vocational Education Act of 1968, Public Law 90–576 (Riverside, Calif.: Riverside City College, 1972).

bers to work harmoniously in the "real world" of their constant interaction and overlapping responsibilities. The highly cooperative nature of each segment's inter-relationships in the Administration of Justice requires more than a cursory orientation of the roles and responsibilities of the other segments. A common reservoir of knowledge would aid measurably in developing and maintaining this cooperative nature.

A common foundation of educational insights into the entire system would assist greatly in developing an understanding and sensitivity to the many difficult problems that face all members within the system. The educational approach needs to be handled on a system-wide basis. This committee has developed a core of five courses with the contents organized to include a "systems approach" to the entire Administration of Justice.

The committee feels that these five courses include a core of knowledge that is common to all segments of the system and will serve as a basic foundation in the building-block concept of the development of a totally integrated system. These courses have been developed with the thought of establishing a proper blend of the liberal arts and behavioral sciences with studies from the justice system.

The program for the Administration of Justice major in a community college should consist of a total of 24 units, including the five core courses contained in this guide, which total 15 semester units. The balance of 9 units on a semester basis should be directed toward one of the sub-system components the student chooses as a specialization within the Administration of Justice programs. Whether the student chooses Law Enforcement, Courts, Corrections, Criminalistics, Industrial Security, or some other specialization will be determined by how he plans the balance of his schedule in addition to the five core courses. The core courses should be introduced at the lower division level in the college program. The five core courses contained in this project are classified as Part I of a multiphased master plan program. Part II will include a course outline guide of elective courses the student may take to complete his major requirements.

The committee does not perceive the five core courses as eliminating any elective courses or major courses within law enforcement, judicial, or corrections. It views the core curriculum as a common starting block, logically leading into the many choices of elective courses.

In the past, police science curriculums as taught in most colleges, have been duplicated in varying degrees in most police academies. There appears to have been a high degree of overlap in the technical training courses and educational offerings. The academic approach seemed to take a back seat in favor of more traditional training methods and course content. The trend currently tends to avoid this particular approach; however, a relatively few institutions still maintain a somewhat parochial viewpoint on this issue.

With a clearly defined set of objectives in mind, the committee carefully studied the current course offerings, selected the major stores of knowledge and specific proficiencies that appeared to be common to the total justice system. The committee's conclusions were based upon their study of the existing courses, the needs of the several types of agencies within the system, and a consensus of the input of their colleagues throughout the state. The effort was cooperative, and the results were five courses now referred to as the five core courses for Administration of Justice.

1. INTRODUCTION TO THE ADMINISTRATION OF JUSTICE

Course Description. The history and philosophy of administration of justice in America; recapitulation of the system; identification of the various subsystems; role expectations and their interrelationships; theories of crime, punishment, and rehabilitation; ethics, education and training for professionalism in the system.

Course Goals:

1. Provide a knowledge of the various agencies encompassing the administration of justice system and the interrelationships between them.
2. Develop the ability of the student to recognize the administration of justice agency best suited to his or her talents and aspirations.
3. Develop an appreciation of the complexity of the total system and the importance and dignity of being a part of the system.

2. PRINCIPLES AND PROCEDURES OF THE JUSTICE SYSTEM

Course Description. An in-depth study of the role and responsibilities of each segment within the administration of justice system: law enforcement, judicial, corrections. A past, present, and future exposure to each subsystem procedures from initial entry to final disposition and the relationship each segment maintains with its system members.

Course Goals:

1. Provide the student with a knowledge of the procedures involved in the justice system from arrest to release.
2. Develop skills in applying this knowledge to an understanding of the operation of the justice system.
3. Develop an appreciation of the necessity for the justice system to operate as a cooperating entity so the most effective handling of cases can be provided.
4. Develop an ability to utilize the material presented in this course in making appropriate, discretionary decisions as to how to proceed while operating as a member of the system.

3. CONCEPTS OF CRIMINAL LAW

Course Description. Historical development, philosophy of law, and constitutional provisions; definitions, classification of crime, and their application to the system of administration of justice; legal research, study of case law, methodology, and concepts of law as a social force.

Course Goals:

1. Provide the student with a knowledge of the historical development of law and the philosophy of law.
2. Familiarize the student with the U.S. Constitution and integrate constitutional provisions with the fundamentals of law.
3. Introduce the student to basic legal definitions and concepts that provide a foundation for law.
4. Develop within the student an appreciation for the value of case study and legal research as a means of interpreting court decisions in relation to the written statutes.

4 LEGAL ASPECTS OF EVIDENCE

Course Description. Origin, development, philosophy, and constitutional basis of evidence; constitutional and procedural considerations affecting arrest, search, and seizure; kinds and degrees of evidence and rules governing admissibility; judicial decisions interpreting individual rights and case studies.

Course Goals:

1. Provide the student with a working knowledge of the rules of evidence, the various kinds of evidence, and the admissibility of evidence.
2. Develop in the student the ability to evaluate the various kinds of evidence available in a given case in order to determine its admissibility in court.
3. Develop an appreciation of the value of all kinds of evidence and the need to use proper procedures and techniques so as to maintain the value and admissibility of evidence.
4. Develop the skill in handling case material so that evidence admissibility will not be destroyed by improper techniques or procedures.
5. Impress upon the student the knowledge that legally admissible evidence is the end product of all the work and effort of the crime investigator, and that it is essential that he possess a sound knowledge of the rules of evidence.

5. COMMUNITY RELATIONS

Course Description. An in-depth exploration of the roles of the administration of justice practitioners and their agencies. Through interaction and study, the student will become aware of the interrelationships and role expectations among the various agencies and the public. Principal emphasis will be placed upon the professional image of the system of justice administration and the development of positive relationships between members of the system and the public.

Course Goals:

1. Acquire a broad base of information regarding the social and ethnic structure of the community and the variety of cultural influences.

2. Develop an awareness of the many real and/or imagined problems of the various segments of the community in relationship to the criminal justice system. This shall be accomplished by means of an opinion survey, survey of available literature, lectures, and guest appearances.

3. Participate in discussions and group projects to acquire an awareness of the social and personal needs of the various individuals and groups of individuals in the modern society that may have previously been foreign to the awareness and experience of the students.

4. Identify conflicts in principles and philosophies of individuals or groups of individuals that contribute to confrontations and physical conflict with different segments of the criminal justice system.

PART TWO OF THE CORE PLAN. During the second year of the task force's existence, which had a nucleus of the original group and other specialists selected because of their unique talents and knowledge,[5] it attacked the study from the point where the basic core curriculum had been developed and went on to develop different tracks of study. Once the students had assimilated the general body of knowledge common to the total system of criminal justice, the next logical direction for their studies to go would be into the specialized areas of their choice. The three major components of law enforcement, judicial process (courts), and corrections were designated as the three tracks. By calling upon their colleagues throughout the state and by studying the occupations involved as well as existing curricula, the task force developed ten courses, three each in law enforcement and corrections, and four in judicial process.

Once the student completes the five core courses he then chooses one of the three tracks. With fifteen semester units from the core, he must choose three courses to total twenty-four semester units for his major, according to the committee. Although they are referred to as *electives,* it appears that the student has little choice once he elects one

[5] The second year's task force included Robert Blanchard of Riverside as the chairman again, Al Nottingham of Modesto, and Tom Adams of Santa Ana of the original group. They were supplemented by Judge F. J. deLarios of the Northern District of San Mateo County, Richard R. Liberty, Clerk of the same court, Douglas C. Oliver of Skyline College in San Bruno, Harold L. Snow of Modesto (currently a Consultant with the California Commission on Peace Officers Standards and Training), James S. Carroll of the San Diego Marshal's Department and Robert W. Reed of Chaffey Community College in Walnut.

of three tracks. Any courses in Administration of Justice beyond those may be taken strictly on an elective basis. Although Part II of this particular program caused some displacement of existing courses, there was no intention to intimidate any college with special needs or interests from designing its own curriculum beyond the uniform program recommended by the committee. The courses developed for Part II include the following:

TRACK ONE: LAW ENFORCEMENT ELECTIVES

1. SUBSTANTIVE LAW

Course Description. An in-depth study of the substantive laws commonly encountered by the municipal, county, or state police officer or investigator or other criminal justice employee. The scope of the course includes misdemeanor and felony violations of the criminal statutes.

Course Goals:

1. Provide a knowledge necessary for understanding the state's codified laws.
2. Provide the student with an overview of case decisions affecting statutory laws.
3. Develop an appreciation for the role statutory law plays in the subsystem of law enforcement in its relationship with the criminal justice system.
4. Develop an ability to exercise correct field level discretionary decisions on behaviors amounting to public offenses.

2. CONCEPTS OF ENFORCEMENT SERVICES

Course Description. Exploration of theories, philosophies, and concepts related to the role expectations of the line enforcement officer. Emphasis is placed upon the patrol, traffic, and public service responsibilities and their relationship to the administration of justice system.

Course Goals:

1. Provide the knowledge necessary for understanding the role expectations of the line officer.
2. Develop the ability to meet the responsibilities of the line officer with respect to his specific functions.
3. Provide the knowledge necessary to analyze the interrelationships between enforcement personnel and the public being served.
4. Develop an appreciation of the interrelationships between the role expectations of the field law enforcement officer and the total administration of justice system.

3. PRINCIPLES OF INVESTIGATION

Course Description. The study of basic principles of investigation of all types utilized in the justice system. Coverage will include human aspects in dealing with the public; specific knowledge necessary for handling crime scenes; interviews; evidence; surveillance and follow-up investigations; technical resources available; and case preparation.

Course Goals:

1. Provide the knowledge necessary to conduct a satisfactory investigation of both criminal and noncriminal matters.
2. Develop the ability to gather facts, analyze the facts, and draw sound conclusions on the basis of the facts that are revealed.
3. Create an appreciation of the complexities involved in dealing with evidence and legal implications in the conduct of an investigation.
4. Develop the necessary proficiencies to conduct an investigation from inception to completion.

TRACK TWO: JUDICIAL PROCESS ELECTIVES

1. JUDICIAL PROCESS IN CALIFORNIA

Course Description. An overview of the system of federal and California courts with a careful examination of the various roles and duties of court-support personnel.. Mock trials and role playing re-create a model court's internal dynamics and its relationship to outside forces. This course is primarily designed for persons seeking or continuing employment in the courts of California.

Course Objectives:

1. Provide the student with an overview of the structure and functions of federal and California courts.
2. Familiarize the student with the nature of American law, the way it compares to other systems of law, and the means by which it is applied through the judicial process.
3. Develop an understanding of the various functions and services needed to operate the judicial process by examining a model court.
4. Develop an awareness of the inputs and outputs of the judicial process in California along with an appreciation of the outside pressures on the process.
5. Promote recognition of communications, human relations, and public relations problems that must be dealt with in the operation of the effective court.

2. PRINCIPLES AND PRACTICE IN CIVIL PROCESS

Course Description. This course is designed to satisfy basic needs of the administrative and enforcement personnel. Civil and small claims matters in the pretrial, trial, and posttrial phases are surveyed. Necessary procedures of the administrative arm and field procedures of the enforcement arm are described in each phase, hence the course is suitable for deputy clerks, marshals, civil division personnel, and persons seeking or continuing work with the courts in a representative, protective, or investigative capacity. Vocabulary, research methodology concepts, and practices in the field of civil process are studied.

Course Goals:

1.   Develop a basic vocabulary of civil and small claims terminology and usage.
2.   Enable students to research case decisions, legal sources, and current rules in civil and small claims courts.
3.   Develop an understanding of the concepts and practices in each stage of a civil or small claims matter.
4.   Promote better understanding of the necessary teamwork required of all the courts' personnel.
5.   Combine theoretical knowledge with practice in activities necessary to smooth functioning of civil and claims court actions.

3. COURT ENFORCEMENT PRINCIPLES

Course Description. An in-depth study of the duties and responsibilities of court enforcement, except those related to civil process. This course is suitable for those planning to begin or continue service in the ranks of uniformed court personnel (constables, marshals, and sheriff's deputies). Included, but not limited to: the bailiff and the warrant functions.

Course Goals:

1.   Provide a knowledge of the enforcement concepts, laws and techniques required of bailiffs.
2.   Develop a thorough knowledge of laws and procedures regarding the care of juries, custody of prisoners, and security of the courthouse.
3.   Develop an understanding of the principles and practices in the service of warrants from issuance through the service or recall.
4.   Infuse attitudes and habits that will promote a healthy working relationship, good public relations, and a spirit of public service.

(or) 3. COURT ADMINISTRATIVE SERVICES

Course Description. This course examines criminal, traffic, juvenile, and various other proceedings from origin to final disposition. Administrative procedures necessary at each step are studied in detail and proficiencies developed in office practices, courtroom clerking and dealing with the public. Principles of calendaring, notification, accounting, and communications are studied. This course is most suitable for those planning to begin or continue employment on the civilian staff of the courts.

Course Goals:

1. Develop an understanding of the stages through which criminal, traffic, juvenile, and other matters may pass in the courts.
2. Develop proficiencies in dealing with the necessary accounting, reporting, calendaring, notification, and supportive services in each stage of the proceedings.
3. Promote attitudes conducive to effective teamwork and a true spirit of public service.

TRACK THREE: CORRECTIONS ELECTIVES

1. FUNDAMENTALS OF CRIME AND DELINQUENCY

Course Description. An introduction to major types of criminal behavior, role careers of offenders, factors that contribute to the production of criminality or delinquency; methods used in dealing with violators in the justice system; the changing roles of police, courts, and after-care process of sentence, probation, prisons, and parole; changes of the law in crime control and treatment processes.

Course Goals:

1. Provide a knowledge of the types of human behavior that constitute violations of legal codes of conduct as declared by authorized agents of a politically organized society.
2. Develop the ability to recognize major role patterns of behavior that amount to public offenses by offenders and an understanding of factors contributing to such acts in a democratic republic.
3. Develop an appreciation of the ethical issues involved in understanding and dealing with public offenders within the justice system; having as primary consideration for legal intervention the protection of society and the rights of all people.

2. INSTITUTIONAL AND FIELD SERVICES

Course Description. Philosophy and history of correctional services. A survey of the correctional subsystems of institutions by type and function, probation concepts, and parole operations. A discussion of correctional employee responsibilities as applied to offender behavior modification via supervisory control techniques. Rehabilitation goals as they affect individual and inmate cultural groups in both confined and field settings.

Course Goals:

1. Provide a basic knowledge of the history of efforts made in various societies to transform public offenders guilty of violations of law into responsible members of the society in the hope of preventing further illegal acts.

2. Develop, with students, an appreciation of the ethical issues involved in dealing with offenders in both open and closed settings in efforts made by institutional and after-release processes to change behavior into lawful patterns.

3. Develop the ability of students to recognize the various types of correctional facilities, such as jails, prisons, halfway houses, and community release centers by philosophy of program and organizational setting, as these factors relate to behavior change goals and objectives for public offenders.

4. Provide the student with an awareness of the role played by institutional and field services in the administration of justice system, and their functions in the subsystem of corrections as they both relate to society.

3. INTERVIEWING AND COUNSELING

Course Description. Introduction to approaches to behavior modification through interviewing and counseling. An overview of the techniques available to entry level practitioners in corrections in counseling and interviewing. Create an awareness of advanced methods utilized by professional counselors. Trace the development of positive relationships between the client and corrections personnel.

Course Goals:

1. Provide the student with a basic knowledge of the theories and contemporary methods utilized by corrections personnel in behavior modification.

2. Develop, through demonstration and participation, the students' rudimentary abilities in the techniques of interviewing and counseling—as performed by line-level personnel in probation, parole, and correctional institutions.

3. Provide the students with a common body of knowledge to serve as a base for further study in the more sophisticated methods of the interviewing and counseling processes.

Universities and State Colleges

The law enforcement curriculum adopted by the University of Maryland [6] reflects a strong orientation in general education and liberal arts. Out of a total of 124 semester units listed in the curriculum, only 30 units of law enforcement courses, or a total of ten courses are listed as required. That curriculum includes the following courses: (1) Introduction to Law Enforcement, (2) Criminal Investigation and Law Enforcement, (3) Criminal Law, (4) Criminal Procedure and Evidence, (5) Advanced Legal Problems, (6) Law Enforcement-Community Relations, (7) Advanced Law Enforcement Administration, (8) Law Enforcement Personnel Supervision, (9) Security Administration, and (10) Directed Independent Research.

Dr. Charles Tenney lists three models for law enforcement curricula, one for the two-year, preservice and in-service (line) program; one for the two-year, in-service staff program; and a four-year program.[7] In addition to the essential courses in Human Relations (an integrated study of the social and behavioral sciences), English, Humanities, and Science, Tenney lists for the preservice and in-service (line) program the following courses in criminal justice: (1) Introduction to Criminal Justice I, (2) Criminal Law and Procedure, (3) Introduction to Criminal Justice II, (4) Police Operations, (5) Evidence, and (6) Skills Development, or Skills Training. The program includes a total of twenty-four semester hours in criminal justice courses out of a total of sixty-one hours. The two-year model for in-service (staff) includes twenty-four of a total of sixty semester hours in the following courses: (1) Police Organization and Administration, (2) Personnel Management, (3) two semesters of Police Operations, (4) Police-Community Relations, and (5) eight units of Skills Development, or Training.

In his plan for the four-year college program, Dr. Tenney again strongly emphasizes the essential general education and liberal arts courses with a total of fifty-three semester hours in criminal justice courses and fifteen hours in electives, which might include criminal justice courses. The courses listed in this model for criminal justice include (1) two courses in Introduction to Criminal Justice, (2) Criminal Law and Procedure, (3) Evidence, (4) Police-Community Relations,

[6] As reported by Peter P. Levins, *Introducing a Law Enforcement Curriculum at a State University* (Washington, D.C.: National Institution of Law Enforcement and Criminal Justice, 1970), pp. 40–42).

[7] Charles W. Tenney, Jr., *Higher Education Program in Law Enforcement and Criminal Justice PR1–2* (Washngton, D.C.: Government Printing Office, 1971), pp. 29–33.

(5) Police Organization and Management, (6) The Patrol Function, (7) Criminalistics, (8) The Investigative Function, (9) Police-Juvenile Problems, (10) The Traffic Problem, (11) Comparative Police Systems, and (12) Skills Development.

Professor James D. Stinchcomb of the Virginia Commonwealth University has developed a baccalaureate program that emphasizes general academic courses during the first two years plus three courses in the School of Community Services Curriculum. The student is required to take (1) Survey of the Administration of Justice and (2) Substantive Criminal Law and Due Process plus (3) an Introduction to the Juvenile Justice System or Introduction to Criminalistics. During the third and fourth years the student chooses one of three options. Stinchcomb describes the options in his program description shown on page 244.

Dr. C. Robert Guthrie, then chairman of the Department of Criminology at California State College (now University) at Long Beach, outlined what he believed to be a comprehensive and workable program for law enforcement education at both two- and four-year institutions.[8]

His recommended curriculum for four-year programs follows:

LOWER DIVISION (FIRST TWO YEARS OF COLLEGE)

Lower Division objectives:

a. Liberal arts background (general education and required courses)
b. Occupational training at performance level (full-time students and officers attending part-time)
c. Provision of a basis for upper division work
d. Provision of a professional career preparation at entrance level
e. Service courses to other college disciplines (Business, Engineering, Government, Journalism)

Criteria for placement at lower division level:

a. Orientation
b. Broad Liberal Arts background
c. Tool or technique type for practitioners

UPPER DIVISION (LATTER TWO YEARS OF COLLEGE)

Objectives:

1. Broad Liberal Arts background
2. Education in theory of supervision and administration

[8] *Police Science Degree Programs Report,* Dissemination Document Project 67–28, June 8–9, 1967 (Washington, D.C.: Office of Law Enforcement Assistance, 1968), pp. 46–50.

PROGRAM OPTION IN CORRECTIONS

THIRD YEAR   CREDITS
- AJP 324 Courts and the Judicial Process — 3
- AJP 351 Correctional Administration — 3
- AJP 352 Crime and Delinquency Prevention — 3
- AJP 431 Criminal Justice: Management Concepts — 3
- AJP 432 Criminal Justice: Organizational Dynamics — 3
- SOC 403 Criminology — 3
- SOC 331 Juvenile Delinquency — 3
- Electives — 3 6

    30

FOURTH YEAR
- AJP 455, RCO 555 Community-Based Correctional Programs — 3
- AJP 460 Evaluation and Treatment of the Offender — 3
- AJP 463 Correctional Law — 3
- AJP 474, URS 574 Correctional Institution Development and Design — 3
- AJP 480 Seminar: Critical Issues in Criminal Justice — 3
- AJP 390 Criminal Justice Internship — 3-6
  - — or —
- AJP 491 Directed Individual Study — 3
- RCO 425 Introduction to Rehabilitation Counseling — 3
- Electives — 6 3

    30

COLLATERAL COURSE WORK

Courses designed to complement the student's specialization area and to broaden his educational perspective may be selected as electives. These courses may be chosen from departments such as: Urban Studies, Political Science, Psychology, Social Welfare, Sociology, Rehabilitation Counseling, and Recreation.

PROGRAM OPTION IN POLICE PLANNING AND MANAGEMENT

THIRD YEAR   CREDITS
- AJP 324 Courts and the Judicial Process — 3
- AJP 360 Comparative Law and Criminal Responsibility — 3
- AJP 342 Public Safety in the Changing Community — 3
- AJP 355 Trends in Police Administration — 3
- AJP 431 Criminal Justice: Management Concepts — 3
- AJP 432 Criminal Justice: Organizational Dynamics — 3
- SOC 403—Criminology — 3
- Electives — 3 6

    30

Additional specialized course work is available in industrial and retail security (AJP 407).

FOURTH YEAR
- AJP 471 Scientific Research and Crime Analysis — 3
- AJP 475 Case Studies in Evidence — 3
- AJP 480 Seminar: Critical Issues in Criminal Justice — 3
- AJP 390 Criminal Justice Field Internship — 3-6
  - — or —
- AJP 491 Directed Individual Study — 3
- URS 321 Planning Information Systems — 3
- URS 422 Programming and Budgeting — 3
- Electives — 6 6

    30

COLLATERAL COURSE WORK

Courses designed to complement the student's specialization area and to broaden his educational perspective may be selected as electives. These courses may be chosen from departments such as: Urban Studies, Political Science, Psychology, Business, and the Physical Sciences.

PROGRAM OPTION IN TRAFFIC AND HIGHWAY SAFETY

THIRD YEAR   CREDITS
- AJP 315 Traffic Planning and Management — 3
- AJP 324 Courts and the Judicial Process — 3
- AJP 342 Public Safety in the Changing Community — 3
- AJP 360 Comparative Law and Criminal Responsibility — 3
- PSY 304 Developmental Psychology — 3
- URS 351 Urban Transportation Systems — 3
- HEN 382 Driver Education — 3
- Electives — 3 6

    30

FOURTH YEAR
- AJP 431 Criminal Justice: Management Concepts — 3
- AJP 432 Criminal Justice: Organizational Dynamics — 3
- AJP 390 Highway Safety Field Internship — 3-6
  - — or —
- AJP 491 Directed Individual Study — 3
- AJP 426 Legal Aspects of Highway Safety — 3
- AJP 437 Accident Analysis and Crash Prevention — 3
- AJP 440 Behavioral Factors in Highway Safety — 3
- AJP 471 Scientific Research and Crime Analysis — 3
- AJP 480 Seminar: Critical Issues in Criminal Justice — 3
- PSY 431 Industrial Safety — 3
- Elective — 3

    30

COLLATERAL COURSE WORK

Courses designed to complement the student's specialization area and to broaden his educational perspective may be selected as electives. These courses may be chosen from departments such as Urban Studies, Political Science, Psychology, Sociology, Safety Education, and Business.

3. Amplification of lower division work through specialized courses
4. Professional career preparation for supervisory and administrative assignment
5. Teacher preparation for academic, state-legislated training programs, junior colleges, colleges, and universities
6. Background for graduate work
7. Opportunity to participate in research
8. Service courses for other disciplines

Criteria for placing in upper division:

a. Advanced or highly specialized
b. Supervisory or administrative in nature
c. Theory and policy courses needed by top-level managers

RECOMMENDED JUNIOR COLLEGE TRANSFER CURRICULUM

A. General Education requirements
B. Major (includes the following courses)
   Introductory or orientation courses
   Law
   Evidence
   Procedure
   Criminal Investigation
   Patrol Procedures
   Traffic Control

Electives should include typewriting, first aid, lifesaving, photography. Liaison between 2 and 4 year institutions is recommended. Coordination is necessary between junior colleges and 4 year colleges in these areas:

1. Relative to courses and units acceptable for transfer from 4 year colleges to 2 year colleges
2. Junior colleges acceptance of academy, institute, or other non-academic, non-accredited, law enforcement training
3. Relative to student counseling terminal versus transfer programs.

In the same publication, Professor Jack A. Mark, Director of the Police Program at Rutgers University, New Brunswick, New Jersey made these recommendations for the Office of Law Enforcement Assistance regarding their funding of educational programs through loans and grants to students:

1. . . . strongly focus on transfer and baccalaureate programs
2. . . . look at funded programs of a terminal nature

3. . . . encourage planning and development of a master plan which seeks to accomplish the following:

    A. Inventory of educational achievement

    B. Coordinated approach in development of programs in police science
leave no gaps and avoid proliferation

    C. A joint and coordinated development of programs in police science so that curricula dovetail and courses provide a logical sequence to one another and supplement each other well

    D. Standardization of course nomenclature, content, and treatment of subject matter to make possible improved course evaluation and student programming

    E. Close liaison between lower and upper division colleges and their chairmen, etc.

    F. Reasonably high standards for the faculty, supporting facilities, equipment, and instructional materials

    G. Sharing of faculty and staff facilities where no conflict exists

    H. Coordinated Participation of faculties of several schools offering programs in Police Science offering specialized institutes and seminars, research cooperaton

    I. High-calibre work-study programs

    J. Winnowing of terminal programs and support only if a richer transfer program cannot meet the needs of the community [9]

Correctional education is unique in some respects, according to Robert Montilla. He states:

Correctional agencies, along with all correctional programs, are part of society's system for the administration of criminal justice (which has its local, state and national dimensions) in which the primary goal is public protection through crime and delinquency prevention and control. Within this system, correctional agencies and programs are associated with police, prosecution and the courts. But correctional agencies and programs are also part of society's "civil" machinery concerned with general health and welfare in which there is also a broad goal of public protection. Here corrections is associated with the fields of medicine, education, social services and a variety of community institutions. The basic, and sometimes conflicting, differences between the two systems are rooted in different orientations of the law: (1) that which relies on punishment of the offender for the purpose of retribution and as a possible deterrence to others, and (2) that which relies on the scientific method to help understand personality, group and environmental factors

[9] *Police Science Degree Programs Report,* pp. 66–68.

that influence human behavior so that those factors can be constructively manipulated to reduce disordered and deviant behavior.[10]

Those observations lend weight to our proposal that there is a common core of knowledge in education of all criminal justice personnel. Beyond the core, then, there must be an array of entirely diverse courses that will be peculiar to only that criminal justice component for which the student becomes more specialized.

Training and Education

Skills development and indoctrination to the routine activities of the occupation are usually assigned the label *training;* while the orientation to philosophy, theories and concepts of the role through intellectualization processes are usually assigned the label *education.* Although it is virtually impossible to distinguish the two in many respects, recent attempts have been made in order that they may be handled differently. A simplified distinction might be to designate training as the process of instructing the individual on how to do the job and providing him with the basic information about the job, and *education* as the process of providing him with a body of knowledge on which he may base his decisions when he is performing the job. While training is generally directly related to the tasks to be performed by the practitioner, the education that he receives should be on a broad base so that he not only understands his own role in society, but that of others who surround him and with whom he interacts.

Charles Tenney defined training in this manner:

A particular subject may be determined to be of the *training* variety if it is directed primarily to the mastery and application of particular rules, to the development of particular mechanical skills in the operation of particular items of equipment, or to the development of a skill in the performance of particular maneuvers concerning which little or no discretion is involved. . . . In other cases, the *manner* in which a course is taught and its *content* will determine its training character. . . . In either case, whether because of the nature of the subject matter itself or because of the manner in which it is taught, little attention is given to the questions of policy, of discretion, or of alternatve methodologies.[11]

[10] Robert Montilla, *Correctional Planning and Resource Guide* (Washington, D.C.: Office of Law Enforcement Assistance, 1969), p. 9.

[11] Tenney, *Higher Education Programs in Law Enforcement and Criminal Justice PR1–2,* p. 8.

Types of Training Programs for Criminal Justice

Following the new employee's appointment and prior to his actual exposure to the job that he will be performing on a regular basis he is given some sort of agency orientation and indoctrination. He is instilled with the pride of membership in this organization in particular and the profession in general. It is, indeed, a proud time, and he is to be reminded that his newly designated power has a set of tremendous responsibilities accompanying that power, and he is given an outline of his limitations as well as the scope of his responsibility. Following that brief induction session, and possibly concurrent with his actual on-the-job participation, the new employee's experiences begin.

Interns and Cadets

As professionalization of the entire field of law enforcement and criminal justice evolves into reality, the academic requirements will doubtlessly increase. Education is a means to an end, however, not an end in itself. Knowing a job and knowing *about* a job are two different situations. You do not learn to swim without getting into the water, nor can you learn the job of *being* a policeman without "getting into the water." During the past several years, various police agencies and colleges have cooperated in a variety of programs that provide to the preservice student practical on-the-job training while still attending college. Two of the more popular programs are internship and cadet training.

How to stimulate and maintain the interest of the young high school graduate during the interim between graduation and his twenty-first birthday has always been a problem. Rather than leave a young man's decision to enter law enforcement to chance, it is more desirable to help him make his choice while still in high school through career guidance programs. It is then necessary that we encourage him for the next few years. The ultimate goal would be entrance into the ranks of law enforcement as an officer, a deputy, or an investigator. But there must be some intermediate goals that are attainable along the way. Without these goals, there is frustration and in many cases a redesignation of goals. Internship and cadet training provide those intermediate goals and emotional satisfaction as well. Additional incentives may be provided in the form of assured acceptance into the sponsoring agency at the completion of the training and financial assistance in the form of nominal pay on an hourly basis.

Internship, or work experience programs, have been in operation within two-year and four-year college programs in California and elsewhere for many years. The student is usually required to attend at least a half-time school schedule and to take a major in the law enforcement program. Some schools include young ladies in their program, but their utilization by cooperating agencies is on a much more limited basis. The student enrolls for the internship, or work experience, course for a specific number of credits (or units) and is required to work and/or observe at a specified cooperating agency for a minimum number of hours. This particular type of course usually does not involve financial remuneration for the student.

Approval of the intern is dependent upon successful completion of a series of entrance examinations and a thorough background investigation conducted by some agencies, and other agencies call for little more than a brief oral interview. In exchange for his hours of work observation, the student receives the credits and grades characteristic of all other college courses. He may be required to prepare periodic reports to both the agency and the college professor in charge of the program and to the agency intern coordinator.

The cadet training program is similar to the internship program, but there is usually an employer-employee relationship between the student and the agency for which he performs. On-the-job supervision in a cadet program is usually the primary responsibility of the employing law enforcement agency. It is possible to assign the cadet to a wide variety of duties throughout the agency in nearly every area except actual enforcement or investigative assignments. Although not operable at the time of the preparation of this manuscript, it is possible that the cadet program could be extended to include the duties of the public service officer in the three-step policeman levels described by the President's Crime Commission and the administration of justice report released in early 1967.

A student attending classes, on a full-time or three-quarter schedule may be scheduled for a twenty-hour week during the school year and a full schedule during school vacation when the officers would be taking their vacations. The most practical method of selection of cadets is to have them go through the identical series of exams and the entire selection process as if they were applying for the policeman position. Later, when the cadet reaches the age of twenty-one and/or completion of his college education and he becomes a candidate for a full-fledged law enforcement officer, only a new medical exam and an oral interview would be necessary. An advantage to completing the selection examination process at the beginning of the cadet's employment in that capacity is that the individual who obviously will not gain eventual employment as a law enforcement officer will know it at that time rather than having the misfortune of spending four years in college only to find out—with degree in hand—that he is not qualified for the job.

Although most of the cadet programs currently in operation are conducted by municipal law enforcement agencies, there is no reason why it should not be extended to include sheriffs' departments, state police, highway patrols, and many state and federal law enforcement and investigative agencies. In order to assure the agency that the program is actually going to produce officers or agents for that agency instead of professional student-cadets, the cadet could be required to sign an agreement that he will apply for the officer or agent position within a reasonable time (specifically stated in the agreement) after he reaches his twenty-first birthday or completes his college training, whichever occurs first, and that his failure to do so will result in his termination as a cadet. This technique would assure a turnover of cadets, limiting their membership to future policemen or investigators only.

Supplementing a paid internship or cadet training program, some colleges use their police science students in a variety of paid police-type activities. Some of those activities include on-campus traffic control, crowd control, and general security. Still another incentive to the future police officer student is the requirement that they wear distinctive uniforms while in class and on campus. Esprit de corps runs high when the students are well trained and strictly disciplined. Entrance into this select group of students should be difficult, with summary expulsion for those who disobey the rules or fail to perform as required.

Basic Training.   The classroom setting with instructors drawn from within the organization to introduce the new employees to the manipulative and procedural functions of his job provides the employee with the basic tools that he must have to function effectively. The classroom instruction may or may not be mixed with field experiences or some laboratory training. This training may last from ten to twenty hours to as much as twenty or more weeks of intensive training in an academy setting.

Escort Training.   Following his basic academy (or whatever other designation the department gives to the basic training), the new employee is now equipped with the knowledge and fundamental proficiencies to do the job, and he is ready for the application phase of his learning process. He must be able to identify the situation and interpret what he must do in his role in the justice system that will correctly address that problem. He is assigned to work with a teammate, a more experienced member of the same organization who has been selected because he performs well on the job, but also because he has the interest and ability to function as a tutor. The relationship is one similar to that of journeyman-apprentice. At the beginning, the tutor demonstrates how to perform the tasks, then he directs the novice to perform them under his surveillance. They discuss the concepts and the actual procedures. This procedure goes on until the trainee is able to function effectively and correctly with the tutor merely looking on and offering only an occasional word of advice or direction. At some time when the tutor feels confident that his charge can "solo," he steps aside and the newly trained employee is on his own. He will continue to be subjected to some supervision and occasional "check-rides" with a senior officer or perhaps another tutor or two to make sure that he has assimilated all of the essential knowledge and improved his basic skills.

Roll call training in progress.
Courtesy, Police Department, Lawton, Oklahoma.

In-Service Daily Training. A specific period of time may be set aside each day for a training session during which the supervisors and training personnel may present formal or informal instructional material to bring the employees up to date on new laws, procedures, new information, or to have some sort of refresher training to assure maximum efficiency on the job. A short film or videotape may be used, or a ten-minute lecture accompanied by some sort of testing to assure the instructor that the information was digested or that the new technique has been mastered by the recipients of the training. Such training is usually related to current problems or current or future needs. Otherwise, the student-practitioners will get little—if any—benefit from the training.

Training Bulletins and Home-Study Material. Professional journals provide excellent sources of information for the professional in the justice system, and libraries will yield more valuable information. The agency may select certain items of interest and essential knowledge for certain individuals or for the entire department membership, and duplicate and disseminate them for home study.

Role Playing as a Training Device. Developed by psychiatrists as a variation of psychodrama in which individuals may act out their feelings and thoughts, utilization of role playing is a form of rehearsal-training that may be quite effective. Simulations of real situations that have occurred, or that frequently occur, or that may never have happened yet, but are anticipated, provide an excellent vehicle for realistic training. The simulation is presented to the student under controlled conditions when the individual is put under artificial stress so that he must make critical decisions, yet be afforded the luxury of making his mistakes while he is performing during the training session rather than in actual situations. The objective is to provide the individual with a series of experiences so that when he is confronted with a real situation under stress he may act as one who has been through similar experiences before, and he should perform with greater confidence and skill.

Seminars and Symposia. Problem-solving groups representing the various agencies of the justice system may meet and discuss their respective problems, and may exchange ideas on their perceptions of the other person's responsibilities. This type of training stimulates greater understanding and cooperation among members of the several components of the justice system. Many of the problems are common to more than one component, and joint symposia creates an awareness that one is not unique in his need for assistance and understanding. This particular method of training session is utilized for problem solving and exchange of information.

Regional Training Centers. All of the components of the justice system have continuous needs for training for both general and special needs. Although the actual course content may vary, the media and facilities, equipment, and support personnel may all be provided at some centrally located resource center. Such a pooling of talents and resources appears to be the trend throughout the nation. Only the largest agencies are able to support such a center by themselves, but when operated under a joint powers agreement, costs are prorated and it is possible for the smaller agencies to benefit from the more advanced forms of training.

Specialized Training. With pooled resources such as those found at regional centers, training programs have been developed to serve agency needs of the many components of the justice system beyond the orientation and apprenticeship levels. Specialized training programs are available for prosecuting attorneys, newly appointed judges, court administrators, as well as many of the different tasks performed by members of corrections and law enforcement professions. The supervisory, mid-management, and executive positions are also recognized by such training courses and seminars in first-line and middle-management supervision, and executive development. Concurrent with management training programs for the incumbents, lower-ranking individuals who have demonstrated promising talents are sent to management training programs and are programmed through a series of learning experiences as a part of a planned executive development schedule.

Summary

What is education and what is training may be a topic for discussion, and there may be some disagreement on definitions, but there is no disagreement that both are equally important and that they are inseparable. In the preceding pages we have covered principles and practices of both education and training, and have briefly touched upon some of the specific developments that have occurred during the past decade. For the serious student, this is only the beginning.

Exercises and Study Questions

1. What is the difference between education and training, as explained in this chapter?
2. Why is there a difference between the application form and the personal history statement?

3. What is the purpose for such a thorough background investigation used by a criminal justice agency prior to employment as a candidate?

4. According to the statement of philosophy, what is the reason for having all Administration of Justice students take "core" courses prior to branching out with one of the tracks that are available to him?

5. The type of training the author called escort training is employed by the prosecuting attorney in which manner when a new prosecutor is placed on the job?

6. Is the internship a valid means of preparing students for criminal justice occupations? Can you explain why you responded to that question as you did?

7. Explain the reason for such a heavy emphasis on liberal arts for Administration of Justice students who are preparing to be police officers.

8. After you have examined the course descriptions of the five core courses, comment on whether you believe those five topics should be core courses, and explain the reasoning for your comment.

9. What courses would you suggest as electives for each of the three justice system components of law enforcement, judicial process, and corrections?

10. List Humanities courses that should be recommended for students preparing for (1) probation officer, (2) federal investigator, (3) group supervisor in juvenile hall, (4) deputy sheriff. If you chose different courses for each of those positions, explain why.

11. For what types of personality characteristics do you believe an individual who is applying for a juvenile probation officer should be excluded if he were screened by a psychologist? Why?

12. Recommended semester project: Work out your own program for the first two years of your educational preparation for your choice of occupation in the justice system. Now, choose an occupation different from your choice and work out a two-year program for that position. List the differences in course selections and explain the reasons why you chose each of those courses. Prepare your materials as if you were going to counsel a student aspiring for the position that is different from your program, and be prepared to defend your recommendation.

Suggested for Additional Study

American Correctional Association, *Manual of Correctional Standards* (3rd Ed.). New York: American Correctional Association, 1966.

CROCKETT, THOMPSON S. and JAMES STINCHCOMB, *Guidelines for Law Enforcement Education Programs in Community and Junior Colleges*. Washington, D.C.: American Association of Junior Colleges, 1968.

Joint Commission on Correctional Manpower and Training, *Manpower and Training in Correctional Institutions.* Washington, D.C.: Government Printing Office, 1969.

PIVEN, HAROLD and ABRAHAM ALCABES, *Probation/Parole: Pilot Study of Correctional Training and Manpower.* Washington, D.C.: Government Printing Office, 1967.

STINCHCOMB, JAMES D., *Opportunities in a Law Enforcement Career.* New York: Vocational Guidance Manuals, 1971.

9

Ethics and Professionalism

Introduction

The many thousands of men and women who occupy the hundreds of classifications of positions in the justice system and its many components serve the public in what I believe to be a position of trust and responsibility. Power vested in these individuals by law is far exceeded by the public's acceptance of their authority. Many of these people are held in awe by the public they serve, and the responsibility to that public is compounded by the pressure to restrain one's self where no external pressures are applied. For example, to the bewildered first-time law violator the police detective who questions him is about ten-feet tall and has total power over his freedom. The investigator has the burden of responsibility to remind the violator that he has the guaranteed right to refuse to answer questions even though he—the investigator—is earnestly seeking those answers. The judge in the courtroom cannot find a person guilty just because the accused person's hair or clothing style is different from that of the judge. He must make his decision solely on the evidence presented to him in a legally prescribed manner, and it can happen that the judge will find someone not guilty even though he may privately or "intuitively" believe that person to be guilty. It is the judge's responsibility to remind the accused as well as the prosecutor and defense attorney that he is innocent until *proven* guilty even though the circumstances may indicate that it is an "open and shut case."

Every individual who is employed within the justice system must adhere to the principles of the codes of ethics of the respective components of the system. Such an individual should not divest himself of his individuality and his personal consciousness of mitigating circumstances that may surround certain actions requiring his intervention, but he must act within the propriety of the ethical requirements of his profession. These codes of ethics may bear the title of Judicial Ethics and may describe the conduct of *judges,* but they apply to every member of that component of the system because they are directly responsible to the same principles and ethics as the judge as his agents and as his direct affiliates. If one of the occupational participants in one of the system's components finds that he cannot operate effectively within the constraints of certain ethical requirements, then he should seek a position in another occupation that will be more compatible with his own philosophy.

The ethical requirements of the law profession provide that an attorney should competently represent his client. If a client is known to be guilty by his own admissions, his attorney is still compelled to provide for his client competent legal services, which may lead to a jury's finding of *not guilty.* The police officer may witness a criminal act that he feels should not be considered a crime, yet he must effect the arrest because of his ethical requirement to serve the *public good* as determined by the legislative branch of government. The probation officer may personally believe that a particular religious philosophy has such a carnival-like aura about it that it is in total disharmony with his personal convictions, yet he is ethically required to try every approach toward the rehabilitation of his client and that may include referral to the spiritual guidance offered by that specific sect.

Professionalism goes along inseparably with ethics. As a matter of fact, one of the requisites of a profession is that it must have a code of ethics and that there must be some provision for the enforcement of those ethical requirements. Professionalization in the justice system has grown immensely in the past two decades, and many new professions have emerged within the system. In this chapter we shall define and discuss *professions* and *professionalism,* and leave the determination up to you—the student—as to whether a particular occupation within the system is a profession. The latter half of the chapter will cover ethics, and we shall present three examples of codes or principles of ethics: the Law Enforcement Code of Ethics, Canons of Judicial Ethics, and the Declaration of Principles of the American Correctional Association, which encompass the professions of probation, parole, and correctional institution management.

Professionalism.   A profession does not suddenly become a profession by proclamation. Although the word has been used in so many different ways, in this chapter the term will apply to those positions that meet the criteria outlined in the paragraphs that follow.

Profession Defined and Discussed

Textbook and dictionary definitions vary, but there seems to be a general agreement on certain factors that distinguish a particular occupation as a profession. Those factors include:

1. A common body of specialized knowledge
2. Minimum education requirements prior to entry into the profession
3. Free exchange of information between individuals and their departments
4. Careful and rigid preemployment screening
5. A code of ethics
6. Recognition by the public
7. Decision-making responsibility and authority

A closer analysis of these seven factors may provide greater insight into many of the occupations in the justice system and enable you to determine whether certain occupations qualify for the classification of *profession*.

1. *A common body of specialized knowledge.* Approximately one thousand educational institutions in the United States offer one or more different programs of education leading to two-year associate degrees, baccalaureate degrees, graduate degrees and doctorates in fields related to the justice system. At the two-year level, a core curriculum may be offered that provides the common body of specialized knowledge in administration of justice, followed by the student's choice of which one of several tracks he wishes to follow. Tracks include Criminalistics, Business and Industrial Security, Law Enforcement, Judicial Process (Courts), or Corrections. The growth of libraries in criminal justice fields, and the diverse backgrounds of their authors further attest to the "body of knowledge" concept. An interesting phenomenon occurs within the justice system educational process: The core at college-entry level provides a common base of information to all participants in the several programs; the students then branch off into tangents related to their own needs and interests; and this is followed by a general transition back toward a second common body of knowledge in organization, management, administrative problems, and the overall aspects of public administration.

2. *Pre-entry education requirements*. There seems to be considerable variance on this qualification. Graduation from high school with no college history at all may be considered sufficient for entry into any of the occupations in prisoner control and in law enforcement. Other occupations, such as judges and lawyers, must have advanced professional degrees, and yet others, such as probation and parole, may require baccalaureate degrees prior to entry into the profession, but that degree may be in any major and/or minor. It appears that there is considerable room for "professional" growth in pre-entry education requirements for virtually all of the justice system professions with the exception of attorneys and judges. Many proponents for advanced education for justice system components encourage support to baccalaureate level degrees for police officers as well as for other professionals in related agencies.

3. *Free exchange of information between individuals and their departments*. Trade secrets are zealously guarded by competing manufacturers of soaps and toys, but what would be the result if the first doctor to successfully transplant a kidney or some other vital organ would forever keep his secret? A true professional is one who makes a discovery that serves mankind in such a beneficial way that it saves lives, or changes lives, and then shares that information with his colleagues by writing papers and conducting a series of lecture-demonstrations. He attempts to disseminate the information, and he assists others in developing the technique so that they may duplicate his successes and may even improve upon them.

In the field of justice administration, the probation officer who develops a technique in which he experiences any degree of success in behavior modification has a professional obigation to tell his colleagues about his new technique. A free-flowing exchange of information throughout the several professions in the justice system is essential to the perpetuation of those professions. Unfortunately, there are some individuals in every profession who may be so greedy, or insecure, or may have some unfulfilled need that they guard their secrets and refuse to share them. The true professional who selflessly devotes his life to the service of others seems also to have the personality characteristics that involve the same selfless exchange of information.

4. *Careful and rigid preemployment screening*. There is a variety of methods of selection utilized by many different agencies. Under the watchful eyes of their respective Peace Officers Standards and Training Commissions, police officers of the several states that have mandated professional standards are subjected to a series of rigid tests. Only a small percentage of candidates who apply are succesful in gaining appointments. Law school is as much a screening process as it is a learn-

ing process, and many aspirants to the legal profession have failed to successfully complete the process, or have had their completion delayed because of some deficiency in their qualifications.

The testing process includes intelligence surveys, attitude and personality screening devices, endurance and agility tests, rigid training schedules, and a probationary period—all designed to eliminate all but the best qualified for the positions involved. Background investigations are conducted for the purpose of determining the candidate's reputation, which is so important to all of the justice system, and to find out whatever possible about the candidate's past performance and attitudes both in his public and his private life.

5. *A code of ethics.* Standards of conduct and specified principles for professional performance provide for the individual a set of guidelines that he may follow as a form of self-discipline, a practice that is essential to any professional person. Within the profession there must also be a prescribed enforcement procedure to assure compliance with the codes of ethics and to assure some form of punitive and corrective action to be taken upon violators of the codes. In this chapter we shall review samples of some of the codes of ethics found in the justice system.

6. *Recognition by the public.* Each of the several professions within the justice system, and other occupations and paraprofessions (or "subprofessions"), is usually viewed separately by the public and holds its own distinctive position of influence in its relationship with the people it serves. A true test of whether a particular calling has attained professional status is to determine how well it is accepted by the public.

7. *Decision-making responsibility and authority.* All professionals, such as those in medicine and law, must make independent decisions based upon their assessment of the situation that confronts them, their education and experiences with similar encounters, the confidence and trust others put in him to make critical decisions, and the authority allowed them to make such decisions. About this particular process involving the police officer, James Q. Wilson made these observations:

> Formally, the police are supposed to have almost no discretion: by law in many places and in theory everywhere, they are supposed to arrest everyone whom they see committing an offense or, with regard to the more serious offenses, everyone whom they have reasonable cause to believe has committed an offense. In fact, as all police officers and many citizens recognize, discretion is inevitable partly because it is impossible to observe every public infraction, partly because many laws require interpretation before they can be applied at all, partly because the police can sometimes get information about serious crimes by overlooking

minor crimes, and partly because the police believe that public opinion would not tolerate a policy of full enforcement of all laws all the time.

In almost every public organization, discretion is exercised . . . but the police department has the special property . . that within it discretion increases as one moves *down* the hierarchy.[1]

Agency Responsibility to the Professional

Part of the public's acceptance of an individual and his occupation as a professional involves the manner in which his own employing agency accepts him and presents him to the public. There are certain factors that comprise the agency's responsibility to the individual. Those factors include the following:

1. *Competent leadership.* The executives and management people in the organization must provide enlightened leadership to the professionals who must respond to their leadership. A good leader must be a model for those he leads, and professional leaders should be no exception. Although he may not have the educational or professional background of the professionals under his leadership, he should recognize those qualities and should strive to get maximum performance from those who have such qualities. Should he possess similar education and experience, which is most desirable, he should maintain an attitude conducive to the encouragement of academic progress and experimentation that accompany professional growth and development, and should refrain from overshadowing his subordinates accomplishments by his own display of skills and talent.

2. *More than adequate facilities.* Although government operations involve public approval for any type of constructions, and then once the decision is made to build, someone who offered to do the work at the lowest bid is chosen, it should be borne in mind that the "bargain basement" is not always the best place to find a bargain. Functional, spacious, and comfortable quarters must be modern and well equipped. Furniture and office equipment, and other operating equipment should be maintained in excellent working condition and nothing should be allowed to fall into a state of disrepair.

3. *Good equipment.* The vehicles, weapons, office equipment, uniforms or other special clothing, and all of the additional equipment that the professional uses should be in excellent shape and capable of serving the purpose for which they are maintained.

---

[1] James Q. Wilson, *Varieties of Police Behavior: The Management of Law and Order in Eight Communities* (Cambridge: Harvard University Press, 1968), p. 7.

4. *Training and educational assistance.* Schedules should be arranged as closely as possible to allow agency members to attend class whenever possible. Arrangements should be made, as nearly as possible, for the agency to at least address the needs of its employees in attempting to upgrade themselves both academically and ethically. In-service training must be arranged, and continuous efforts should be made to make training for criminal justice agencies meaningful and actually productive in accordance with an agency's needs. Schedules should be arranged so that the interested employees may continue their educational pursuits without the work and the school attendance interfering with each other. Financial incentives could be used—and are used by many agencies— to stimulate interest in continuing one's educational pursuits.

5. *Recognition.* Individual employees should have a team spirit and strive to present an image of the department that will enhance the individual's status with colleagues and the public. Although it may not be wise to emphasize private gain as an end result, there should be realistic incentives and rewards that will encourage the employees to earn recognition for extra efforts toward improvement of techniques in performing one's tasks. Constructive changes that lead to actual improvement are healthy, but changes that are made strictly for the sake of change may lack the same vitality.

6. *Remuneration.* Professional people must be paid wages appropriate to professional positions. Pay should be comparable to the performance as well as the competence and skill of the professional who is being paid.

The Individual's Responsibility to the Profession

"Devotion to duty" should describe the professional's attitude and actions. If he is to earn for himself and his colleagues the status of a professional, he has certain obligations to his employing agency and, above all, to the profession itself.

1. Positive attitude. The chronic complainer and the drone have no place in the administration of justice. The individual's attitude must be one of optimism and enthusiasm. By his own enthusiasm, he will generate the same feeling in the people with whom he works.

2. Industriousness. The highly individualized professional should be able to work on his own. Success in any profession requires intelligence and energy. Criminal justice is no exception.

3. Loyalty. The professional must be loyal to his God, his country, and to his community. The public good is the primary concern of the Constitution; his concern should be the same.

4. Competence. The individual must achieve and maintain minimum performance standards. The "twenty-year company man" may or may not be a true professional.

Ethics

Every profession has its canons, or code of ethics that it uses to identify its principles, its goals, and general rules of ethical conduct. Such an instrument is used as a self-management tool that acts as a gauge by which an individual may measure his own standards and mode of operation. Development and maintenance of some sort of uniformity in minimum standards of conduct by all members of the profession involve the utilization of a statement of ethics to articulate what those standards are and how they may be maintained. The errant member of the profession who fails to adhere to the minimum standards and to the codes of conduct stated in the canons may be reminded by his peers of such standards, and his deliberate or continued violation of those standards may ultimately be utilized as a means of denying the individual the privilege of continuing his practice in the profession.

The several components of the justice system have their respective canons and codes of ethics. Because there are so many individual professions within the system, there are many more than the few that you will find in this chapter. For example, attorneys have canons of ethics; court administrators, legal secretaries, court reporters, and many others likewise have their own special codes of ethics. In this chapter, we shall discuss the Law Enforcement Canons and Code of Ethics, the Canons of Judicial Ethics, and the Declaration of Principles of the American Correctional Association. Each of these represents the types of professional statements and standards that are characteristic of the several professions represented in the justice system.

Law Enforcement Canons and Code of Ethics

LAW ENFORCEMENT CODE OF ETHICS [2]

As a Law Enforcement Oficer, my fundamental duty is to serve mankind; to safeguard lives and property; to protect the innocent against

[2] Adopted in 1956 by the California Peace Officers Association, and in 1957 by the International Association of Chiefs of Police.

deception, the weak against oppression or intimidation, and the peaceful against violence or disorder; and to respect the Constitutional rights of all men to liberty, equality and justice.

I will keep my private life unsullied as an example to all; maintain courageous calm in the face of danger, scorn, or ridicule; develop self-restraint; and be constantly mindful of the welfare of others. Honest in thought and deed in both my personal and official life, I will be exemplary in obeying the laws of the land and the regulations of my department. Whatever I see or hear of a confidential nature or that is confided to me in my official capacity will be kept ever secret unless revelation is necessary in the performance of my duty.

I will never act officiously or permit personal feelings, prejudices, animosities, or friendships to influence my decisions. With no compromise for crime and with relentless prosecution of criminals, I will enforce the law courteously and appropriately without fear or favor, malice or ill will, never employing unnecessary force or violence and never accepting gratuities.

I recognize the badge of my office as a symbol of public faith, and I accept it as a public trust to be held so long as I am true to the ethics of the police service. I will constantly strive to achieve these objectives and ideals, dedicating myself before God to my chosen profession . . . law enforcement.

CANONS OF POLICE ETHICS [3]

Article 1.   Primary Responsibility of Job

The primary responsibility of the police service, and of the individual officer is the protection of the people of the United States through the upholding of their laws; chief among these is the Constitution of the United States and its amendments. The law enforcement officer always represents the whole of the community and its legally expressed will and is never the arm of any political party or clique.

Article 2.   Limitations of Authority

The first duty of a law enforcement officer, as upholder of the law, is to know its bounds upon him in enforcing it. Because he represents the legal will of the community, be it local, state or federal, he must be aware of the limitations and prescriptions which the people, through law, have placed upon him. He must recognize the genius of the American system of government which give to no man, groups of men or institution, absolute

[3] Composed in 1957 by a Committee of the International Association of Chiefs of Police, Inc. consisting of the following: Andrew J. Kavanaugh, Franklin M. Kreml, and Quinn Tamm.

power, and he must insure that he, as a prime defender of that system, does not pervert its character.

Article 3. Duty to be Familiar with the Law and with Responsibilities of Self and other Public Officials

The law enforcement officer shall assiduously apply himself to the study of the principles of the laws which he is sworn to uphold. He will make certain of his responsibilities in the particulars of their enforcement, seeking aid from his superiors in matters of technicality or principle when these are not clear to him; he will make special effort to fully understand his relationship to other public officials, including other law enforcement agencies, particularly on matters of jurisdiction, both geographically and substantively.

Article 4. Utilization of Proper Means to Gain Proper Ends

The law enforcement officer shall be mindful of his responsibility to pay strict heed to the selection of means in discharging the duties of his office. Violations of law or disregard for public safety and property on the part of an officer are intrinsically wrong; they are self-defeating in that they instill in the public mind a like disposition. The employment of illegal means, no matter how worthy the end, is certain to encourage disrespect for the law and its officers. If the law is to be honored, it must first be honored by those who enforce it.

Article 5. Cooperation with Public Officials in the Discharge of Their Authorized Duties

The law enforcement officer shall cooperate fully with other public officials in the discharge of authorized duties, regardless of party affiliation or personal prejudice. He shall be meticulous, however, in assuring himself of the propriety, under the law, of such actions and shall guard against the use of his office or person, whether knowingly or unknowingly, in any improper or illegal action. In any situation open to question, he shall seek authority from his superior officer, giving him a full report of the proposed service or action.

Article 6. Private Conduct

The law enforcement officer shall be mindful of his special identification by the public as an upholder of the law. Laxity of conduct or manner in private life, expressing either disrespect for the law or seeking to gain special privilege, cannot but reflect upon the police officer and the police service. The community and the service require that the law enforcement officer lead the life of a decent and honorable man. Following the career of a policeman gives no man special prerequisites. It does give the satisfaction and pride of following and furthering an unbroken tradition of safeguarding the American republic. The officer who reflects upon this tradition will not degrade it. Rather, he will so conduct his private life that the public will regard him as an example of stability, fidelity, and morality.

Article 7. Conduct Toward the Public

The law enforcement officer, mindful of his responsibility to the whole community, shall deal with individuals of the community in a manner calculated to instill respect for its laws and its police service. The law enforcement officer shall conduct his official life in a manner such as will inspire confidence and trust. Thus, he will be neither overbearing nor subservient, as no individual citizen has an obligation to stand in awe of him nor a right to command him. The officer will give service where he can, and require compliance with the law. He will do neither from personal preference or prejudice but rather as a duly appointed officer of the law discharging his sworn obligation.

Article 8. Conduct in Arresting and Dealing with Law Violators

The law enforcement officer shall use his powers of arrest strictly in accordance with the law and with due regard to the rights of the citizen concerned. His office gives him no right to prosecute the violator nor to mete out punishment for the offense. He shall, at all times, have a clear appreciation of his responsibilities and limitations regarding detention of the violator; he shall conduct himself in such a manner as will minimize the possibility of having to use force. To this end he shall cultivate a dedication to the service of the people and the equitable upholding of their laws whether in the handling of law violators or in dealing with the lawabiding.

Article 9. Gifts and Favors

The law enforcement officer, representing government, bears the heavy responsibility of maintaining, in his own conduct, the honor and integrity of all government institutions. He shall, therefore, guard against placing himself in a position in which any person can expect special consideration or in which the public can reasonably assume that special consideration is being given. Thus, he should be firm in refusing gifts, favors, or gratuities, large or small, which can, in the public mind, be interpreted as capable of influencing his judgment in the discharge of his duties.

Article 10. Presentation of Evidence

The law enforcement officer shall be concerned equally in the prosecution of the wrong-doer and the defense of the innocent. He shall ascertain what constitutes evidence and shall present such evidence impartially and without malice. In so doing, he will ignore social, political, and all other distinctions among the persons involved, strengthening the tradition of the reliability and integrity of an officer's word.

The law enforcement officer shall take special pains to increase his perception and skill of observation, mindful that in many situations his is the sole impartial testimony to the facts of a case.

Article 11. Attitude Toward Profession

The law enforcement officer shall regard the discharge of his duties as a public trust and recognize his responsibility as a public servant. By diligent study and sincere attention to self-improvement he shall strive to make the best possible application of science to the solution of crime, and, in the field of human relationships, strive for effective leadership and public influence in matters affecting public safety. He shall appreciate the importance and responsibility of his office, and hold police work to be an honorable profession rendering valuable service to his community and his country.

CANONS OF JUDICIAL ETHICS [4]

Canon 1. A judge should uphold the integrity and independence of the judiciary.

Canon 2. A judge should perform the duties of his office fairly and diligently.

Canon 3. A judge may engage in activities for the improvement of the law, the legal system, and the administration of justice.

Canon 4. A judge should regulate his extra-judicial activities to minimize conflict with his judicial duties.

Canon 5. A judge should avoid impropriety and the appearance of impropriety in all of his activities.

Canon 6. A judge should publicly report compensation received for quasi-judicial and extra-judicial activities.

Canon 7. A judge should not engage in political activity except to the extent necessary to obtain or retain judicial office through an elective process.

DECLARATION OF PRINCIPLES OF
THE AMERICAN CORRECTIONAL ASSOCIATION [5]

PREAMBLE

The American Congress of Correction, to reaffirm the basic ideals and aspirations of its membership, to encourage a more enlightened criminal

[4] Presented by United States Supreme Court Chief Justice Warren E. Burger at Williamsburg, Virginia in March, 1971. Prepared by a Committee of the American Bar Association in February, 1971, this was presented as the sixth draft of that document. Taken from: *Addresses and Papers of the National Conference on the Judiciary, March 11–14, 1971 at Williamsburg, Virginia* (Washington, D.C.: Government Printing Office), *Justice in the States*, p. 25.

[5] American Correctional Association, *Manual of Correctional Standards* (College Pk., Md.: American Correctional Association, 1959), pp. XIX–XXIV. The document was first prepared by the American Prison Association in 1870. It was revised and reaffirmed in 1930 and again in 1960 by the American Correctional Association.

justice in our society, to promote improved practices in the treatment of adult and juvenile offenders, and to rededicate its membership to the high purposes stated by its founding leaders in 1870, does adopt this revised Declaration of Principles.

Principle I

The prevention and control of crime and delinquency are urgent challenges to the social sciences. The growing body of scientific knowledge, coupled with the practical wisdom and skill of those professionally engaged in society's struggle with the problem of criminality, provide the soundest basis for effective action.

Principle II

The forces for the prevention and control of crime and delinquency ultimately must find their strength from the constructive qualities of the society itself. The properly functioning basic institutions—such as the family, the school and the church, as well as the economic and political institutions—and a society united in the pursuit of worthwhile goals are the best guarantees against crime and delinquency. The willingness of the society to maintain a rationally organized and properly financed system of corrections, directed toward the reclamation of criminals and juvenile delinquents, is a prerequisite of effective control.

Principle III

Both punishment and correction are at present our methods of preventing and controlling crime and delinquency. Further improvement and expansion of the correctional methods should be the generally accepted goal, fully in line with the spirit of the penal reform of the past century and our current correctional progress.

Principle IV

Traditionally, violators of the criminal law have been differentiated into those who are mentally sick and should be handled as such and those who are considered criminally responsible. The best legal and psychiatric knowledge should be employed to define this distinction.

Principle V

Until the guilt of the suspected offender has been established in the course of due process of law, he should be considered innocent and his rights as a free citizen should be respected, except for such restraints as are indispensable to insure the proper investigation and trial.

Principle VI

If, as a result of a miscarriage of justice, an individual has been made to suffer, he should receive reasonable indemnification.

Principle VII

The correctional facilities, comprising both institutional and non-institutional treatment—probation and parole—should be planned and organized as an integrated system under a central authority responsible for guiding, controlling, unifying, and vitalizing the whole.

Principle VIII

The variety of treatment programs corresponding to the different needs of the offenders suggests a diversification of correctional institutions resulting in a system of specialized institutions so classified and coordinated and so organized in staff and program as to meet the needs of those offenders who present specific problems. The spirit of continued experimentation with new types of institutions and agencies which show promise of more effective results should be encouraged and supported.

Principle IX

Repeated short sentences imposed for recurring misdemeanors or petty offenses, are ineffective, both as means of correction and as a punitive deterrent. These sentences often are a contributing factor in the career of the petty recidivist. An integrated system of control by means of special institutional facilities and community supervision is essental for the solution of this problem. Further research and experimentation with agencies and institutions of other than the conventional type offer the greatest promise.

Principle X

The architecture and construction of penal and correction institutions should be functionally related to the programs to be carried on in them. The great variety of existing programs, to be further diversified in the future, indicates the need for a similar variety and flexibility of architectural design and type of construction. The building standards and technological advances of the day should be reflected in these institutions. The current scepticism about inordinately large institutions suggests the desirability of institutions of moderate size, which may be more costly to build and operate, but which lend themselves better to the fulfillment of the objectives of a good correctional institutional program.

Principal XI

The organization and administration of correctional institutions and agencies is one of the more complex. areas of public administration and deals with one of the most involved of social problems. It is essential that the administration of the correctional agencies meet the highest standards of public administration and that all employees be selected in accordance with the best available criteria and serve on the basis of merit and tenure systems.

Principle XII

The special and complex problems characteristic of criminal and delinquent behavior imply the need for suitable personality traits and specialized skills on the part of the personnel and hence the need for special professional education and training of a high standard, including preservice and continued in-service training.

Principle XIII

Correctional institutions and agencies can best achieve their goal of rehabilitation by focusing their attention and resources on the complete study and evaluation of the individual offender and by following a program of individualized treatment.

Principle XIV

The sentence or disposition determining the treatment for the offender should be based on a full consideration of the social and personality factors of the particular individual.

In the many jurisdictions these investigations may be made at different levels, so long as the essential information is available to the court or treatment authority at the time crucial case decisions are to be made.

Principle XV

A punitive sentence should properly be commensurate with the seriousness of the offense and the guilt of the offender. Inequality of such sentences for the same or similar crimes is always experienced as an injustice both by the offender and the society. On the other hand, the length of the correctional treatment given the offender for purposes of rehabilitation depends on the circumstances and characteristics of the particular offender and may have no relationship to the seriousness of the crime committed. In a correctionally oriented system of crime control, the indeterminate sentence administered by qualified personnel offers the best solution.

Principle XVI

The principles of humanity and human dignity to which we subscribe, as well as the purposes of rehabilitation require that the offenders, while under the jurisdiction of the law enforcement and correctional agencies, be accorded the generally accepted standards of decent living and decent human relations.

Their food, clothing and shelter should not be allowed to fall below the generally accepted standards, and they should be afforded the conventional conveniences made possible by our technological progress. Their health needs—both physical and mental—should be met in accordance with the best medical standards. Recreation should be recognized as a wholesome element of normal life.

Principle XVII

Religion represents a rich resource in the moral and spiritual regeneration of mankind. Especially trained chaplains, religious instruction and counseling, together with adequate facilities for group worship of the inmate's own choice, are essential elements in the program of a correctional institution.

Principle XVIII

Rewards for conformance to the highest values of our culture should be given precedence over fear of punishment in guiding the development of human character in correctional systems as well as in society at large. Enlightened self-interest must be emphasized and made operative at all times.

Principle XIX

No law, procedure or system of correction should deprive any offender of the hope and the possibility of his ultimate return to full, responsible membership in society.

Principle XX

Moral forces, organized persuasion and scientific treatment should be relied upon in the control and management of offenders, with as little dependence upon physical force as possible.

Principle XXI

The task of evaluating the individual offender and developing the most appropriate treatment program must draw upon all the available knowledge and professional skill represented by sociology, psychology, psychiatry, social case work and related disciplines. Specialists and technicians from these fields must be welded into a diagnostic and treatment team by competent administrators, so that the disciplines they represent may become the core of the correctional treatment program.

Principle XXII

To assure the eventual restoration of the offender as an economically self-sustaining member of the community, the correctional program must make available to each inmate every opportunity to raise his educational level, improve his vocational competence and skills, and add to his information meaningful knowledge about the world and the society in which he must live.

Principle XXIII

To hold employable offenders in correctional institutions without the opportunity to engage in productive work is to violate one of the essential objectives of rehabilitation. Without in any way exploiting the labor of involuntary confines for financial gain, or unduly interfering with free enterprise, it is not only possible but imperative that all governmental jurisdictions give full cooperation to the establishment of productive work programs with a view to imparting acceptable work skills, habits, attitudes and work discipline.

Principle XXIV

Some of the criminal law violators who are found by the courts to be criminally responsible, but who are abnormal from the point of view of the modern disciplines of psychiatry and psychology, are in need of psychotherapy. Diagnostic and treatment facilities for such mentally abnormal offenders should be further developed at the appropriate stages of the correctional process.

Psychiatric and psychological services should be provided for the pre-sentence investigations of the courts; out-patient clinics for the use of the non-institutional treatment agencies—probation and parole; and psychiatric and psychological services within the penal and correctional institutions, even to the extent of developing special institutions for this type of offender.

Principle XXV

Recent research in the community aspects of the institutional populations suggests the importance of the group approach to the problem of correctional treatment. There is a need for more attention to the implications of this new method as well as the need to support and promote experiments and demonstration projects.

Principle XXVI

The exercise of executive clemency in the pardon of criminals is a question of great delicacy and difficulty. The use of this power should be limited largely to cases of wrongful conviction, or of excessive sentences constituting injustice, or, in rare instances, where extreme hardship is involved and executive dispensation is warranted. The practice of releasing large numbers of prisoners by executive clemency is generally condemned. The use of executive clemency or pardon to restore civil rights to a fully rehabilitated person who has established a record of responsible living for a period of years is, on the other hand, to be commended.

Principle XXVII

Suitable employment for a discharged or paroled offender is one of the major factors in his rehabilitation and the regaining of his lost position in society. The most forceful efforts and comprehensive methods should be exercised to secure such work. An understanding, favorable attitude and the participation of organized labor and management should be actively sought.

Principle XXVIII

Probation has come to be accepted as the most efficient and economical method of treatment for a great number of offenders. To enhance the achievement of the full potentialities of probation, mandatory exceptions to the use of probation with respect to specific crimes or to types of offenders should be eliminated from the statutes.

Current research indicates great possiblities for developing specific types and degrees of probationary supervision adapted to the needs of the individual offender.

Principle XXIX

With a few possible exceptions, all offenders released from correctional institutions should be released under parole supervision, and parole should be granted at the earliest date consistent with public safety and the needs of rehabilitation. Decisions pertaining to an individual's parole should be made by a professionally competent board. The type and degree of supervision should be adapted to the needs of the individual offender.

Principle XXX

The collection and publication of criminal statistics designed to provide information on the extent and nature of criminality and juvenile delinquency and on the various phases of the correctional process is indispensable for the understanding of crime and for the planning and evaluation of correctional and preventive measures.

Such statistics are necessary and should be developed on the national, state and local levels and should consist of statistics of the offenses known to the police, arrest statistics, judicial statistics, probation, institutional and parole statistics as well as criminal career records.

Principle XXXI

Research and the scientific study of the problems of juvenile delinquency and criminality and of the methods of dealing with these are essential prerequisites for progress. Through its educational, research and governmental institutions society should sponsor, finance and carry out both basic and applied research in this area. The law enforcement and correctional institutions and agencies should lend their support, take initiative and themselves engage in appropriate research as an indispensable part of their effort to improve their performance.

Principle XXXII

In a democracy the success of any public agency, including that of correctional institutions and agencies, depends in the final analysis on popular support. An adequate financial base, emphasis on the adequacy of personnel and, in general, insistence on an alert and progressive administration in corrections is the responsibility of the public and a function of its enlightened concern with crime and delinquency problems.

Principle XXXIII

The correctional process has as its aim the re-incorporation of the offender into the society as a normal citizen. In the course of non-institutional treatment the offender continues as a member of the conventional community. In the course of his institutional stay constructive community contacts should be encouraged. The success of the correctional process in all its stages can be greatly enhanced by energetic, resourceful and organized citizen participation.

Summary

Professionalism involves more than the completion of a college baccalaureate program. There is a personal commitment also involved, which extends beyond the normal "job requirements" of any occupation. A common body of knowledge is essential to provide the base for the profession, a minimum educational requirement is imposed to assure acquisition of that body of knowledge, and along with the assimilation of information and development of proficiencies required of the profession there is a free exchange of information concerning techniques and procedures, including what might be considered in business and industry as "trade secrets." A true professional zealously exchanges information as the possessor of a trade secret zealously guards its confidentiality. Selection of individuals who are to become members of a profession, and regulation of the membership through enforcement of rigid professional standards are prime requisites for professionalism. Many of the occupations in the justice system already meet the specifications of true professions according to the prerequisites discussed in this chapter, and as illustrated in their codes of ethics or statements of principles. Many other occupations are emerging as professions.

Ethics of professionals include attitudes as well as personal and public commitments to service. There is a general preparation statement in the code of ethics, which involves an attitude of "service above self," or "equal service to all people," or—as stated in the Law Enforcement Code of Ethics—"my fundamental duty is to serve mankind; to safeguard lives and property; to protect the innocent against deception, the weak against oppression or intimidation, and the peaceful against violence or disorder; and to respect the Constitutional rights of all men to liberty, equality, and justice." Other aspects of professionalism that are articulated through the media of statements of principles and codes of ethics involve selflessness, exemplary morality, serving as a model to aspirants to the same profession and an example of the profession to the community. Use of one's professional status to gain special favors, gratuities, or positions of advantage is similarly forbidden by one's professional membership. In addition to the profession itself recognizing certain individuals as "professionals," there is an extremely important consideration: public acknowledgement.

Exercises and Study Questions

1. What are the factors that distinguish a *calling* as a *profession?*

2. Do you agree with the statement that professionals should not zealously guard trade secrets as one would do in business and industry?

3. Why is it so important that individuals in the justice system professions be so careful about the conduct of their private lives?

4. What are the pre-entry educational requirements for the profession you have selected for your occupational goal?

5. Regarding the decision-making prerogative of a professional, is it wise to extend this prerogative to the field police officer and allow him to make the decision whether to prosecute someone for a felony?

6. Continuing with the decision-making prerogative of a professional, what types of constraints should be imposed upon the police officer? the prosecuting attorney? the judge? the probation officer?

7. List at least three things that the agency should provide for its employees in recognition of their professional stature.

8. How would you distinguish between a true professional compared with another type of employee?

9. Give an example of how acceptance of a gratuity could later "backfire."

10. Explain the general theme of each of the professional ethics and/or principles of each of the three components of the justice system: law enforcement, judicial process, and corrections.

11. Recommended semester project: Write a paper on professionalization as it affects one of the components of the justice system.

Suggested for Additional Study

ADAMS, THOMAS F., *Criminal Justice Reading*. Pacific Palisades, Calif.: Goodyear Publishing Co., Inc., 1972. A section of this book of carefully selected readings is devoted to police professionalism.

American Correctional Association, *Manual of Correctional Standards*. College Park, Md.: American Correctional Association, 1959.

LaFAVE, WAYNE R., *Arrest: The Decision to Take a Suspect into Custody*. Boston: Little, Brown, and Company, 1965.

SKOLNICK, JEROME, *Justice Without Trial: Law Enforcement in Democratic Society*. New York: John Wiley & Sons, Inc., 1966.

WILSON, JAMES Q., *Varieties in Police Behavior: The Management of Law and Order in Eight Communities*. Cambridge: Harvard University Press, 1968.

WILSON, O. W., *Police Planning* (2nd Ed.). Springfield, Ill.: Charles C Thomas, 1962.

10

Constitutional Considerations
in Justice Administration

Introduction

When John Hancock and his colleagues signed the Declaration of Independence on July 4, 1776, it included an extensive list of grievances against the tyranny of King George III. The purpose of the document was to declare the independence of the Colonies from England and the King's oppression. The document also included a statement supporting the new nation's secession from the mother country that in effect stated that governments should not be changed for "light and transient causes," but "when a long train of abuses and usurpations, pursuing invariably the same Object evinces a design to reduce them under absolute Despotism, it is their right, it is their duty, to throw off such Government, and to provide new Guards for their future security." The Declaration reflected the philosophy of the men who fashioned the framework for the newly formed independent government: "We hold these truths to be self-evident, that all men are created equal, that they are endowed by their Creator with certain unalienable Rights, that among these are Life, Liberty, and the pursuit of Happiness.—That to secure these rights, Governments are instituted among Men, deriving their just powers from the consent of the governed. . . ."

The statesmen who took part in the framing of the Declaration of Independence also set about the task of establishing the new government of the United States of America with the following selfless pledge: "And for the support of this Declaration, with a firm reliance on the protection of Divine Providence, we mutually pledge to each other our

Lives, our Fortunes and our sacred Honor." Those same men had very definite ideas as to the rights and privileges of the individual in this great new country and his relationship with his government "of the people, by the people, and for the people." The purpose of government is to insure all people in the nation that they shall equally enjoy the rights of "Life, Liberty and the pursuit of Happiness." The right of the government to govern comes from the will of the people, it was also pointed out in the document.

The people in the United States of America have the fundamental right to be free and enjoy their liberties but also the right to be secure and have protection against others who would interfere with their rights to "Life, Liberty, and the pursuit of Happiness." When the authors of the United States Constitution met, they obviously had those rights in mind, as reflected in the Preamble:

> We the people of the United States, in Order to form a more perfect Union, establish Justice, insure domestic Tranquility, provide for the common defence, promote the general Welfare, and secure the Blessings of Liberty to ourselves and our Posterity, do ordain and establish this Constitution for the United States of America.

By virtue of police power, the nation's hundreds of thousands of local, state, and federal criminal justice professionals have the responsibility and the authority to maintain an ordered liberty through the exercise of their respective duties. They must enforce the Constitution, and they, too, must be governed by its requirements. In their respective duties, the individuals in the justice system should be guided by this statement by Justice Brandeis in *Olmstead* v. *United States*.[1] Frequently referred to in recent cases, this has been considered a guiding view in judicial philosophy. Justice Brandeis wrote these words in his dissenting opinion:

> Decency, security and liberty alike demand that government officials shall be subjected to the same rules of conduct that are commands to the citizen. In a government of laws, existence of the government will be imperilled if it fails to observe the law scrupulously. Our Government is the potent, the omnipresent teacher. For good or for ill, it teaches the whole people by its example. Crime is contagious. If the Government becomes a lawbreaker, it breeds contempt for law; it invites every man to become a law himself; it invites anarchy. To declare that in the administration of the criminal law the end justifies the means—to declare that the Government may commit crimes in order to secure the conviction of a

[1] 277 U.S. 438,485.

private criminal—would bring terrible retribution. Against that pernicious doctrine this Court should resolutely set its face.

The U.S. and State Constitutions

For the purpose of restricting the material to the subject of the text, let us study those portions of the constitutions that are related to the law enforcement and criminal justice role and begin with the U.S. Constitution, which is the supreme law of the land.

Sections 8 and 9, Article I, list many of the powers of Congress, so that they may provide for the common defense and general welfare of the United States. Among those laws are the powers to fix the standard of weights and measures, to provide for punishment of violators of laws prohibiting counterfeiting U.S. coins or securities, copyright and patent law, to define and punish for violations of the laws on the high seas, and to provide for organizing a militia and for calling it forth in times when it is needed to suppress insurrections and repel invasions. The Constitution also provides that the privileges of the writ of habeas corpus shall not be suspended unless the public safety may require it in cases of rebellion or invasion. The Congress may also make any laws necessary to carry out the many powers vested by the Constitution in the Government of the United States or any of its officers.

Section 2 of Article IV provides for interstate extradition of a person charged in any state for treason, a felony, or any other crime who flees from justice and is found in another state. On demand of the executive authority of the state from which he fled, the person shall be delivered to a representative of that authority so that he may be returned to the state having jurisdiction over the crime. The same section provides that the citizens of each state shall be entitled to all privileges and immunities of citizens in the several states, which is repeated and broadened in the Fourteenth Amendment.

The various state constitutions are separate and distinct from the United States Constitution. For many years, it was the interpretation of the Supreme Court that the specific provisions of the Constitution, particularly the Bill of Rights, applied only to judicial affairs of the United States courts and not to the individual states. During the past three decades, however, there have been some significant changes. The philosophy during recent years has been that the United States Constitution and its Amendments are to be enforced by state legislation and by the state judicial and police officers. This trend will be particularly noticeable when we discuss later the provisions of the Bill of Rights.

The state constitutions are each original documents and vary in language and total content, but they are basically similar in that they set forth the mechanics for the government, and they also include sections that are similar to the first ten amendments to the United States Constitution, the Bill of Rights. For example, the California Constitution contains a Declaration of Rights in Article I. Some of the sections deal with the following rights:

> *Section 1.* All men are by nature free and independent, and have certain inalienable rights; among which are those of enjoying and defending life and liberty; acquiring, possessing, and protecting property; and pursuing and obtaining safety and happiness.

This section provides for the police power of the state, and case decisions have held that the exercise of police power by a state is solely for the welfare of the *public* as opposed to individuals. Persons and property are subject to certain restraints and burdens to secure the general welfare of the state.

> *Section 2.* All political power is inherent in the people. Government is instituted for the protection, security, and benefit of the people, and they have the right to alter or reform the same whenever the public good may require it.

Cases related to this section point out that an individual who becomes a member of the society under our form of constitutional government does surrender some of his personal rights but only to the extent that such relinquishment may be necessary for the common good.

Section 3 declares that the State of California is an inseparable part of the American Union, and the Constitution of the United States is the supreme law of the land. State sovereignty is defined as the role of the states and their relationship with the federal government.

> To the Federal Government is delegated the exercise of certain rights or powers of sovereignty; and the exercise of all other rights of sovereignty, except as expressly prohibited, is reserved to the people of the respective states, or vested by them in their local governments.

Section 4 provides for religious freedom, and Section 5 provides that the privileges of the writ of habeas corpus shall not be suspended except when such suspension shall be necessary because of a rebellion or invasion. Section 6 prohibits excessive bail, unusual punishment, and the detention of witnesses in places where criminals are imprisoned.

Other sections of the California constitution bear a remarkable resemblance to certain portions of the United States Constitution, and are duplicated—in philosophy rather than in exact words or the same location in the documents—in numerous other constitutions. These provide for the right to trial by jury, freedom of speech and of the press, and the right to assemble and petition. Due process of law and its administration according to the legal and proper rules is required by the Constitution, as are the right to a speedy trial and protection against unreasonable search and seizure.

Police Power

There is no single document in the United States system of government that provides for police power. The federal police power is described in the Constitution, which lists the specific instances under which certain laws found in Section 8 of Article I are made and enforced. Primary police power in the United States rests with the individual states, which have the inherent power to legislate for the preservation of peace and protection of the public health, morals, safety, and welfare.

The states depend upon the county and city governments and their police agencies to enforce the major portion of the laws enacted by the states and to pass local ordinances to meet the needs of the respective jurisdictions, providing that the local laws are not in conflict with the state laws. During recent years, many local ordinances have been declared null and void on the premise that specific areas have been preempted by state laws and, therefore, the local government cannot enact new laws in those areas because of the conflicting problems involved in their enforcement. Most of those laws have been in the categories of vice and disorderly conduct.

Within the limitations provided by the Constitution, the state legislatures are responsible for defining the police powers in each respective state. What is "public welfare" is for the courts to decide, and the ultimate determination as to whether or not the laws enacted by the legislative police power and enforced by the many governmental enforcement agencies—and the criminal justice system in general—are reasonable and consistent with the Constitution and public policy also rests with the courts. As it was pointed out earlier in this chapter, use of the police power must be for the public good. The principal control designed to assure the people that there shall not be excessive use or abuse of police power is Section 1 of the Fourteenth Amendment to the U.S. Constitution, which states in part:

> . . . No State shall make or enforce any law which shall abridge the privileges or immunities of citizens of the United States; nor shall any

State deprive any person of life, liberty, or property, without due process of law; nor deny to any person with in its jurisdiction the equal protection of the laws.

The Bill of Rights

The first ten amendments to the U.S. Constitution are better known as the Bill of Rights and were added to the original document just a few months after ratification of the Constitution itself. They include some of the unalienable rights that were alluded to in the Declaration of Independence written several years earlier. They should be zealously guarded by everyone in the United States, particularly the local police departments who have the sworn duty to preserve the public peace and to protect lives and property. One very important fact that should never be overlooked with respect to the Bill of Rights is that along with the rights goes a corresponding set of responsibilities to assure liberty to others as well as to self. Madison said: "Liberty may be endangered by the abuses of liberty as well as by the abuses of power." And Oliver Wendell Holmes, Jr. illustrated the premise that all rights are relative, not absolute, and must be exercised within limits, by stating that freedom of speech does not include the right to falsely shout, "Fire!" in a crowded theater.

> *Article I.* Congress shall make no law respecting an establishment of religion, or prohibiting the free exercise thereof; or abridging the freedom of speech, or of the press; or the right of the people peaceably to assemble, and to petition the Government for a redress of grievances.

Free speech is limited in such cases when such speech or publications are obscene, or tend to disturb the peace, or advocate the overthrow of the established government. The freedom also does not include speech or publications that are designed or intended to incite to treason, rebellion, the commission of crimes, of disobedience of or disrespect for the law. A person may speak of his intense hatred, but he may not incite others to commit such acts as to riot. People may assemble to picket in a peaceful manner and shall not be inhibited except when they commit some criminal act, such as trespass on private property, or do malicious mischief to personal property, or when their gathering purpose shows evidence of changing its nature to one with the purpose of committing some criminal act. In the latter case, the assembly becomes an unlawful assembly.

The police role with respect to Article I involves one of visiting or observing an assemblage of people to ascertain its lawful nature.

The police are responsible for the maintenance of peace, and there may be good cause for the officers to remain present or nearby to assure the continued peaceful and lawful nature of the assembly. Published material is of no official concern to the police unless there is a violation of the law involved. The police are not censors, nor should they be. It is merely the responsibility of the police to enforce the law as it is written and intended. Pornography is illegal filth, but just exactly where the separation lies between what is pornographic and what is acceptable is a matter of interpretation, and the interpretations vary with the changing times and the interpreters. Many supreme and lesser courts have repeatedly stated that "pornography" is virtually impossible to define. Recent trends have been to gauge "decency" on local *community standards,* whatever they might be at a given time and place.

> *Article II.* A well regulated Militia, being necessary to the security of a free State, the right of the people to keep and bear Arms, shall not be infringed.

The courts have held that the right to bear arms means that a person has the right to possess firearms and to use them in defense of self or property. The courts have also held that the states may make whatever laws they deem necessary to regulate the possession and carrying of firearms, such as the prohibition against aliens or felons possessing or carrying guns. Carrying certain weapons concealed or mere possession of certain other types of weapons, such as machine guns without specific legal cause or compliance with other regulations, is not unlawful for the various legislative bodies to prescribe or proscribe. When the public safety demands it, the police have a duty to search persons known or suspected of having weapons on their person or in their possession, to confiscate the weapons, and to arrest the persons for violations of the laws.

> *Article III.* No soldier shall, in time of peace, be quartered in any house without the consent of the owner, nor in time of war but in a manner to be prescribed by law.

This article of the Bill of Rights was intended to prohibit the quartering of military troops in private residences, in the manner practiced by the British Army in the American Colonies. It would apply equally to any police agency that would entertain any inclinations of a similar nature.

> *Article IV.* The right of the people to be secure in their persons, houses, papers, and effects, against unreasonable searches and seizures, shall not

be violated, and no Warrants shall issue, but upon probable cause, supported by Oath or affirmation, and particularly describing the place to be searched, and the persons or things to be seized.

The article was originally designed as a protection against abusive practices that had been the rule rather than the exception for the British Army and from which the framers of the Bill of Rights sought protection. The purpose for such a rule was explained in 1948 by the Supreme Court in *United States* v. *DiRe,* 332 U.S. 581, 595:

> . . . the forefathers, after consulting the lessons of history, designed our Constitution to place obstacles in the way of a too permeating police surveillance, which they seemed to think was a greater danger to a free people than the escape of some criminals from punishment.

The provision requiring an affidavit for a search warrant was designed to prevent the practice of police "fishing expeditions."

A key word in the article is "unreasonable," which is sometimes erroneously used synonymously with the word "illegal." The officer's actions in situations involving searches must be based upon "probable" or "reasonable" cause, and those two words may be used interchangeably. For many years, until 1961 actually, the states each had the complete freedom to make their own rules on search and seizure and were not directly involved with the specific wording of federal rules. Although some states had previously had state supreme court rulings that applied the federal rule as to the reasonableness of searches and seizures, it was not until 1961 when the United States Supreme Court ruled in *Mapp* v. *Ohio,* 367 U.S. 643 that, as a matter of constitutional law, the federal "exclusionary rule" [2] applied to the several states as well as the agencies of the federal government. The states may continue to rule on their own specific cases, but they shall not violate the standards in the Fourth Amendment, so stated the court.

John Edgar Hoover, late Director of the Federal Bureau of Investigation and defender of positive police practices under the law, wrote in the *Iowa Law Review* (Winter 1952): "Law enforcement, however, in defeating the criminal, must maintain inviolate the historic liberties of the individual." Judge Lewis, of the Tenth U.S. Circuit Court of Appeals, wrote in *Anspach* v. *United States* 305 R. 2d48 (1958):

> But the prevention and detection of crime is not a polite business and we see no need or justification for reading into the Fourth Amendment

---

[2] The exclusionary rule referred to in this instance is that evidence that is acquired by means of an unreasonable search shall be "excluded" or held inadmissable at the trial.

a standard of conduct for law enforcement officials which would leave society at the mercy of those dedicated to the destruction of the very freedoms guaranteed by the Constitution. The "pursuit of happiness" referred to by Justice Brandeis in Olmstead can be destroyed by idealistic theory that shuns the deadly realism of crime.

A police chief wrote this about the police process of arrest and search:

> The importance of arrest, and the search incident thereto, cannot be overemphasized. Arrest affects fundamental individual rights to personal liberty and privacy. The strict and technical laws of arrest and search are an effort to balance the right of society, through government, to protect itself and its members against the right of the individual to life, liberty, and the pursuit of happiness. Because of their importance and complexity, the subjects of arrest, search, and seizure have generated a major training problem. Twenty years ago a police recruit would be told all he needed to know about his arrest powers in a few hours.[3]

> *Article V.* No person shall be held to answer for a capital, or otherwise infamous crime, unless on a presentment or indictment of a Grand Jury, except in cases arising in the land or naval forces, or in the Militia, when in actual service in time of War or public danger; nor shall any person be subject for the same offense to be twice put in jeopardy of life or limb; nor shall be compelled in any criminal case to be a witness against himself, nor be deprived of life, liberty, or property, without due process of law; nor shall private property be taken for public use, without just compensation.

The self-incrimination and "due process" clauses of this article are those that affect the police on a more regular basis than the other clauses. The "due process" provision is a reference to the normal and legal procedure, which may not be bypassed for any purpose. Federal police agencies were the first to be instructed and required not only to respect an individual's right against self-incrimination, but they were also required to orally admonish him as to his rights against making any statements that could be used against him in a court of law. This federal rule became known as the McNabb-Mallory Rule, based on two cases in 1943 and 1957 respectively.

A series of cases in various states eventually led to what is now known as the Miranda Rule of the U.S. Supreme Court, rendered by that body on June 13, 1966. The rule applies to the admissibility in court of a person's statements made during a custodial police interrogation, .

---

[3] John P. Howard, "Arrest: An Administrator's View," *Police Work,* April 1971, p. 13.

which means a questioning session during which the subject being questioned was the suspect of a criminal case and the investigation had focused on him at the time. The Supreme Court ruled that the Fifth and Sixth Amendments shall directly be applied to all the states, and that the police shall comply with the rule in the case of all custodial interrogations. The subject must be advised as follows, and he must understand the meaning of what he is being told:

> You have the absolute right to remain silent. Anything you say can, and will, be used against you in court.
>
> You have the right to consult with an attorney, to be represented by an attorney, and to have one present before I ask you any questions.
>
> If you cannot afford an attorney, one will be appointed to represent you before you are questioned, if you desire.

The subject may then waive these rights, and the waiver must be made "voluntarily, knowingly, and intelligently." The Court's rule requires that the officer proceed only after asking the subject: With these rights in mind, are you ready to talk with me about the charges against you? The subject must then reply with an oral affirmative before the officer proceeds. After the interview begins, the subject is given continued protection against himself and any statements he may make by the Court's direction: "If, however, he indicates in any manner and at any state of the process that he wishes to consult with an attorney before speaking there can be no questioning. Likewise, if the individual is alone and indicates in any manner that he does not wish to be interrogated, the police may not question him. The mere fact that he may have answered some questions or volunteered some statements on his own does not deprive him of the right to refrain from answering any further inquiries until he has consulted with an attorney and thereafter consents to be questioned."

> *Article VI.* In all criminal prosecutions, the accused shall enjoy the right to a speedy and public trial, by an impartial jury of the State and district wherein the crime shall have been committed, which district shall have been previously ascertained by law, and to be informed of the nature and cause of the accusation; to be confronted with the witnesses against him; to have compulsory process for obtaining witnesses in his favor, and to have the Assistance of Counsel for his defence.

The speedy trial provision is met by the police officers' taking the suspect before a magistrate without undue delay and filing charges against him. State law requires that the subject of an arrest be specifically advised of the crime for which he is being charged, except that in some cases this advisement may be waived when it is understood exactly why the arrest is being made, such as when an officer arrests the defendant during the actual commission of a crime or following a pursuit immediately following the act. The witnesses against the defendant are presented in court to give their testimony, and at that time may be cross-examined by the defendant or his attorney.

At the outset of the investigation when an identification may be made by a witness from behind a screen or other device that hides the identity of the witness from the suspect, such a procedure is in the best interest of the safety of the witness and it is not a violation of the defendant's rights under authority of the Sixth Amendment. His attorney may utilize an "early discovery" rule that many states have that allows the defense to demand, and receive, copies of statements made by witnesses in a specific case.

There are times when the identity of confidential informants are the source of information that may lead to the institution of an investigation, and for public safety reasons—such as sustaining the life of the informant—the informant is never identified. In this type of case, however, there must be evidence independent of the informant's information that will stand on its own merits and sustain a conviction of the defendant.

> *Article X.* The powers not delegated to the United States by the Constitution, nor prohibited by it to the States, are reserved to the States respectively, or to the people.

Article Ten provides for the primary police power to be vested in the individual states, which are sovereign in our system of government in the United States.

Major Court Decisions

Since its promulgation the Constitution has been the subject of clarification, explanation, and interpretation. Many times the enforcement of law and related police conduct has been the subject of *judicial review*. The activity has been particularly noticeable during the past two decades. The following list outlines a few of the cases that had their most significant effect on police practices. They only illustrate the complexity of a police officer's responsibility to the law through the Bill of Rights.

> *Weeks* v. *United States*, 232 U.S. 383 (1914). Rendered inadmissable any evidence seized by federal agents in violation of search and seizure rules (Fourth Amendment).

Powell v. *Alabama*, 287 U.S. 45 (1932). A defendant's right to counsel at a trial (Fifth and Sixth Amendments).

McNabb v. *United States*, 318 U.S. 322 (1943). Requires a prompt arraignment and "aims to avoid all the implication of secret interrogations of persons accused of crime." A rule for federal officers (Fifth Amendment).

Rochin v. *California*, 342 U.S. 165 (1952). Excludes evidence seized by officers whose conduct "shocks the conscience" according to the courts. Reasonableness of the search must be weighed with other factors, in this case a stomach was pumped to obtain swallowed morphine (Fourth Amendment).

Mallory v. *United States*, 499 (1957). Another case like McNabb involving federal agents that required them to arrest on probable cause, to arraign the accused without unnecessary delay, and to interrogate without delay (Fifth Amendment).

Roviaro v. *United States*, 353 U.S. 53 (1957). When the disclosure of an informant's identity becomes essential for a fair trial or is helpful to the defense, the government must disclose the identity of the informer.

Mapp v. *Ohio*, 367 U.S. 643 (1961). Prohibited unconstitutional searches and seizures by state or local officers, similar to the exclusionary rule set in Weeks in 1914. Applied federal rules to state officers (Fourth and Fourteenth Amendments).

Robinson v. *California*, 370 U.S. 660 (1962). Narcotic addiction is an illness not a crime. A state law that imprisons as a criminal a person thus afflicted inflicts a cruel and unusual punishment in violation of the Fourteenth Amendment.

Gideon v. *Wainright*, 372 U.S. 335 (1963). Right to be represented by an attorney and at state expense if the defendant cannot afford one (Sixth Amendment).

Escobedo v. *Illinois*, 378 U.S. 478 (1964). Right to counsel during private interrogation by the police (Sixth Amendment).

Massiah v. *United States*, 377 U.S. 210 (1964). A defendant has a right to an attorney at any time during or before a trial where the counsel's absence might deprive the accused of a fair trial (Fifth and Sixth Amendments).

Miranda v. *Arizona*, 384 U.S. 436 (1966). Rules established for custodial interrogation and the individual's right to counsel during the accusatory stage (Fifth and Sixth Amendments).

Gilbert v. *California*, 388 U.S. 263 (1967). Handwriting exemplars may be required of a suspect. They are nontestimonial, identifying physical characteristics outside the protection of the Fifth Amendment.

Gault v. *Arizona*, 387 U.S. 1 (1967). Juvenile has a right to be informed of the specific charge against him, a right to counsel, a privilege not to incriminate himself, and a right to due process including cross-examination and confrontation of the witness (Fifth and Sixth Amendments).

United States v. *Wade,* 388 U.S. 218 (1967). Legal counsel should be available to the accused during a lineup for identification (Sixth Amendment).

Terry v. *Ohio,* 392 U.S. 1 (1968). Reinforces the duty requirement of a police officer to stop and frisk a person for weapons under certain conditions. Distinguishes a "stop" from an "arrest" and a "frisk" from a "search" (Fourth Amendment).

Chimel v. *United States,* 395 U.S. 752 (1970). Limits the extent of a search incidental to an arrest without a search warrant, provides for judicial review prior to searching (Fourth Amendment).

Summary

At no other time in the history of the United States has the Constitution played such a leading role in the process of law enforcement. The police officers walk a thin tightrope while preserving the peace and protecting life and property. They, too, must operate within the law and according to the provisions of the Constitution and the Bill of Rights. They have no time to ponder the finer points of constitutional law, and they must act with speed and decisiveness when the occasion arises. When they effect an arrest of a person or a search of his person or property, they must be acting upon good faith and reasonable cause or by authority of a warrant that must be based upon information from a reliable source and with good cause.

The freedom of man is sacred, but liberty is relative and there are certain obligations to other persons and their liberty as well. Each person must meet these obligations if his own liberty and safety are to be preserved and protected. The police power within the United States that is not specifically delegated to the federal government by the Constitution is inherent within the individual states. They have the right and the duty to legislate for the preservation of peace and protection of the public health, morals, safety, and welfare of the community. The police agencies and their officers are responsible for enforcing the police power but with wisdom and proficiency so as to do the most efficient job within the guidelines established by law and the decisions of the Supreme Court.

Exercises and Study Questions

1. Commit to memory (again) the Preamble to the Constitution.
2. Define "police power."

3. The police are the enforcement arm of which branch of government?

4. Of what significance is the Fourteenth Amendment?

5. What is "due process" and how does it involve a criminal investigation?

6. List and discuss at least three examples of abuse of the right to free speech.

7. Of what significance was *Mapp* v. *Ohio* to local law enforcement agencies?

8. What is the Miranda Rule?

9. What is meant by the term "judicial supremacy"?

10. Recommended semester project: List and discuss the major decisions of the U. S. Supreme Court during the past fifteen years. Describe the case in point and discuss the implications of each decision regarding all future police actions.

Suggested for Additional Study

A political science textbook of your choice. Study the Constitution and the Bill of Rights and the courts in the American system of jurisprudence.

The Bill of Rights, A Source Book for Teachers. Sacramento, Calif.: Department of Education, 1967.

LEVY, LEONARD W., *Judicial Review and the Supreme Court.* New York: Harper Torchbooks, Harper and Row, 1967.

SKOLNICK, JEROME H., *Justice Without Trial: Law Enforcement in Democratic Society.* New York: John Wiley and Sons, Inc., 1966.

WESTON, PAUL B. and KENNETH M. WELLS, *Criminal Evidence for Police.* Englewood Cliffs, N.J.: Prentice-Hall, Inc., 1971.

WILSON, JAMES Q., *Varieties of Police Behavior, The Management of Law and Order in Eight Communities.* Cambridge: Harvard University Press, 1968.

11

The Justice System
and the Community

Introduction

Each one of the components of the justice system is a direct representative, an extension, of the public it serves. Responsibility to that public plays a significant part in the discretionary judgment of the individual police officers, judges, institutional employees, probation and parole officers, and the prosecuting attorney, to mention a few. The justice system is providing a series of services for the public, and it must maintain an open line of communications with the individuals in that public to have an exchange of ideas as to the needs and wishes of both practitioner and public. It is a multidirectional communications requirement. I use the word *individual* in this paragraph to emphasize the distinct individuality of the practitioners in the justice system as well as the individuality of the public, which is actually a conglomeration of many publics: the taxpaying public, the parent public, the law-violating public, the law-abiding public, the middle-class public, the rich public, the poor public, the advantaged public, the disadvantaged public, and many composite publics representing two or more classifications of publics. The mere explanation of "public" becomes complex, as it also involves "community," which may be similarly discussed to emphasize the intense individuality of the people who make up the public or the community.

If we expect the people to understand *what* we are doing and *why*, it is our responsibility to explain it to them. After all, it is their interests that we are looking after. Professional prosecutors, judges, police officers, parole and probation officers, court administrators, investigators, and other individuals working in the field of criminal justice have been employed to perform their services in accordance with their respective proficiencies and their discretionary powers. The work is not one for amateurs, and most of the people in the community know that. When the many jobs are being done correctly in an acceptable manner, the general public does not attempt to interfere. There are detractors, of course, and those who will criticize regardless of what is being done, or how.

It is when the police officer, or the judge, or the prosecutor "pulls a boner," or a series of errors that the publics begin expressing their concern. If we are to expect the people who comprise the publics to be able to tell the difference between correct and incorrect procedure, there must be an ongoing educational and informational process so that the people have the information and knowledge that they need. If the justice system provides this information correctly, the agency relationships with the community are enhanced and it is possible to have actual community involvement as well as understanding.

In this chapter we shall discuss the topic of community and justice system relationships from two basic premises: public relations, and community relations. Although the distinction may seem artificial or arbitrary —or both—the deliberate distinction is intended to classify community involvement and interaction as *community relations,* and the usually one-sided public speaking and press-agentry aspects of presenting information to the public as *public relations.*

Community Relations

Mere use of the words seems to imply that some sort of human interaction is involved, that there is some face-to-face, give-and-take interfacing on a "no-host" basis. In this environment of informality and spontaneity the objective of community relations activities is to achieve a mutual understanding between the people in the community and the justice system people who serve them. There can be no single program or activity that is expected to meet this objective. The process is continuous, it is diversified, it is fluid and interrelated with the entire agency's activities, and it involves people in these activities as individuals.

Self-evaluation. Before an agency attempts to widely disseminate details of its activities, there should be a careful study of those activities to determine that they are well-defined and well done. The image that the agency wishes to present should be one that involves both facilities and personnel. Personal conduct should be pleasant and inoffensive. When one has to exercise his authority to accomplish a task it is possible to speak confidently and forcefully without taking on an officious air that will sound pompous and more of a caricature rather that a serious act. Roles are important to social interaction, and it is important that the actors in their respective roles do convincingly look the parts they are playing. Their dress, personal grooming, physical appearance, and mannerisms must be representative of the roles they play if the people are to accept them in those roles.

The building and its offices should be pleasant and nonthreatening, and certain parts of the building should be designed to evoke appropriate responses. For example, the courtroom has many traditions and its design tends to cause its occupants to act in a more subdued manner than they would act in the hallway. The raised bench and the traditional positions for the people who spend their days in the courtroom perpetuate the ceremonial atmosphere of the room and tend to encourage dignified and "courtly" conduct.

Cultural Awareness. Every racial or ethnic culture is steeped in rich tradition that distinguishes that culture from all others, however subtle the differences may seem. Genuine sincerity in attempts to develop an understanding in a culture other than one's own is an admirable trait. It is not enough for a justice system practitioner to refrain from demonstrating prejudicial views, or to be tolerant of others; what he must do is to actually make it a point to develop his own awareness of the cultures and traditions of people with whom he works and for whom he serves in his public service occupation. Along with this understanding, it is extremely important that there be a deliberate avoidance of the use of "trigger words," or those words that tend to evoke the ire of those to whom the words may apply—by inference if not by actual intention.

Professional Conduct. Both on and off the job, the professional should continue to play the role, which means that he or she is under close observation by everyone who knows him or her as a representative of the justice system. There is a quiet dignity to the professional when the role is cast in the theater. The public that is responsible for payment of a professional's salary similarly expects the "real-life" players to possess similar qualities. If those qualities are unrealistic and need modification, then it is time that the actual players in the process bring about that change.

An objective, impartial attitude may be reflected in the individual's actions, and he must refrain from a display of personal involvement in someone's personal problems that present themselves to him while he

is working. A calm and detached manner is far more effective than subjective emotionalism. Gratuities and special favors should not be accepted
because of the ethical considerations involved, in addition to other considerations. The justice system practitioner must be approachable and a
good listener, and should avoid being a "busybody" or meddler.

Community Assistance.   If we are to effectively serve the community on the basis of real needs that the people have identified to the
different components of the justice system, we must have the community's
assistance. Use of advisory committees to determine the temper and
priorities that exist in the eyes of the community is an effective method
for getting feedback from the community. Careful selection of community representatives is critical. Unless the selection method is designed
to choose true leaders in the community, the agency doing the selecting
may discover that it is creating its own "community representatives" who
represent no one but themselves. Such a selection may also tend to
alienate those so-called leaders from the community they are supposed
to represent, while a true leader in the community would probably
not suffer from alienation. In fact, his position may be strengthened by
such an affiliation, because the people he represents would be confident
that he would not serve as a "rubber stamp" for anyone.

Volunteers.   The use of volunteers or similar aides in some paraprofessional capacity stimulates community interest in many of the
criminal justice operations that would otherwise go unnoticed. The utilization of interns, cadets, or community service representatives within the
agency also provides financial assistance to students who are preparing
for professional positions within the system. The individual who is employed by an agency and who finds that his work is rewarding and challenging does not have to be sold on the value of his input nearly as
much as if he were on the outside looking in.

Political Activity.   Partisan political activity on the part of the
public servants in the justice system is a dangerous game to play. One
of the disadvantages is whatever one does in the line of his normal responsibilities may be interpreted through partisan viewpoints. There
are other ways to engage in political activity, however, that will produce
a positive effect on the system's community image. When a particular
law is unenforceable, for example, or is ambiguous and impossible to
interpret objectively, then it would be most desirable to have someone
in the system to speak out in behalf of either changing the law or eliminating it completely. If enforcement of a particular law is unpopular, it
may not be eliminated, but an officer may advise (through his department) the legislature of the problems encountered in that law's enforce-

ment. The legislators could then study the law in light of the feedback they receive from the enforcement officers, and take whatever steps they believe necessary. The *intent* of the law may be to solve a certain type of social problem or to respond to some sort of pressures on legislatures to make the law. If, after a careful study, the legislators decide that the law should continue to be enforced, then it would be their responsibility to "sell" the idea to their constituents, who are the same constituency served by the justice system.

Community Participation by Agency Members. As private individuals, the police officer, or court clerk, or parole officer, or any other people in the justice system professions and paraprofessions have private lives to lead as neighbors, parents, spouses, and they may worship if and how they choose, hold memberships in whatever organizations they wish, and actively participate in community affairs. Such activity and membership should be extended whenever possible to get maximum community involvement.

Address Criticism. The stoic position of certain agencies in the face of criticism must give the leaders of those agencies a certain feeling of satisfaction in knowing that the criticism is incorrect and they are secure in the knowledge that what they are doing is correct. Unfortunately, however, there are many people who believe that one's refusal or failure to deny certain accusations is the equivalent to confessions of culpability, or tacit admissions. Sometimes the charge itself causes damage, and then a stand of silence may reinforce that damage. Any criticism or accusations of improper conduct should be carefully studied, and accompanied by careful self-analysis at the same time to determine the degree of truth or accuracy—if any—of the charges. The sources of rumors and gossip, and false accusations should be ferreted out and identified. Then it is advisable to attempt to widely disseminate the true facts that will answer the distorted facts, or the lies that have been circulated. There are times when the accused may use the press media as a platform for widely disseminating proclamations of his innocence and to plead for the sympathy on the part of the public, while at the same time the prosecutor must remain silent and present the evidence only in court to assure the accused his constitutionally guaranteed right to a fair trial, due process, and his posture of innocence until he is proven guilty.

Communicators Are Essential. By both oral and written methods, it is necessary that the police officer, the judge, the attorney, or any other professional in the justice system have the ability to communicate effectively. An articulate man or woman can win a conviction with the support of sufficient evidence, prevent a riot, arbitrate a family dispute, settle complaints, and accomplish many of the agency's objectives through the use of persuasive communications.

Public Relations

As used in this chapter, the term *public relations* implies more of a formalized one-way communicative process in which the justice system and its operants present their agencies to the public at an advantage through the media of mass communications and in personal presentations, but less on a give-and-take basis than through community relations processes. The public relations process involves press-agentry, salesmanship, image-building, and all of the other techniques that most business and industrial enterprises employ to present their products or services in the best possible light. Presidents are elected, milk regains its popularity, books are sold, colleges become internationally famous, entertainment celebrities attain stardom, and justice system agencies gain ACCEPTANCE when they employ public relations methods. The individual who becomes the greatest in any profession gains that stature because he: first, does something that causes the world to know of his unusual talents and accomplishments; second, he continues to demonstrate his greatness; and, third, his feats are publicized so that the world will know of him and his stature of greatness. Without the correct type of publicity, for example, the Los Angeles Police Department would be just another name on a list of names. Think about it; even a church has a bell to remind people of its existence. "It pays to advertise" is not a hollow slogan.

It is necessary to continually strive for public recognition and to try to get extensive dissemination of information about an agency's efforts if the public is to understand what a criminal justice agency is doing. Each actor must play his role in a convincing manner, and there should be some concerted effort to continuously be active in matters of public relations. It is not unusual for any agency of any size that can support the expense to employ a full-time public relations expert. Among his other responsibilities, the program developed by such an expert would include the following:

1. Publication of policies and philosophies of the department. Whenever the agency in question takes a stand, such as a hard line by the courts on violators of pedestrian right-of-way in which many people have lost their lives during a recent period of time, the public should

Community relations activities (above) of the police department include community involvement. Courtesy, Police Dept., St. Louis, Missouri.

The officer in this photo is accepting printed material from Mr. Darling and Councilman Fischer for the "Officer Bill" program which involves the children of San Jose. Courtesy Police Dept., San Jose, California.

know of the court's attitude on the matter. A statement by the judge that he believes his actions will serve to deter more deaths, and that he intends to send some people to jail for the offense should be publicized and may help solve the problem. A police department might advertise that citations will be issued for all littering violations and might help to keep the city cleaner. A prosecutor whose philosophy is to aggresively seek out and prosecute violators of consumer fraud laws should educate the public through publicity on the types of activities that might be used to bilk them out of their money; at the same time the criminals are publicly notified that they should either comply with the laws or find their victims elsewhere.

2. Regular publications. Annual reports, budget statements, special information bulletins, printed brochures, and press releases may all be used to an advantage by agencies of the justice system, provided the materials are factual, accurate, and interesting. A well-written press release about some item of public interest will quite probably be printed by at least one of the papers and is likely to be used by the other media as well. Editors often keep a ready supply of filler material—stories and items of interest that do not have to be dated—that can be used to fill a space or time frame when the opportunity presents itself. The material is of extra value if someone does not have to rewrite it.

3. Radio and television appearances. This is an excellent opportunity for the introduction of a new procedure or what might amount to a "crackdown" on some type of criminal activity. Sometimes an opportunity like a radio or television interview is the chief executive's only opportunity to explain a procedure or a philosophy in his own words without modification.

4. Personal visits to the homes of new residents. New arrivals to a community are often visited by representatives of several of the local merchants, sometimes by a young lady operating a welcome wagon, armed with free gifts and introductory discounts. Such an opportunity may be used by the local police department or sheriff in providing the new resident some printed information about procedures for reporting crimes or for home protection. Some departments have their "beat officers" visit the new residents so that the officers and the people may get acquainted. The personal touch has a salutory effect, providing the visit is timed right and the resident is not sensitive to the visit. The uniformed officer and the visibly marked car may be alarming to some people, but if such a practice is commonplace, then there should be no embarrassment by having a police car parked out front.

5. Public speaking programs. Entertainment committee chairmen

are hard-pressed for original and entertaining programs for their organizations. It is not unusual for the chairman for some breakfast or luncheon club to call his local police department, sheriff, or district attorney with a fervent plea for a speaker to fill in for some other speaker who had to cancel at the last minute. Speeches and programs may be prepared well in advance by the agency's public relations officer, who can call on a specialist in some area virtually at the last minute. Armed with the standard prepared material, the expert can embellish and expand, and once again sell his department.

There are many different types of special occasions when the justice system may comfortably take part in ceremonies without being out of place, such as Law Day, Armed Forces Day, and Labor Day events. Shortly before heavy shopping seasons, a program on bad checks and shoplifting is quite popular with merchants and other businessmen. Vacation time calls for special presentations on driving and security tips for the motorist or traveler. Special problems created by natural weather phenomena, such as snow and ice, or flash floods, provide an excellent opportunity for the agency to perform genuine public services and at the same time score successfully for the image of the agency.

How does one sell a prison to a group of local businessmen? It may be necessary to assure them that the institution is not unfairly competing for their markets, and at the same time demonstrate the skills and talents of convicted prisoners who are in need of employment to assure their success on parole once released. An example of the type of public relations work that may be done with some success may be to have a professional burglar demonstrate how easy it is to break into the average home, but how difficult a certain local security product makes the task of committing burglary. In order to avoid getting into the middle of what might be a condition of fierce competition between two neighboring manufacturers, it may be an effective public relations device to have the inmates who have been convicted for burglary serve as an advisory board or "testing laboratory" for certain security device manufacturers. Various other types of criminal specialities may be used as topics for crime prevention seminars and public relations programs. It will serve as an informative tool for the public and a form of catharsis for the participants who may use his public-speaking tour as a rehabilitation tool.

A series of well-prepared, half-hour programs involving interesting visual aids and other multimedia supplements to the prepared speech by a well-trained agency representative can do a great deal of good for the agency. The nature of the business—jails and institutions, law enforcement, the courts, and field casework—makes it somewhat difficult to allow public access into some institutions (impossible in some cases) or to ride along during the average work day. Motion pictures, videotapes, and slide programs can be used as a vehicle to transport the audience on a vicarious tour through the labyrinths of the instituiton that stands at the outskirts of town, and such a tour may serve to dispel some of the myths about what goes on inside the walls. Some of the community residents may become so interested in some phase of a rehabilitative process, for example, that they may volunteer to help with the program.

6. Positive action programs. An ethnic minority may be aggrieved about alleged or real problems of discrimination. While carefully avoiding any "showcase" attempt to display a fair and unbiased attitude on the part of the department, it may be possible to make positive efforts to employ representatives of the minority population, or to direct a series of programs to specifically overcome whatever barriers or difficulties that may have existed. Sometimes a mere shifting of priorities in the agency's public relations program may solve a problem that may exist because one facet of the program was incorrectly placed on the priority list. This is one occasion when the utilization of an advisory committee would be helpful.

7. Participation in youth activities. The agency may sponsor a youth organization as an extension of its own regular responsibilities, such as an explorer post, youth athletic league, or youth employment service. Positive results may be obtained by a genuine display of interest in the community as a responsible part of that community.

8. Enlist spokesmen. Within the community it is not difficult to encounter someone who feels strongly about the police, or the courts, or probation in a positive way. They are genuinely concerned that innuendos and unfounded slander about the agency or any of its members may be perpetuated beyond our wildest imagination. There are times when such a spokesman who speaks from a vantage point outside the agency will have a greater effect than some agency representative, who may be accused of "whitewashing" a situation because of his protective attitude from inside the agency.

9. Rumor control. When emotions are keyed up and tempers flare some inconsequential incident may run rampant and almost spontaneously get out of control like a brushfire in a dry canyon. By suggestion, and sometimes by deliberate implantation at the appropriate time, unfounded bits of information might be disbursed and then the rumors begin to fly, grossly exaggerated bits of lies and half-truths. The damage is sometimes irreparable. If possible, indigenous leaders of the com-

munity should be informed of the facts and—if a rumor control procedure has been established—they may be able to squelch the rumor before it gets too far.

10.   Attempts to overcome community indifference. Sometimes an
antagonistic individual is easier to cope with than one who displays no
interest in a situation at all. Special interest groups, both pro- and anti-
criminal justice system, are vocal and manage to be heard. What is
really difficult is to prod the indifferent and apathetic people in the
community into expressing their likes or dislikes. If the entire community is to be served, then it is imperative that we find out how and
what the community at large is thinking. Surveys, questionnaires, and
other forms of opinion analyses may be utilized to determine community
standards for courtroom documentation that a certain type of entertainment, for example, is contrary to local mores. Personal visits to the homes
and businesses of many of these silent residents may prove beneficial
both to the agency and to the people they are serving.

11.   Public image. It is important to establish a businesslike operation and present an image to the public that convinces them that their
justice system is operating efficiently and that their taxes are well spent.
Telephone courtesy and personal contacts in office reception areas should
be as important to the criminal justice agency as it is to the automobile
sales agency, which considers every caller or visitor a potential buyer.
There is a difference between an individual who speaks with authority
and the one who speaks as an officious martinet who mouths words in
such a manner that he evokes resentment and anger. People should be
treated with courtesy and respect, and with dignity.

Summary

In this brief chapter we have outlined some of the basic considerations
for community and public relations and the justice system. Because of
the diversity of agencies and communities throughout the nation, it is
virtually impossible to prescribe a precise program for any single agency.
There are certain guidelines that apply almost universally, however. As
with any business or government operation, the criminal justice agency
must have a good public relations program, and it must involve itself
with the community it serves as a part of that community rather than
apart from the community. As continuously pointed out in this chapter,
if there were two words to describe community and public relations they
would be EFFECTIVE COMMUNICATIONS.

Exercises and Study Questions

1. Define *public relations.*

2. Define *community relations.*

3. Now that you have defined the two terms, what is the difference, if any?

4. Why is it imperative that an agency self-evaluate?

5. Give an example of how an officer of a police department may demonstrate his desire to gain cultural awareness.

6. In what way would you utilize an advisory committee to assist in the operation of a medium security prison?

7. In what capacity would you place a volunteer citizen in a probation department?

8. How may a police officer engage in politics and not involve himself in partisanship?

9. If you were a police officer visiting a new resident on your beat, what types of information about the department do you believe he should have?

10. Recommended semester project: Develop a five-point plan for a community relations program for each of the following: probation department, police department, sheriff's department, and the district attorney. Prepare the plan as though you had been employed as the public relations expert for each of these departments and your plan is intended to solve the major communications problems with the community.

Suggested for Additional Study

ADAMS, THOMAS F., Ed., *Criminal Justice Readings.* Pacific Palisades, Calif.: Goodyear Publishing Co., Inc., 1972.

HEWITT, WILLIAM H. and CHARLES L. NEWMAN, *Police Community Relations. An Anthology and Bibliography.* Mineola, N.Y.: The Foundation Press, 1970.

STRECKER, VICTOR G., *The Environment of Law Enforcement: A Community Relations Guide.* Englewood Cliffs, N.J.: Prentice-Hall, Inc., 1971.

12

Trends in
Justice Administration

Introduction

Progress in law enforcement and the entire criminal justice system, which encompasses law enforcement, the courts, and corrections as presented in this text, is absolutely essential if our modern society is to keep from strangling itself. In this chapter, it would be impossible to enumerate all of the innovations in police administration and the related fields. What we will cover are some of the highlights, beginning with the President's Crime Commission study and all of its reports that were released for public ingestion in early 1967. Prior to that time the police, the courts, corrections, and all of the related agencies and their processes were of little direct concern to anyone except those who were directly involved with the system.

The "business" of criminal justice is similar to many other businesses that deal in services. The significant difference is that none so directly and dramatically affect the lives and reputations of many of the individuals we contact. A decision has tremendous impact, whether it be to arrest or release, file a complaint or not file, cite or not cite, shoot or not shoot, or simply prepare and file a report.

Recognizing the need for innovation and improvement, the criminal justice practitioner must first identify and analyze the problem. Once he has done that, he can address the problem. By now, it seems, we have identified enough problems to keep us busy for at least the next century. In this chapter we will articulate some of those problems and list some of the things we have done to address them.

President's Crime Commission

On July 23, 1965, President Lyndon B. Johnson assembled together a panel of people representing divergent views and a variety of backgrounds and created a committee with a single objective: to study the criminal justice system for the purpose of making a series of recommendations for improvement of the system. Officially named the President's Commission on Law Enforcement and Administration of Justice, the commission, its consultants, and its staff compiled in a series of publications, task force reports, and its major publication, *Challenge of Crime in a Free Society,* a wealth of information that previously had been available to the people in a piecemeal fashion. Little of the information was new, just the method of collecting and disseminating it and putting it into focus.

The President's Crime Commission made more than two hundred recommendations for change in every facet of the criminal justice system. Not only did the commission recommend action to be taken by the public segment of our society but also the private segment in a massive cooperative effort. All of these publications are available for nominal prices through the U.S. Government Printing Office and should find their way into your library.

For the purpose of this chapter's theme, some of the commission's most significant recommendations are recounted. Study the recommendations carefully and compare them with the actual policies and procedures of the various agencies in your own city, county, and state.

CRIME IN AMERICA

The Commission Recommends:

* Those cities that have not already done so should adopt centralized procedures for handling the receipt of reports of crime from citizens and institute and staff controls necessary to make those procedures effective.

* The present index of reported crime should be broken into two wholly separate parts, one for crimes of violence and the other for crimes against property.

JUVENILE DELINQUENCY AND YOUTH CRIME

The Commission Recommends:

* Efforts, both private and public, should be intensified to:
  Prepare youth for employment.
  Provide youth with information about employment opportunities.

Reduce barriers to employment caused by discrimination, the misuse of criminal records, and maintenance of rigid job qualifications.

Create new employment opportunities.

° To the greatest feasible extent, police departments should formulate policy guidelines for dealing with juveniles.

° All officers should be acquainted with the special characteristics of adolescents, particularly those of the social, racial, and other specific groups with which they are likely to come in contact.

° Custody of a juvenile (both prolonged street stops and station house visits) should be limited to instances where there is objective, specifiable ground for suspicion.

° Every stop that includes a frisk or an interrogation of more than a few preliminary identifying questions should be recorded in a strictly confidential report.

° Police forces should make full use of the central diagnosing and coordinating services of the Youth Services Bureau. Station adjustment should be limited to release and referral; it should not include hearings or the imposition of sanctions by the police. Court referral by the police should be restricted to those cases involving serious criminal conduct or repeated misconduct of a more than trivial nature.

° Communities should establish neighborhood youth-serving agencies —Youth Services Bureaus—located if possible in comprehensive neighborhood community centers and receiving juveniles (delinquent and nondelinquent) referred by the police, the juvenile court, parents, schools, and other sources.

° Juvenile courts should make fullest feasible use of preliminary conferences to dispose of cases short of adjudication.

° The movement for narrowing the juvenile court's jurisdiction should be continued. (Specifically, the commission recommends a list of changes, primarily limiting the jurisdiction of the juvenile court to only those acts of a juvenile that would be criminal acts if committed by an adult.)

° Counsel should be appointed as a matter of course wherever coercive action is a possibility, without requiring any affirmative choice by child or parent.

° Notice should be given well in advance of any scheduled court proceeding, including intake, detention, and waiver hearings, and should set forth the alleged misconduct with particularity.

° Adequate and separate detention facilities for juveniles should be provided.

° Legislation should be enacted restricting both authority to detain and the circumstances under which the detention is permitted.

THE POLICE

The Commission Recommends:

* State legislatures should enact statutory provisions with respect to the authority of law enforcement officers to stop persons for brief questioning, including specifications of the circumstances and limitations under which stops are permissible.

* The police should formally participate in community planning in all cities.

* Police departments in all large communities should have community-relations machinery consisting of a headquarters unit that plans and supervises the department's community relations programs. It should also have precinct units, responsible to the precinct commander, that carry out the programs. Community relations must be both a staff and a line function. Such machinery is a matter of the greatest importance in any community that has a substantial minority population.

* In each police precinct in a minority-group neighborhood there should be a citizen's advisory committee that meets regularly with police officials to work out solutions to problems of conflict between the police and the community. It is crucial that the committees be broadly representative of the community as a whole, including those elements who are critical or aggrieved.

* It should be a high-priority objective of all departments in communities with a substantial minority population to recruit minority-group officers and to deploy and promote them fairly. Every officer in such departments should receive thorough grounding in community-relations subjects. His performance in the field of community relations should be periodically reviewed and evaluated.

* Every jurisdiction should provide adequate procedures for full and fair processing of all citizen grievances and complaints about the conduct of any public officer or employee.

* Police departments should develop and enunciate policies that give police personnel specific guidance for the common situations requiring exercise of police discretion. Policies should cover such matters, among others, as the issuance of orders to citizens regarding their movements or activities, the handling of minor disputes, the safeguarding of rights of free speech and free assembly, the selection and use of investigative methods, and the decision whether or not to arrest in specific situations involving specific crimes.

* Each municipality, and other jurisdiction responsible for law enforcement, should carefully assess the manpower needs of its police agency on the basis of efficient use of all its personnel and should provide the resources required to meet the need for increased personnel if such a need is found to exist.

* Basic police functions, especially in large and medium-sized urban

departments, should be divided among three kinds of officers, here termed the "community service officer," the "police officer," and the "police agent."

* Police departments should recruit far more actively than they do now, with special attention to college campuses and inner-city neighborhoods.

* The ultimate aim of all police departments should be that all personnel with general enforcement powers have baccalaureate degrees.

* Police departments should take immediate steps to establish a minimum requirement of a baccalaureate degree for all supervisory and executive positions.

* Until reliable tests are devised for identifying and measuring the personal characteristics that contribute to good police work, intelligence tests, thorough background investigations, and personal interviews should be used by all departments as absolute minimum techniques to determine the moral character and the emotional and intellectual fitness of police candidates.

* Police departments and civil service commissions should reexamine and, if necessary, modify present recruitment standards on age, height, weight, visual acuity, and prior residence. The appointing authority should place primary emphasis on the education, background, character and personality of a candidate for police service.

* Police salaries must be raised, particularly by increasing minimums. In order to attract college graduates to police service, starting and maximum salaries must be competitive with other professions and occupations that seek the same graduates.

* Salary proposals for each department within local government should be considered on their own merits and should not be joint with the demands of other departments within a city.

* Promotion eligibility requirements should stress ability above seniority. Promotion "lists" should be compiled on the basis not only of scores on technical examinations but on prior performance, character, educational achievement and leadership potential.

* Personnel to perform all specialized police functions not involving a need for general enforcement powers should be selected for their talents and abilities without regard to prior police service. Professional policemen should have the same opportunities as other professionals to seek employment where they are most needed. The inhibitions that civil service regulations, retirement plans, and hiring policies place on lateral entry should be removed. To encourage lateral movement of police personnel, a nationwide retirement system should be devised that permits the transferring of retirement credits.

* All training programs should provide instruction on subjects that prepare recruits to exercise discretion properly, and to understand

the community, the role of the police, and what the criminal justice system can and cannot do. Professional educators and civilian experts should be used to teach specialized courses—law and psychology, for example. Recognized teaching techniques such as problem-solving seminars should be incorporated into training programs.

* Formal police training programs for recruits in all departments, large and small, should consist of an absolute minimum of 400 hours of classroom work spread over a four- to six-month period so that it can be combined with carefully selected and supervised field training.

* Entering officers should serve probation periods of, preferably, eighteen months and certainly no less than one year. During this period the recruit should be systematically observed and rated. Chief administrators should have the sole authority of dismissal during the probation period and should willingly exercise it against unsatisfactory officers.

* Every general enforcement officer should have at least one week of intensive in-service training a year. Every officer should be given incentives to continue his general education or acquire special skills outside his department.

* Every state, through its commission on police standards, should provide financial and technical assistance to departments to conduct surveys and make recommendations for improvement and modernization of their organization, management, and operations.

* Every medium- and large-sized department should employ a skilled lawyer full time as its legal adviser. Smaller departments should arrange for legal advice on a part-time basis.

* Police departments must take every possible step to implement the guiding organizational principle of central control. Specialist staff units for such matters as planning, research, legal advice, and police personnel should include persons trained in a variety of disciplines and should be utilized to develop and improve the policies, operations, and administration of each function.

* Every department in a big or medium-sized city should organize key ranking staff and line personnel into an administrative board similar in function to a corporation's board of directors, whose duty would be to assist the chief and his staff units in developing, enunciating, and enforcing departmental policies and guidelines for the day-to-day activities of line personnel.

* Every department, regardless of size, should have a comprehensive program for maintaining police integrity and every medium- and large-sized department should have a well-manned internal investigation unit responsible only to the chief administrator. The unit should have both an investigative and preventive role in controlling dishonest, unethical, and offensive actions by police officers.

* Police departments should commence experimentation with a team-policing concept that envisions those with patrol and investigative duties combining under unified command with flexible assignments to deal with the crime problems in a defined sector.
* A comprehensive regulation should be formulated by every chief administrator to reflect the basic policy that firearms may be used *only* when the officer believes his life or the life of another is in imminent danger, or when other reasonable means of apprehension have failed to prevent the escape of a *felony* suspect whom the officer believes presents a serious danger to others.
* States should assume responsibility for assuring that area-wide records and communications needs are provided.
* In every metropolitan area the central city or the state should provide laboratory facilities for the routine needs of all the communities in the area. State or multistate laboratories and the FBI laboratory should continue to provide the necessary research to make available to all laboratories more sophisticated means of analysis.
* Specialized personnel from state or metropolitan departments should assist smaller departments in each metropolitan area on major investigations and in specialized law enforcement functions.
* Each metropolitan area and each county should take action directed toward the pooling, or consolidation, of police services through the particular technique that will provide the most satisfactory law enforcement service and protection at lowest possible cost.
* Police standards commissions should be established in every state, and empowered to set mandatory requirements and to give financial aid to governmental units for the implementation of standards.

THE COURTS

The Commission Recommends:
* Felony and misdemeanor courts and their ancillary agencies—prosecutors, defenders, and probation services—should be unified.
* As an immediate step to meet the needs of the lower courts, the judicial manpower of these courts should be increased and their physical facilities should be improved so that these courts will be able to cope with the volume of cases coming before them in a dignified and deliberate way.
* Prosecutors, probation officers, and defense counsel should be provided in courts where these officers are not found, or their numbers are insufficient.
* The states and federal government should enact legislation to abolish or overhaul the justice of the peace and U.S. commissioner systems.
* Each state should enact comprehensive bail reform legislation. . . .

* Each community should establish procedures to enable and encourage police departments to release, in appropriate classes of cases, as many arrested persons as possible promptly after arrest upon issuance of a citation or summons requiring appearance.

* Prosecutors and defense counsel should in appropriate cases share information they secure independently at all points in the process when such sharing appears likely to lead to early disposition.

* Police, prosecutors, bar associations, and courts should issue regulations and standards as to the kinds of information that properly may be released to the news media about pending criminal cases by police officers, prosecutors, and defense counsel. These regulations and standards should be designed to minimize prejudicial statements by the media before or during trial, while safeguarding legitimate reporting on matters of public interest.

* States should reexamine the sentencing provisions of their penal codes with a view to simplifying the grading of offenses, and to removing mandatory minimum prison terms, long maximum prison terms, and ineligibility for probation and parole. In cases of persistent habitual offenders or dangerous criminals, judges should have express authority to extend prison terms. Sentencing codes should include criteria designed to help judges exercise their discretion in accordance with clearly stated standards.

* The question whether capital punishment is an appropriate sanction is a policy decision to be made by each state. . . .

CORRECTIONS

The Commission Recommends:

* Parole and probation services should be available in all jurisdictions for felons, juveniles, and those adult misdemeanants who need or can profit from community treatment.

* Every state should provide that offenders who are not paroled receive adequate supervision after release unless it is determined to be unnecessary in a specific case.

* Probation and parole services should make use of volunteers and subprofessional aides in demonstration projects and regular programs.

* Probation and parole officials should develop new methods and skills to aid in reintegrating offenders through active intervention on their behalf with community institutions.

* Case loads for different types of offenders should vary in size and type and intensity of treatment. Classification and assignment of offenders should be made according to their needs and problems.

* Correctional authorities should develop more extensive community programs providing special, intensive treatment as an alternative to institutionalization for both juvenile and adult offenders.

* Federal and state governments should finance the establishment of model, small-unit correctional institutions for flexible, community-oriented treatment.
* Graduated release and furlough programs should be expanded. They should be accompanied by guidance and coordinated with community treatment services.
* Local jails and misdemeanant institutions should be integrated into state correctional systems. They should not be operated by law enforcement agencies. Rehabilitative programs and other reforms should be instituted.
* Wherever possible, persons awaiting trial should be housed and handled separately from offenders.
* Universities and colleges should, with governmental and private participation and support, develop more courses and launch more research studies and projects on the problem of contemporary corrections.

ORGANIZED CRIME

The Commission Recommends:
* At least one investigative grand jury should be impaneled annually at each jurisdiction that has major organized crime activity.
* Congress should enact legislation dealing specifically with wiretapping and bugging.
* Every attorney general in states where organized crime exists should form in his office a unit of attorneys and investigators to gather information and assist in prosecution regarding this criminal activity.
* Police departments in every major city should have a special intelligence unit solely to ferret out organized criminal activity and to collect information regarding the possible entry of criminal cartels into the area's criminal operations.
* The prosecutor's office in every major city should have sufficient manpower assigned full time to organized crime cases. Such personnel should have the power to initiate organized crime investigations and to conduct the investigative grand juries mentioned above.
* The federal government should create a central computerized office into which each federal agency would feed all of its organized crime intelligence.
* Groups should be created within the federal and state departments of justice to develop strategies and enlist regulatory action against businesses infiltrated by organized crime.
* Private business associations should develop strategies to prevent and uncover organized crime's illegal and unfair business tactics.
* Enforcement officials should provide regular briefings to leaders at all levels of government concerning organized crime conditions within the jurisdiction.

NARCOTICS AND DRUG ABUSE

The Commission Recommends:

* Research should be undertaken devoted to early action on the further development of a sound and effective framework of regulatory and criminal laws with respect to dangerous drugs. In addition, research and educational programs concerning the effects of such drugs should be undertaken.
* The enforcement and related staff of the Bureau of Customs should be materially increased.
* The enforcement staff of the Bureau of Narcotics should be materially increased. Some parts of the added personnel should be used to design and execute a long-range intelligence effort aimed at the upper echelons of the illicit drug traffic.

DRUNKENNESS OFFENSES

The Commission Recommends:

* Drunkenness should not in itself be considered a criminal offense. Disorderly and other criminal conduct accompanied by drunkenness should remain punishable as separate crimes. The implementation of this recommendation requires the development of adequate civil detoxification procedures.
* Communities should establish detoxification units as part of comprehensive treatment programs.
* Research by private and governmental agencies into alcoholism, the problems of alcoholics, and methods of treatment should be expanded.

SCIENCE AND TECHNOLOGY

The Commission Recommends:

* Police call boxes should be designated "public emergency call boxes," should be better marked and lighted, and should be left unlocked.
* Whenever practical, a single police telephone number should be established, at least within a metropolitan area and eventually over the entire United States, comparable to the telephone company's long-distance information number.
* Frequencies should be shared through the development of larger and more integrated police mobile radio networks.
* Police departments should undertake data collection and experimentation programs to develop appropriate statistical procedures for manpower allocation.
* A National Criminal Justice Statistics Center should be established in the Department of Justice. The center should be responsible for

the collection, analysis, and dissemination of two basic kinds of data:

Those characterizing criminal careers, derived from carefully drawn samples of anonymous offenders.

Those on crime and the system's response to it, as reported by the criminal justice agencies at all levels.

* A federal agency should be assigned to coordinate the establishment of standards for equipment to be used by criminal justice agencies and to provide those agencies technical assistance.

* The federal government should encourage and support the establishment of operations research staffs in large criminal justice agencies.

* A major scientific and technological research program within a research institute should be created and supported by the federal government.

* Criminal justice agencies, such as state court and correctional systems and large police departments, should develop their own research units, staffed by specialists and drawing on the advice and assistance of leading scholars and experts in relevant fields.[1]

Results

What is your opinion of each one of those recommendations individually? What do you believe to be their general value and effect? Following this series of recommendations, we have seen the implementation of literally dozens of these recommendations. Certainly not to be ignored are the significant advances made by individual criminal justice agencies for decades in a successive progression of events prior to the commission's study and recommendations. In fact, many of those recommendations were based on ongoing programs within specific agencies contacted during the commission's fourteen months of operation. However, it cannot be denied that both personal and financial attention toward the problems of the criminal justice system were much more generous following the commission's reports.

Law Enforcement Assistance Administration

One of the more visible results of the recommendations of the President's Crime Commission was the establishment of the Law Enforcement As-

---

[1] President's Commission on Law Enforcement and the Administration of Justice, *Challenge of Crime in a Free Society* (Washington, D.C.: Government Printing Office, 1967).

istance Administration.[2] *Law Enforcement,* in the context of the Omnibus Crime Bill of 1968 and the Law Enforcement Assistance Act is the term used to describe all of the components of the system of justice administration, including the fields of law enforcement, corrections, and the courts. Congress established LEAA to channel funds to states through their respective State Planning Agencies, and to carry out certain other activities involving research and improvement of law enforcement systems. The funds available through this source were as follows: [3] Fiscal Year 1968, $100,111,000; FY 1969, same as 1968; FY 1970, $300,000,000; FY 1971, $650,000,000; FY 1972, $1,150,000,000; and FY 1973, $1,750,000,000.

The Attorney General's Annual Report explains the background of the Law Enforcement Assistance Administration:

> The Law Enforcement Assistance Act of 1965 (P.L.89–197) established a program of funding research and demonstration projects to improve law enforcement, crime prevention and administration of criminal justice.
>
> The policy of providing Federal funds for state efforts in law enforcement and criminal justice received strong endorsement in 1967 from the President's Commission on Law Enforcement and Administration of Justice. That Commission said it perceived a need for a Federal assistance program "on which several hundred million dollars annually could be profitably spent over the next decade."
>
> Basic Act. The following year, Congress established the nation's first large-scale comprehensive program attacking crime and delinquency. That program was embodied in the Omnibus Crime Control and Safe Streets Act of 1968 (P.L.90–351).
>
> Congress said in that Act that it found "a high incidence" of crime that threatened the "peace, security, and general welfare" of the nation. It said that law enforcement needed to be better coordinated, intensified, and more effective at all levels of government. Further, Congress found that "crime is essentially a local program that must be dealt with by state and local governments if it is to be controlled effectively."
>
> Congress said its declared policy was "to assist state and local governments in strengthening and improving law enforcement at every level by national assistance."
>
> It said the Act had the threefold purpose to: "(1) encourage States and units of general local government to prepare and adopt comprehensive plans based upon their evaluation of State and local problems of law enforcement; (2) authorize grants to States and units of local government in order to improve and strengthen law enforcement; and (3) encourage

---

[2] Law Enforcement Assistance Administration, *3rd Annual Report of the Law Enforcement Assistance Administration Fiscal Year 1971* (Washington, D.C.: Government Printing Office, 1972), p. 3.

[3] President's Commission, *Challenge of Crime in a Free Society,* p. 5.

research and development directed toward the improvement of law enforcement and the devolopment of new methods for the prevention and reduction of crime and the detection and apprehension of criminals."

The Act further called for special efforts in the areas of organized crime and civil disorders; it established a National Institute of Law Enforcement and Criminal Justice to conduct research; it established an academic assistance program to further education among law enforcement personnel; it directed LEAA to collect, evaluate, publish and disseminate statistics and other data on the condition and progress of law enforcement in the nation; and it authorized expenditures of $100,111,000 for the first two years, FY 1968 (or the portion thereof remaining) and FY 1969.

The Act was approved by the Senate on May 23, 1968, and by the House of Representatives on June 6, 1968. It was signed into law by the President on June 19, 1968. Congress approved appropriations for FY 1969 on August 9, 1968, and on October 21, 1968, LEAA formally came into being as the first Adminstrators took office under recess appointments. By December 19, 1968, all states had established State Criminal Justice Planning Agencies (SPA).

Congress amended the basic Act in the Omnibus Crime Control Act of 1970 (P.L.91–644), which was signed into law by the President on January 2, 1971.[4]

An Ongoing Program

Literally billions of dollars previously not available to the several components of the justice system are being poured into their jurisdictions to fulfill research, training, and operational needs, as well as special crime-related projects to meet the demands caused by the growing problems of crime and its prevention, criminals and their rehabilitation, and the system and its management. Just a listing of the many topics covered in the President's Crime Commission Report of 1967 indicates the scope of projects that LEAA funding would be directed toward during the next few years.

To enumerate names, dates, and places in this chapter would date this publication because of the constantly changing picture in this category. Rather than specifically list new products, changes in procedures, innovative programs, or recent studies, what we shall do is list some of the topics that were listed in the commission's recommendations in which significant changes may or may not have taken place during the past

[4] President's Commission, *Challenge of Crime in a Free Society,* p. 5.

few years. Filling in the details of precisely what has been done—if anything—will be left to you, the reader.

* Improvements in crime reporting procedures.
* Policy guidelines for dealing with juveniles.
* Police referrals to the youth services bureau of delinquents and near-delinquents.
* Neighborhood police youth services bureaus.
* Separate detention facilities for juveniles.
* "Stop and frisk" legislation and guidelines.
* Police involvement in community planning.
* Innovative community relations programs.
* Citizens advisory groups to work with police agencies.
* Recruitment of officers from minority group heritage.
* Guidelines for officers in matters in which the officer has wide discretionary powers.
* Different levels of entry into police service.
* Recruitment of police officer candidates on college campuses.
* Educational upgrading for police entrance and promotion requirements.
* Improved selection methods.
* Modifications of physical requirements for police service.
* Pay and promotion on the basis of ability and merit.
* Lateral movement of qualified police personnel.
* Upgrading of training to include discretionary decision making.
* Minimum of 400 hours basic training combined with additional time for actual training in the field.
* One week refresher training at least once a year.
* Probationary period for minimum of one year to eighteen months.
* Establishment of procedures to process and investigate grievances and complaints about the conduct of any department employee.
* Internal affairs units to assure honesty and integrity of personnel.
* Team-policing concept for maximum effectiveness.
* Improvement in utilization and deployment of manpower.
* Consolidation of some police services to improve service with economy.
* Community detoxification centers for alcoholics.
* Standardization of information releases about arrested persons and pending cases to assure a fair trial for defendants.
* New methods for probation and parole.
* Community-based treatment centers for criminal offenders.
* University and college involvement in criminal justice education and training.
* Special intelligence units to ferret out and combat organized crime.

* Consolidation and coordination of police information systems and computerization where applicable.
* Establishment of research and development units in local, state, and federal agencies of criminal justice.

During the early stages of development of the newly formed Law Enforcement Assistance Administration and at about the same time when the requests for funding had begun to gain momentum, that agency produced several documents relating to guidelines on the process of making applications for funding. Among those documents was the *Correctional Planning and Resource Guide*.[5] The following statement appeared in the introduction:

To be comprehensive, law enforcement planning must include all elements of the criminal and juvenile justice system. Further, comprehensive planning will require inter-relating of the separate law enforcement elements—police, courts, corrections, the criminal law and a variety of environmental factors and conditions. Among these are population growth and characteristics, socio-economic conditions, employment, education, mental and physical health.[6]

Referring to the President's Commission on Law Enforcement and the Administration of Justice, previously referred to also as the President's Crime Commission, the *Guide* continues:

Despite the seriousness of the crime problem today and the increasing challenge in the years ahead, the central conclusion of the Commission is that a significant reduction in crime is possible if the following objectives are vigorously pursued:

First, society must seek to prevent crime before it happens by assuring all Americans a stake in the benefits and responsibilities of American life, by strengthening law enforcement, and by reducing criminal opportunities.

Second, society's aim of reducing crime would be better served if the system of criminal justice developed a far broader range of techniques with which to deal with individual offenders.

Third, the system of criminal justice must eliminate existing inequities if it is to achieve ideals and win the respect and cooperation of all citizens.

Fourth, the system of criminal justice must attract more people and better people—police, prosecutors, judges, defense attorneys, probation

---

[5] Law Enforcement Assistance Administration, *Correctional Planning and Resource Guide* (Washington, D.C.: Government Printing Office, 1969).

[6] LEAA, *Correctional Planning and Resource Guide,* p. 1.

and parole officers, and corrections officials with more knowledge, expertise, initiative, and integrity.

Fifth, there must be more operational and basic research into the problems of crime and criminal administration, by those both within and without the system of criminal justice.

Sixth, the police, courts and correctional agencies must be given substantially greater amounts of money if they are to improve their ability to control crime.

Seventh, individual citizens, civic and business organizations, religious institutions, and all levels of government must take responsibility for planning and implementing the changes that must be made in the criminal justice system if crime is to be reduced.

Essential to the achievement of these objectives is the need to overcome the fragmentation, disunity and operations of programs at cross purposes by the multitude of agencies and jurisdictions which are essential supports to law enforcement and corrections.[7]

Trends for the Future

The past few years have witnessed literally thousands of studies and experiments in all of the areas of justice administration. Because a textbook is a semipermanent document once the manuscript is submitted to the publisher and many innovations at the time of the writing may have been tried or abandoned, or modified many times, or may have become "traditional" by the time the text reaches the classroom, this particular section of the book must necessarily be open-ended. You, the reader and student, are challenged to write the conclusions for this chapter based on your inquiries of your local justice system agencies and your research on what has become of the crime commission's recommendations and the many thousands of studies and innovations in methods and equipment that have occurred since that commission's report was first disseminated.

To stimulate the further study of this tremendous boon to the system, following is a brief list of just a few of the LEAA funded projects, and other projects that have been carried out concurrently with other funds as sources of support during recent years. From your local criminal justice agencies, find out what they have been doing and see what you can add to the list. As a part of your participation in writing this chapter in the annals of criminal justice, prepare a paragraph about each item on this list and then discuss them in class with your instructor and fellow students.

[7] LEAA, *Correctional Planning and Resource Guide,* p. 3.

Law Enforcement

Enlightened, more "humanistic" approaches to personnel management.

Changes in weaponry, including nonlethal projectiles and tear gas that can be directed toward its target more selectively.

Computer-based information systems.

Hand-held portable radios for foot beat officers.

Tracking systems for radio-equipped police cruisers.

Atomic research in criminalistics.

"Systems" approach to police training, defining objectives based on task analyses and teaching toward those objectives with prescribed minimum performance levels.

"Civilianizing" certain police positions that do not require peace officer powers or qualifications, such as clerical and statistical positions.

Changes in entrance requirements, such as the height, dental, and visual acuity restrictions.

Entry into police service at different levels, depending on experience, education, and age factors.

Lateral transfer of experienced personnel from one agency to another without loss of rank, longevity, or retirement benefits.

Building security studies.

Family crisis intervention experiments.

Ultra-high frequency radio equipment and teleprinters in vehicles.

Organized crime task forces that work cooperatively to address a mutual problem.

Electronic analysis and retrieval of criminal histories, providing information about crimes and the people who commit them.

Law enforcement education program, including loans and grants to students.

Disadvantaged persons trained for law enforcement.

Police corruption and organized crime.

Law enforcement standards laboratories for study of new equipment.

Police air mobility in helicopters and fixed wing aircraft.

Electronic surveillance and intelligence equipment.

Unification of services, consolidating several smaller agencies into one metropolitan agency.

Police legal advisors.

Universal police emergency telephone number: 911.

Alarm systems evaluation and improvement.

Private police and their training.

Corrections

Prison legal-aid programs.

Training for jail and prison personnel.

Uniform inmate grievance procedures.

Father's day and special family activities, conjugal visits.

Probation subsidy as an alternative to imprisonment.

Short-term leaves prior to parole, with an objective of making the re-integration process an easier transition.

Alcoholic detoxification centers.

Correctional supervision and management training.

Modifications in correctional facility architecture.

Parole decision-making.

Community-based corrections.

Drug abuse rehabilitation.

Parole computerized data bank.

Juvenile corrections studies.

Reduced case loads.

Success predictability for parolees.

Special casework approaches.

Summer excursions for juvenile probationers and near-delinquents.

Interagency cooperative projects in training and casework management.

Courts

Bail reform studies.

Bail investigation and "recognizance releases" pending hearings and trials.

Use of hearing officers or commissioners to relieve load on judges.

Reduction of delays on pretrial procedures.

Court administrators to replace judges for court management.

Executive training for court administrators.

Uniform codes and standards.

Recruitment and training of prosecutors.

Specialized training for judges.

Improvement in court paper-work procedures.

Automated transcription systems.

Improvements in court security.

Selection and utilization of juries with less delay.

Automated records for the courts.

Extension of public defender services for the indigent.

Consolidation and coordination of court bailiff responsibilities.

Statewide court systems, including phasing out of the justice court.

Summary

In this chapter we have merely scanned the trends in justice administration in the United States, particularly some of the things that have taken place during the turbulent and extremely demanding years of the past decade. Since the inauguration of the Law Enforcement Assistance Administration and State Planning Agencies, and the infusion of billions of dollars previously not available for research, education, and training, we have witnessed thousands of experiments and innovations. At the present time we are in a constant state of modification and realignment. The nature of law enforcement and criminal justice agencies as community service organizations, which must be responsive to the changes of the demands of society, has made it necessary for such dynamic efforts to evaluate and reevaluate, modify, change or retain, and to generally update the system to best serve the needs of the people. We have merely exposed you to the data. Now it is your responsibility as the student to complete the chapter.

Exercises and Study Questions

1. Visit your local police agency. From your observations, list at least three positions currently being filled by sworn police officers that could be handled just as well—if not better—by civilian counterparts.

2. In class, discuss the relative merits of internship training programs for college students.

3. What is "lateral entry," and of what value is it to the professional?

4. When the author stated that there is a "more humanistic approach to criminal justice management," what did he mean?

5. What was the purpose for creation of the President's Crime Commission?

6. What is the purpose for the Law Enforcement Assistance Administration?

7. What dramatic improvements have been made in the local law enforcement picture where you live as a direct or indirect result of the special funding made possible through the Law Enforcement Assistance Administration?

8. What is "community-based corrections," and what is different about it when compared with institution-based corrections?

9. Is there any difference in the operation of the courts in your jurisdiction as a result of funding through LEAA or other sources?

10. Recommended semester project: From the recommendations of the President's Commission on Law Enforcement and the Administration of Justice listed in this chapter and in the commission's report, choose any twenty recommendations and list them. Write your justification for each. Survey the criminal justice agencies in your geographical area and find out what changes, if any, have taken place with respect to the twenty recommendations you have chosen. Prepare a paper on your findings.

Suggested for Additional Study

President's Commission on Law Enforcement and the Administration of Justice, *Challenge of Crime in a Free Society.* Washington, D.C.: Government Printing Office, 1967.

Index

Ability tests, preemployment screening and, 260
Accountants, licensing of, 138
Adjutant general (state), 131-32
Administrative hearings, 10, 171
Administrative Office of U.S. Courts, 196
Administrative police boards, 109-10
Advisory Commission on Intergovernmental Relations, 2, 111
Advisory committees, community relations and, 293
Affirmative action requirements, 212
Age, criminal activity related to, 49, 51
Aggravated assault, Crime Index listing of, 77, 79
Aggressive tendencies, criminality and, 42
Agility tests for justice system applicants, 216
Air Force, Office of Special Investigations (OSI) within, 145
Air National Guard, organization of, 131
Alcabes, Abraham, 206
Alcaldes (magistrates), 112
Alcohol, Tobacco, and Firearms Division, Treasury Department, 139, 140
Alcoholic beverage control agencies (state), 8, 119, 134-35
Alcoholics Anonymous, 95, 189
Alcoholism
  decriminalization of, 197
  President's Crime Commission recommendations on research into, 30, 311
Alfred, King of England, 101
American Bar Association (ABA)
  Committee on Crime Prevention and Control of, 20, 86, 87-88, 89

American Bar Association (ABA) (*cont.*)
  criminal justice system criticism of, 1-2
  probation standards of, 181
  on victimless crimes, 65
American Correctional Association, Declaration of Principles of, 257, 267-73
American Law Institute, model penal code of, 90
Amnesty of prisoners, 15
Ancient civilizations, law enforcement in, 100-1
Anglo-Saxon law, 101-2, 115
Annual reports, 297
Anspach v. United States, 283-84
Appellate courts, 8, 112
  federal, 156
  function of, 159
  jurisdiction of, 160
Application forms, for justice system positions, 212-13
Architecture of correctional institutions, 269
Arizona Rangers, 130
Armed Forces Day, 298
Army, Counter-Intelligence Corps (CIC) of, 145
Arrests
  Canons of Police Ethics on, 266
  Federal Bureau of Investigation records for, 141
  of justice system applicants, 225-26, 227
  juvenile, 220-21
  Mallory v. United States on, 287
  searches and, 284
  state agency records of, 128

322